Southeastern Flies

Southeastern Flies

A Collection of Flies, Fly Tying, and Fly Fishing Tips for Use on the Tailwaters, Streams, and Lakes of the Southeastern United States

L. J. DeCuir

Printed in the United States of America.
Published by Menasha Ridge Press.
First Edition, First Printing.

Library of Congress Cataloging-in-Publication Data:
DeCuir, L.J.
Southeastern flies : a collection of flies, fly tying & fly fishing tips for use on tailwaters, streams & lakes of the southeastern United States / by L. J. DeCuir.
cm.
Includes bibliographical references (p. 281) and index.
ISBN 0-89732-304-1
1. Flies, Artificial—Southern States 2. Fly Tying—Southern States I. Title.
SH451.D43 1999
688.7'9124—dc21 99-27801
CIP

Photos and art by the author unless otherwise credited.
Typography and design by Robert Clay White, Manuscript Ink.™
Cover photo by © David Brownell, 1997.
Cover design by Grant Tatum.

Menasha Ridge Press
700 28th Street South, Suite 206
Birmingham, Alabama 35233

Table of Contents

Fly Fishing in the Southeast

The Southeast United States holds one of the greatest variety of waters anywhere in the country for the fly fisher. The mountain streams of the Southern Appalachians abound in native Brookies and introduced Brown and Rainbow Trout. In addition there are a large number of tailwaters below impoundments that offer trout fisheries that sustain populations of large Rainbows and Browns rivaling those to be found anywhere in the United States. The U.S. record Brown Trout was only recently taken from one of these Southeastern tailwaters. For those interested in fly fishing for other species, the Southeast has little rival in the number of fisheries of Smallmouth, Largemouth, and inland Striped Bass. This does not even begin to take into consideration the salt and brackish water fisheries along the coasts. The best part of all of this, however, is that because of the moderate climate throughout most of the Southeast the vast majority of these fisheries are available year-round or nearly so. In the mountains of the Southeast the Spring thaw comes in March instead of May or June and there are not many rivers in the world other than the Saluda or the Chattahoochee where you can fish for trout in January AND get your fly hung up on Spanish Moss hanging from a Live Oak. When our Northern cousins, sometimes affectionately known as Yankees (or even Dammyankees), are holed up at their tying desks with feet of snow on the ground and frozen lakes and ponds many of us Southerners are out fishing.

There are several pioneering works that have provided anglers with information on fly fishing in the Southeast to which this author owes a debt of gratitude. Don Kirk's *Smoky Mountains Trout Fishing Guide* was one of the first books to deal with the wealth of habitat available in the Great Smoky Mountains National Park and remains the definitive guide to fishing that area. Jimmy Jacobs has likewise provided us with two outstanding works on fishing the Southeast with *Trout Streams of Southern Appalachia* and *Tailwater Trout in the South* as has Harry Slone in his *Virginia Trout Streams.* All of these authors suggest specific flies that either were developed in the Southeast United

States or though they originated elsewhere are effective in the Southeast. None of them, however, provide the fly fisher and fly tyer with detailed information on the patterns for these flies and instructions on how to go about tying them, or other than general information on fishing these specific patterns. Harry Murray in his two books *Trout Fishing in the Shenandoah National Park* and *Fly Fishing for Smallmouth Bass* does provide some excellent patterns for flies. Harry's focus, however, is upon the locations and conditions to be found in Virginia's Shenandoah Valley and National Park. If you are interested in fishing these areas his two works are invaluable.

This work seeks to explore the effective patterns for the Southeastern United States in much more depth. All of the patterns found in this book have been seriously field tested on Southeastern Trout, Smallmouth, Largemouth, Stripers, and a variety of Panfish both by myself and a number of other Southeastern fly fishers. Many of these patterns were developed in the Southeast and as one would expect work extremely well there. Others hail from the East, West, or even outside of the United States. What all of these patterns have in common is that they will catch fish in the Southeast. This is not just a book of patterns, however; it also presents detailed tying instructions for each of the patterns represented that have been verified on the tying bench and seeks to give you a guide as to where, when and how to present the fly for best results. At the back of the book you will also find information to aid the novice fly tyer in their first efforts at fly tying.

Serious fly fishers have long been aware that there is considerable regional variation in the insect life upon which trout feed and which we seek to imitate with our flies. The "sulphur" mayfly found on the Clinch River in Tennessee can vary considerably from the "sulphur" to be found in other areas of the county. A fly pattern that is deadly in New England may be totally ignored when fished on the Rapidan in Virginia. Many flytying books seem to either ignore or only give lip service to this basic fact of fly fishing life known to almost all experienced anglers. With the expansion of the popularity of fly fishing throughout the United States and in the Southeast it is time to recognize which patterns are effective in this region. Many flytying books have long distinguished between "Eastern" and "Western" patterns. This book makes a first attempt at that recognition for the Southeastern United States.

While it is true that there are certain patterns that are effective primarily in certain regions, it is also true that there are some patterns that can be almost universal in their ability to catch fish. There are a number of those patterns in this book as well. The Woolly Bugger, for example, is one of those patterns that has proven to be an outstanding fly no matter where it has been tried. What I have also attempted to do in this work is to give you variations on many universal patterns such as the Woolly Bugger that have proven to be useful in the Southeast.

For those of you from outside the Southeast there are some patterns in this book that are native to the region with which you may not be familiar such as the Yallerhammer. I would like to suggest that you give some of these a try in your own areas as well. You will most likely have some surprises in store when you do. On a recent trip to New England I found that Yallerhammers were just as effective on Vermont trout as they have long been on Southeastern ones.

There is no question that the Southeast offers the fly fisher more fishable days per year than almost any other region of the United States on a wide variety of species of fish. As more and more anglers from other parts of the country seek a location to enjoy their sport without having to resort to the extremes of geography such as Easter Island or New Zealand, the popularity of this region as a refuge from snowdrifts and frozen fingers will undoubtedly increase. My hope is that this work will help make the efforts of visiting anglers more enjoyable as well as providing a basis from which the native angler can expand their own knowledge of the area.

Acknowledgments

A list of all of the people who have been involved in creating and testing the patterns in this book would be so long that I could not even begin to list them here. Most of the people responsible for the patterns have been mentioned in the text of the specific patterns themselves. To all of you I give my heartiest thanks. In addition I would like to mention that the Listserv FLYFISH@ on the Internet has proven to be an incredibly valuable resource for locating and testing of these patterns. A large thank you is also deserved by "Listmeister" Danny Walls and all of the subscribers to FLYFISH@. If you are interested in more information, drop by the listserv's homepage at http://www.uky.edu/~agrdanny/flyfish/main.htm.

When you start thanking people who have helped, you realize that it is impossible to mention everyone who has been involved in a project such as this, so I must also include a general thank you to all of you whom I have not specifically mentioned, but who have been invaluable to the assembly of this work. Believe me, all of you have been appreciated. There are a few specific people that especially deserve my thanks. These are folks who have provided assistance above and beyond the call of duty in joining me on fishing trips and in long discussions of the patterns and problems encountered in fishing the Southeast. You will find David Allerton's name mentioned on numerous of the patterns presented in this book. David and I have personally either tested, adapted, and/or created the vast majority of these patterns. David has also been responsible for doing much of the research into the origins of many of these patterns and tying methods. Without David's unstinting help, this book would never have gotten to where it is today. I'd also like to thank Bob Miller and his wife Diane for joining me in numerous fishing trips and discussions, Bob Gartner for providing an incredible resource of patterns and advice, Dave Cox for first introducing me to fly tying, and H.B. McCowan, Pat Proffitt, Bill Murphy, Leon Gyles, Walt Winter and others for putting me up and/or putting up with me on any number of occasions. Finally, I have also got to mention the unbelievable tolerance, patience, and other saintly qualities of my wife Mari. This is a woman who has become a legend herself in fly fishing when she insisted that I NOT postpone a Steelhead trip in spite of the fact that she was in a hospital bed at the time. Without all of the help that I have received, this book would never have been realized.

Everyone should also note that this is a work in constant progress. If I've left out one of your favorite patterns, please let me know about it. There are a lot more great *Southeastern Flies* out there.

L J. DeCuir
ldecuir@utkux.utcc.utk.edu

Fishing is not a
matter of life and death.
. . . It's much more
important than that!

—L. J. DeCuir

Introduction

This book is primarily intended as a collection of patterns, tying tips and information on tying and fishing fly patterns that are effective in the Southeastern United States. There are also a number of articles that include more general information pertinent to fly fishing in the area as well. These patterns have been collected over a number of years from a wide variety of sources. Some of these patterns are traditional patterns that have been used in the Southeastern U.S. for so long that in some cases no one even remembers exactly who was the original tyer. Other patterns have been developed by residents of the Southeast, myself included, specifically for fishing in the area. Yet others of these patterns were originated by fly tyers from a variety of parts of the U.S. and even the rest of the world, but have been proven highly effective on fish in the Southeast. No matter where the patterns were originally developed there is one thing that holds them all together as a group—they all catch fish in the Southeastern United States. A number of other Southeastern fly fishers and myself have demonstrated this again and again over years of fishing.

The patterns are written in a manner and using terminology that will be familiar to those experienced in fly tying. This method of presenting a pattern is one that has been developed over a long period of time by many fly tyers and as such has been long recognized as a concise and effective means of communicating the information needed to construct the fly. It is, however, a somewhat specialized language that may initially be somewhat daunting to the neophyte. When I simply say "whip finish", for example, exactly how do you go about doing that? To assist those who may be less than fully experienced fly tyers, I have also included a number of sections at the end of the book.

If you come across a term such as "whip finish" with which you are not familiar, please flip back to the Glossary (p. 243) to find an explanation of the term and, if it is a technique, information on how it is done. There are also drawings included with information on the Parts of the Hook (p. 241) to help you visualize these parts. A Hook Equivalency Chart (p. 268) is there to help you try to make sense out of the fact that no two hook manufacturers use the same terminology. Information on the Proportions of Flies (p. 241) comprises yet another section to give you a reference for the relative sizes of parts of various flies. Drawings of the Parts of Flies (p. 242) makes up one more section at the rear of the book to help you identify these parts and there is a section on Basic Fly Tying Tools (p. 230) for the beginner who hasn't yet acquired these important items. For those interested in beginning fly tying on a truly modest budget there is also a section on tools and materials that can be found around the house: The Anarchist Fly Swap (p. 234). While all of these things may be second nature to the experienced fly tyer, they can be extremely confusing to the beginner.

Before tackling any of the patterns there are a few other pieces of information of which you should be aware. As with all well written patterns the materials listed under Pattern: are given in the order in which they are initially tied onto the hook. A ribbing material, for example, is usually tied onto the hook early in the flytying process. It is then allowed to hang there while two or three other steps in the process are completed and only then is wound forward to provide an imitation of a segmented body. So when you see an item such as ribbing in the Pattern: this tells you when to first attach it to the hook. Follow the Tying Instructions: in the sequence given so that every step will be completed in the proper order. When tying a fly it is just as important to follow the correct sequence as it is to use the correct material.

Most of the materials called for in this book are readily available at a well stocked flyfishing store, or for those of you who don't have one nearby are obtainable through one of the numerous flyfishing mail order houses around the country. Unlike classic Salmon Flies there are no materials used that are so exotic that they should be difficult to locate. In many cases I have also offered suggestions for substitutions that are just as acceptable. I would encourage you to look around for other substitutions that you may have available. Read the article on "The Anarchist Fly Swap" (p. 234) to get some ideas of what I mean by this. Often there are materials just lying around the house that will form an excellent substitute for a more expensive commercial product.

Most of the patterns in this book also have a section on the variations that are possible with the pattern. There is no pattern that has ever been developed that hasn't been adapted in some way or another by different fly tyers. As you gain more experience in fly fishing and fly tying you will also want to experiment with your own adaptations of patterns. Conditions within the Southeast also change from one location to another and variations on patterns help you as a fly fisher adapt to these varying conditions.

I have tried with the majority of these patterns to include a section on fishing the fly that is intended to help you get the most effective results out of each pattern's possibilities. Because fly fishing is such a diverse and individualized sport, none of the above should be taken as gospel. Just because it has finally made it into print does not mean that it is carved in stone. I'll be trying out new variations on patterns, new materials for tying them, and new ways of fishing them almost every time that I'm on the water. You'll learn a great deal about the possibilities and the limitations of any pattern or technique by doing the same yourself. The best of luck with all of these patterns and "tight lines and screaming reels" to each and every one of you.

Dry Flies and Emergers

The dry fly is the kind of fly that most people who are not fly fishermen associate with the sport. This is the classic fly fishing presentation that has come down to us from Isaac Walton and through hundreds of years of hoary tradition. And there is indeed something heart thrilling and wonderful about watching a trout take a dry fly from the surface of the water whether he is doing it with a spectacular splash or a delicate sip. Actually seeing the fly disappear and then lifting the tip of the rod and feeling that throbbing tug on the end of the line is an experience that many feel is the quintessential essence of fly fishing. Never mind that it is far from being the most productive method of catching fish day in and day out. Never mind that it is often the most difficult of the various techniques of fly fishing to master. Never mind that it is frustrating, unproductive, and reeks of snobbery and elitism. This is the way that it is done on the Test, the Itchen, and the other hallowed chalk streams of England. This is the way that it was done by the Dettes and the Wullfs up in the Catskills. This is the way that it is done!

Gimme a break, guys! Dry flies are fun when they produce fish, but there is a heck of a lot of the time that they just don't, and that is when the complete fly fisherman breaks out the other weapons in his or her arsenal. So while this chapter covers the hallowed classics (and some not so hallowed newcomers) don't neglect the other flies in the book as well. You'll probably end up catching a lot more fish on the other flies than you do on the dries.

There is no denying, however, that the dry fly is one of the most fun ways of catching a fish ever devised by man. As a result, many of the flies in this chapter have been catching fish for over a hundred years and are just as effective today as they were when they were first developed. For those of you from outside the Southeast you will probably meet some old friends here like the Adams. Many of the classics work just as well in the Southeast as they do elsewhere—that's how they became classics. However, you will also find some flies that are probably unfamiliar like the Thunderhead and the Mr. Rapidan that were developed specifically for conditions in the Southeast. If you've tied up a mix of both the classics and some of the specifically Southeastern flies you'll have a fly box that is probably pretty well equipped to handle most of the conditions that you will encounter.

Hair Winged Caddis (EHC and others)

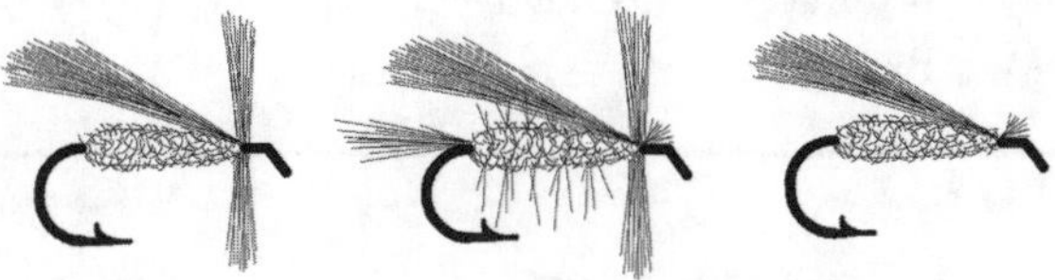

The Hair Winged Caddis is one of the most versatile patterns available to the fly fisher. Although originally intended to imitate the Caddis Fly, it serves so well as an imitation of a wide variety of insect life that it can even be used effectively on streams that have no Caddis present.

The wing from which the Hair Winged Caddis derives its name is a clump of stacked hair that is tied in at the front of the body and behind the eye of the hook. One of the oldest versions of this fly is the famous EHC or Elk Hair Caddis. This version of the Hair Winged Caddis is so well known now that almost any Caddis imitation that uses a hair wing is referred to as an EHC. In fact, the wing does not have to be of Elk Hair, but can be made from any hair with good flotation. The next most important factor in choosing hair is to use a hair that works best with the size of the hook being tied. The smaller the hook the finer the hair necessary. In the smallest sizes I have even used poly yarn as a substitute.

Variations on the basic pattern are too numerous to even begin to enumerate here, but fall into four general categories: 1) The Palmered Rib, used in the original EHC by Al Troth, 2) The Standard Hackle, often attributed to Polly Rosborough, 3) A Combination of Palmered Rib and Standard Hackle and 4) No Hackle. You will also find patterns in which a tail or trailing shucks are incorporated and body materials such as quill or floss are used rather than dubbing.

Proportions are usually given as follows: Body: Reverse taper to eye, Wing: Slightly longer than the hook shank (often by as much as one-third), Hackle: Tips as high as three-quarters of hook shank length, Palmered Rib: One size smaller than gap size, Tail: (if any) usually one-third shank length past bend.

Bucktail Caddis This pattern uses both a standard and palmered hackle.

Hook:	Mustad 94840 or Tiemco 100 (#10-18)
Thread:	Brown
Tail:	Natural Brown/Gray Deer Hair tied short
Palmer Rib:	Brown Hackle palmered through body
Body:	Brown, Green, Tan, Gray or Black dubbing
Wing:	Natural Brown/Gray Deer Hair
Hackle:	Brown

Tying Instructions

These instructions are for tying the Bucktail Caddis and includes all of the techniques used in the other patterns. For tying the simpler patterns just omit the appropriate steps.

1 Start the thread at the front of the hook close to the eye and then wind it all the way back to the bend. This will provide a thread underbase that will make tying on the wing easier by helping to keep it from "spinning."

2 Cut off a small amount of hair for the tail (for a #16 hook this would be 4-5 hairs). Clean the fuzz from the clump of hair with a toothbrush and stack it tips first in your hair stacker. Tie it on at the bend of the hook as a tail. Note that the first couple of wraps should be a little loose to keep the hair from flaring, then you can gradually tighten the wraps of thread as you spiral the thread forward to about ½ the body length. Cut off the excess butts and then use the thread to bind down any flared hairs. Return the thread to the bend of the hook.

3 Tie in a hackle feather, the barbules of which are slightly smaller than the hook gap. This feather should be tied in by its tip with the feather extending back of the fly. It will later be used to form the Palmered Rib.

4 Dub the thread with the appropriate colored material. I recommend a poly dubbing or a coarse "nymph" style dubbing rather than a fine "dry"

style dubbing. Form the body with the dubbing in a reverse taper—that is, heavier near the bend and narrower as it approaches the eye of the hook. Stop the dubbing short of the eye of the hook and let the thread hang.

5 Grasp the hackle feather previously tied in with a pair of hackle pliers and wind it forward in an open spiral to about 1/4 hook shank length back of the eye. Take a couple of wraps at this point with the thread. Cut off the excess butt of the Palmered Rib feather. The thread should be at the point where the wing will be attached, approximately 1/4 hook shank length back of the eye.

6 Cut a larger bunch of deer hair for the wing (for a #16 hook this would be about the size of a wooden matchstick). Clean this hair and stack it by the tips. Grasp the stacked hair at slightly behind the point at which it will be attached to the hook shank. Attach the hair wing to the top of the hook shank with three wraps of thread. The butts of the hairs will be hanging over the front of the hook. Use your scissors to cut off the butts at an angle parallel with the eye of the hook. At this point you may find it useful to apply a drop of head cement to the thread windings, securing the wing to keep it from shifting on you later in the procedure.

7 If you do not desire a flared head on the fly, now trim the wing butts and wrap them down with the thread, returning the thread to the base of the wing. If you desire a flared head then trim the wing butts to shape.

8 (* See Glossary on Preparing Hackle) Select two hackle feathers which measure slightly less than would normally be used for the related hook size and tie them in by the butts. Wind the hackle collar one feather at a time. Use two turns of thread to secure each of the collar feathers in place after they are wound forward and trim the excess tips. Whip finish just behind the eye and apply a little head cement if desired.

Variations

Patterns: The patterns given below are an example of the many different kinds of Hair Winged Caddis. Each pattern is given in tying order, as are all patterns in this book: the order of materials listed is the order in which they are tied in.

Dubbing color for the Hair Winged Caddis can be anything from the most subtle imitations to the most blatant attractor colors that you find to be effective. Black, Olive, Green, Gray, Brown and Tan are the most common colors used, but I have also found Red, Yellow and Orange to be highly effective.

Hook sizes can vary from as small as #22 to as large as #4. In the smaller sizes they can be used to fish midge hatches, in the larger sizes to imitate hoppers and in between to imitate Caddis and a variety of terrestrials. Pinch the body in the middle and you have an ant.

Fishing the Fly

These patterns are usually fished as a dry fly, but can be fished in a variety of styles. Twitching the line to cause it to "skitter" across the water, for example, can be very effective when fishing it as a Caddis. The no hackle version can be used as an Emerger and when drowned can be fished down and across or on a slow retrieve like a wet fly. Add a small amount of weight to the tippet 6" in front of the fly and you have a "diving Caddis."

Bucktail Caddis This pattern uses both a standard and palmered hackle.

Hook: Mustad 94840 or Tiemco 100 (#10-18)
Thread: Brown
Tail: Natural Brown/Gray Deer Hair tied short
Palmer Rib: Brown Hackle palmered through body
Body: Brown, Green, Tan, Gray or Black dubbing
Wing: Natural Brown/Gray Deer Hair
Hackle: Brown

Black Caddis This is an example with a standard hackle.

Hook: Mustad 94840 or Tiemco 100 (#12-18)
Thread: Black
Body: Black Dubbing Fur
Wing: Black Mink Tail Guard Hair Fibers
Hackle: Black

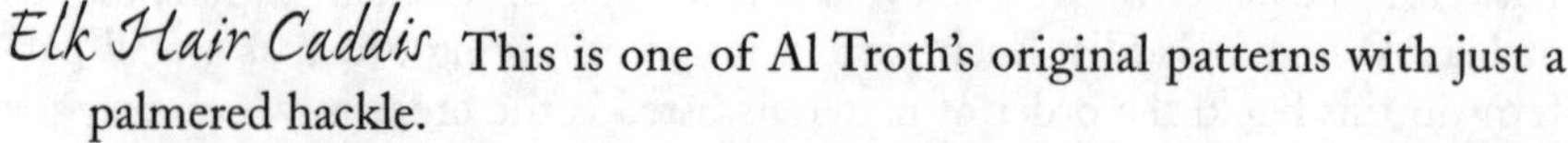

Elk Hair Caddis This is one of Al Troth's original patterns with just a palmered hackle.

Hook: Mustad 94840 or Tiemco 100 (#10-20)
Thread: Tan or Brown
Palmer Rib: Brown Hackle palmered through body
Body: Hare's Ear & Mask Dubbing Fur

Wing: Tan Elk Hair
Head: Trimmed Butts of Elk Hair Wing

No Hackle Caddis (Orange)

The simplest and often most versatile of all.

Hook: Mustad 94840 or Tiemco 100 (#10-22)
Thread: Orange
Body: Orange Poly Dubbing
Wing: Tan Coastal Deer Hair or Gray Poly Yarn

Quill Bodied Caddis

This version was contributed by Don Yelton.

Hook: Mustad 94840 or Tiemco 100 (#10-22)
Thread: Black
Body: Stripped quill (peacock herl, hackle quill, etc.)
Wing: Elk hair or fine deer hair

The Henryville Special

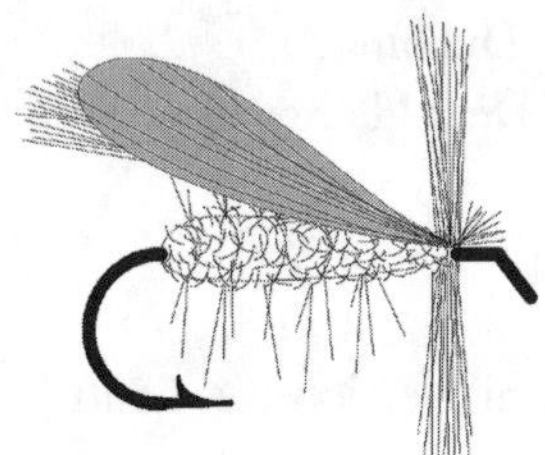

The Henryville Special has been used to imitate Caddis flies throughout the U.S. and the world. Originated by Hiram Brobst in the Henryville section of Broadhead Creek in Pennsylvania, it has spread from there throughout the Southeast as well. While the olive body given here is probably the most popular, it can be tied in a wide variety of other colors. Red, green, yellow and burnt orange are popular variations. The pattern was originally tied with a floss body, but this variation uses antron dubbing instead.

Hook:	Mustad 94840, TMC 100 #12-18
Thread:	Olive
Rib:	Grizzly hackle palmered forward (one size smaller than the regular hackle)
Body:	Olive antron or poly dubbing
Under Wing:	Wood duck flank fibers
Wing:	2 mallard wing quill sections tied down wing style
Hackle:	Brown dry fly hackle

Tying Instructions

1 Tie in the hackle to be used for the ribbing at the bend of the hook.

2 Dub the body forward to a position about 1/3 hook shank behind the eye.

3 Palmer the ribbing forward to the end of the dubbing, tie off and trim excess.

4 Trim the hackle flush with the top of the body.

5 Tie in a few wood duck flank fibers to form an underwing. These are tied in just at the forward end of the body with the tips about on line with the bend of the hook.
Note: See the section on Quill Winged Flies (p. 38) before preparing the quill wings for step 6.

6 Position the duck quill section to form the far side of the wing and secure it in place with a couple of turns of thread. The end of this wing section should be just slightly beyond the end of the hook

7 Position the duck quill section to form the near side of the wing and secure it in place with a couple of turns of thread.

8 Take a couple more turns of thread to secure them well in place. When this is done properly, it will also cause the wings to slightly flare away from each other. Trim off the front section of the quills used to form the wings.

9 (* See Glossary on Preparing Hackle) Tie in a brown dry fly hackle in front of the wing and wrap it a couple of times around the hook shank. Tie off. Trim the excess and whip finish.

Fishing the Fly

The Henryville Special is a Caddis imitation that works extremely well on fast water. The combination of Palmered and standard hackle means that it takes a lot of work to sink this fly. This is a great fly for Trout in the mountains of the Southeast. What a lot of folks don't realize about the Henryville, though, is that it is also a dynamite panfish and Bass fly. Because it is a hard fly to sink you can work this baby around lilypads as noisily as you want when going after Bass and, when landed with a plop it will quickly stir the interest of Bluegills and Bream.

The Parachute

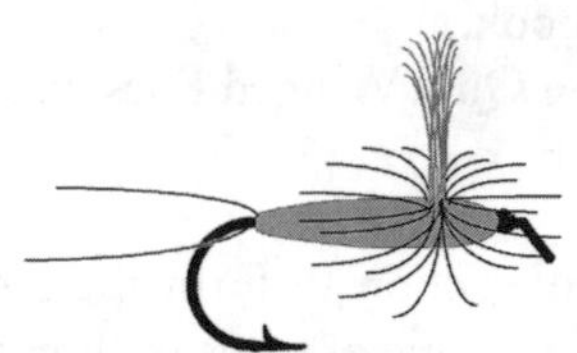

The idea of tying a dry fly with the hackle wound on a horizontal plane with the shank of the hook rather than perpendicular to it has been with us for some time, but has only become very popular in moderately recent times. This method of tying a fly brings the body of the fly closer to the water and thus presents (many believe) a better silhouette to the fish. Parachute flies also have the advantage of almost never landing upside down, on their sides, on their heads, etc., as well as just about always landing gently. They make a very realistic presentation. These are great flies for the tailwaters of the Southeast and have proven to be equally popular in some of the mountain areas as well. This particular version of the Parachute was taught to me by Jim Shea.

The Adams

Hook: Mustad 94840, TMC 100, etc. #12-22
Thread: Black
Wing: Post wing of white or dun polyester yarn
Tail: 2 microfibbets tied in as a split tail, or brown & grizzly hackle fibers
Body: Muskrat dubbing (natural or artificial)
Hackle: 1 Brown, 1 Grizzly hackle wound parachute style around the post wing

Parachutes can be tied in a wide variety of colors to represent nearly any mayfly that you would like just by varying the materials that are used. The basic pattern that I'm giving below is for the Adams, but also listed are versions for a Sulphur, a Blue Winged Olive and a number of others.

Tying Instructions

1 Start the thread just behind the eye of the hook and wind it ⅓ of the way toward the bend.

2 Tie in a piece of polyester yarn of the appropriate diameter at this point (trim to length later). Pick up the end of the polyester yarn toward the front of the hook and take several thread wraps in front to hold it upright as a post wing.

3 Trim the back of the piece of yarn so that it forms a taper that ends just before the bend of the hook, then work your thread back to the bend of the hook, forming the base of a tapered body with just one turn of thread at the bend of the hook.

4 Tie in two microfibbets as a split tail or tie in several brown & grizzly hackle fibers as a straight tail. Many patterns call for building up a "bump" of thread at the bend to aid in tying in the microfibbets. I prefer to lay one piece at an angle across the hook and take one turn of thread over the top of it. Then to lay the second piece in place and carefully take one turn over it. Then I adjust the length and angle of the microfibbets. Finally, I take a careful turn to hold both in place and then several more, working my way up the hook to secure them firmly. Finish with the thread at the bend of the hook.

5 Dub muskrat fur (natural or artificial) forward to just behind the wing, forming a tapered body.

6 (* See Glossary on Preparing Hackle) Tie in the two hackle feathers with the butt pointing toward the eye of the hook and the tip of the feather angling over and along the abdomen that you have just formed with the dubbing.

7 Dub muskrat fur forward of the post wing to form the thorax of the fly to just behind the eye of the hook.

8 Holding the post wing upright, wind one of the hackle feathers two to three times around the base of the post wing, forming the "parachute."

9. Tie off the leftover end of the hackle feather just behind the eye of the hook.

10. Trim off the excess feather and then repeat with the second feather.

11. Trim the post wing to the desired height.

12. Whip finish or finish with several half hitches. With the hackle in the position that it is for a parachute, it usually is easier to use several half hitches to finish the fly rather than a whip finish. If you do want to use a whip finish, many people like to use a hackle guard in the whip finish process to hold the hackle out of the way. If you don't have a hackle guard, one can be easily fashioned from a circle of stiff plastic with a hole in the center and a slit cut from the edge to center. Making it out of clear plastic has the added advantage of letting you see what you are doing better.

Fishing the Fly

The Parachute in one of its many guises is a great fly for dealing with slow water, still water or highly selective Trout. You can easily achieve a very delicate presentation with this fly that does not spook the fish and it shows a highly realistic silhouette as well. This is one of my favorite tailwater dries. One of the great things about the Parachute as a style of fly tying though is that the poly post wing also makes it a fly with excellent flotation properties—which means that it is useful on the mountain streams of the Southeast as well.

Other Parachute Patterns

The Sulphur

Hook: Mustad 94840, TMC 100, etc. #14-18
Thread: Pale Yellow
Wing: Post wing of white or dun polyester yarn
Tail: 2 pale yellow to tan microfibbets tied in as a split tail, or cream hackle fibers
Body: Pale yellow to dirty orange dubbing
Hackle: Cream hackle wound parachute style around the post wing

The Blue Winged Olive (BWO)

Hook: Mustad 94840, TMC 100, etc. #16-20
Thread: Olive

Wing: Post wing of white or dun polyester yarn
Tail: 2 medium to dark dun microfibbets tied in as a split tail, or dun hackle fibers
Body: Olive, olive-brown, or olive-gray dubbing
Hackle: Medium to dark dun hackle wound parachute style around the post wing

The Mr. Rapidan

Hook: Mustad 94840, TMC 100, etc. #12-18
Thread: Tan
Wing: Post wing of yellow polyester yarn
Tail: 2 stiff dark moose or elk hairs tied in as a split tail
Body: A blend of fine dubbing (50% Quill Gordon, 50% March Brown)
Hackle: One brown, one grizzly hackle wound parachute style around the post wing

The Light Cahill

Hook: Mustad 94840, TMC 100, etc. #12-18
Thread: Pale yellow-cream
Wing: Post wing of dun or white polyester yarn
Tail: 2 cream to tan microfibbets tied in as a split tail, or dark cream hackle fibers
Body: Creamy, yellow fine dubbing
Hackle: Dark cream hackle wound parachute style around the post wing

The March Brown

Hook: Mustad 94840, TMC 100, etc. #12-18
Thread: Orange or Brown
Wing: Post wing of white or dun polyester yarn
Tail: 2 ginger microfibbets tied in as a split tail, or ginger hackle fibers
Body: “March Brown” fly dubbing (tannish-brown with a hint of red)
Hackle: One ginger, one grizzly hackle wound parachute style around the post wing

The Biot-Bodied Parachute

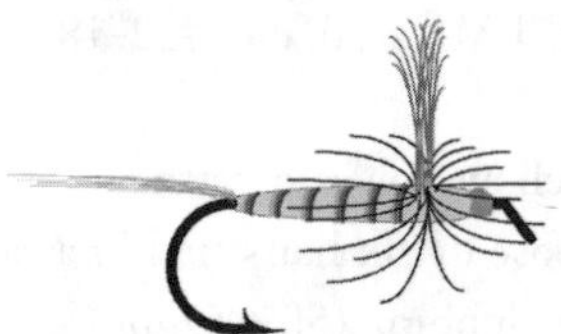

This variation of the Parachute was developed by Steve Davenport of Atlanta and uses biots to form the body of the fly rather than quills or dubbing. Biots are available dyed in a wide variety of colors. They create a body with a segmented look much like a quill body, but considerably tougher. Rather than imitating a specific mayfly, this pattern is generic and can be used to imitate most smaller mayflies by altering the component colors. For the past several years Steve has hosted NEG-Clave, a Conclave on the Chattooga down on the GA–SC border that has attracted a small, but devoted group of attendees who come to fish the river where *Deliverance* was filmed, scarf down some of Don Yelton's canollis and generally swap lies and ideas about fishing in the Southeast.

Hook:	Mustad 94840, TMC 100 #12-18
Thread:	Color to match body
Tail:	Microfibbets, color to match natural
Body:	Turkey biot for #14 and larger, goose biot for #16 and smaller, dyed to match natural
Wing:	Post wing made from Poly Yarn: white, hi-vis, or color similar to natural
Hackle:	Color to match legs of natural

Tying Instructions

1 Before beginning tying, pull an appropriate number of biots from the quill (1 per fly) and place them in a cup of water to soak.

2 Tie in thread just behind the eye and wrap an underbody to the tailing point. Note: The underbody will provide a small amount of bulk beneath the biot so the fly's body is not too narrow.

3 Tie in the microfibbet tail. For a #16 fly use 4 microfibbets (vary for other hook sizes) To tie the fly with split tails, make a small thread ball at the tailing point consisting of 3-4 thread wraps. Tie in 2 microfibbets at an angle on either side of the thread bump. The tails should angle up slightly as well as angle to either side of the body. Secure the tails in place with 2 thread wraps. Do not trim the microfibbets.

4 Tie in the biot by its tip at the tailing point. The biot should be at an angle to the hook when tying in. Examine the biot carefully and you will note a difference between the two edges. One edge is smoother, the other has fine fibers coming off of it. As you wind the biot forward later to form the body, the trailing edge will cover the leading edge of the previous wrap. Which edge of the biot that you use as the trailing edge will give you either a smoother body or a body with more pronounced segmentation.

5 Wrap thread back to the hook eye over the microfibbets, keeping the microfibbets on top of and parallel to the hook shank. If the microfibbets are allowed to twist around the shank, the fly's body will be deformed. The thread will overwrap the microfibbets and will add just a little more bulk to the body.

6 Trim off the microfibbet butts about $\frac{1}{2}$ hook eye length behind the hook eye.

7 Wrap the biot toward the hook eye with each wrap slightly overlapping the previous wrap. Wrap the biot all the way to the hook eye. Secure the biot butt with a couple of thread wraps and trim the tag end.

8 Return the thread to immediately behind the hook eye and wrap a layer of thread over the trimmed biot to form a smooth layer of thread back to about one hook eye width behind the eye.

9 Prepare the post wing by splitting a length of poly yarn (about $1\frac{1}{4}$ to $1\frac{1}{2}$ inches) into a bundle with a diameter roughly equal to the body of the fly.

10 To tie in the post wing, hold the bundle of poly yarn parallel to the hook shank so that the midpoint is over the rear edge of the tag end of the biot. Secure the post material to the hook with 3 wraps of thread.

11 To finish the post, pull the two ends of the poly yarn upward and hold them together. Make 3 to 4 loose turns of thread around the base of the post and then tighten. Wrap the thread up the post about 1/16 of an inch, holding the post and tightening the wraps about every three to four turns. Then wrap the thread back down the post and once around the hook shank to secure.

12 Prepare the hackle by trimming a portion (approximately 1/2 inch) of the barbules of each side of the butt end of the feather. Trim an additional 1/8 inch worth off the side that will be the inside of the first hackle turn on the post.

13 Hold the hackle so that the quill is parallel to the hook shank and in front of the post. Be sure that the side of the prepared feather with the extra trimmed barbules is adjacent to the post. Secure the hackle feather to the hook shank in front of the post.

14 At this point, if the thread color does not closely match the color of the thorax of the natural, a narrow thorax may be added immediately behind and in front of the post with dubbing.

15 Wrap the hackle onto the post, starting at the top and working down. Three to four turns of hackle is plenty. Secure the hackle against the hook shank behind the eye. Trim off the excess hackle and any stray barbules.

16 Finish the fly with 3 to 5 half hitches or whip finish and trim off the thread. Add a drop of head cement to the wraps if desired.

The Comparadun

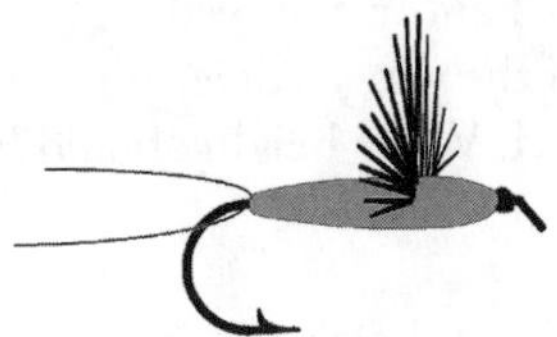

The Comparadun, like the Parachute, is a dry fly that sits low in the water. Unlike the Parachute it has no hackle, but instead has a fan shaped deer hair wing. The name was originally coined by Al Caucci and Bob Nastasi in their book *Hatches*. It has become a very popular Southeastern Fly in recent years, though the idea of a hackle-less fly goes back to the 1930s with Ray Bergman and Herb Howard. The Comparadun is a style of fly tying that can be used to imitate many different mayflies. The version given here is for a Sulphur, but there are variations listed for an Adams, a Blue Winged Olive and others.

The tricky part of tying this pattern is in setting the wing. I would recommend using a fine deer hair or elk hair for the wing. The color of the hair can be varied to suit the fly that you are trying to imitate.

The Sulphur

Hook: Mustad 94840 or TMC 100 #14-18
Thread: Pale yellow, cream or dirty orange
Wing: Light coastal deer
Tail: 2 Pale yellow, tan or dirty orange microfibbets or a few hackle fibers
Body: Pale yellow to dirty orange dubbing

Tying Instructions

1 Start the thread at the bend of the hook and wind it all the way forward to the eye, forming a thread underbody. Wind it $\frac{1}{3}$ of the way back between the eye of the hook and the bend.

2 Clean and stack a clump of deer hair about the diameter of a wooden kitchen match for a #16 hook. For larger or smaller hooks, adjust the size of the clump of deer hair appropriately.

3 Lay the clump of deer hair on top of the hook with the tips pointing forward. The height of the wing is determined by how much of the tips is forward of the thread. Wing height should be approximately $1\frac{1}{2}$ to 2 times gap width.

4 Grasp the deer hair so that the clump is on top of and extending down both sides of the hook shank, but not going around the bottom of the hook shank.

5 Take 4-5 turns of thread around the deer hair. You are tying the clump of fibers to both sides and the top of the hook shank.

6 Lift the deer hair to a vertical position and then take a good number of turns of thread directly in front of the base of the fibers. Continue to push the deer hair upward as you are winding the thread. They will flare upward and outward, forming an arc of 180 degrees on both sides and on top of the hook shank. If this isn't quite happening, help it along with a little pulling and tugging on the deer hair as you wind the thread. Any deer hair that drops below the bottom of the hook shank can be trimmed off.

7 When you have the wing set to your satisfaction, bring the thread to a position behind the deer hair.

8 Trim and taper the butts of the deer hair to form the base for a tapered body. Wind the thread over these trimmed butts to the bend of the hook.

9 Lay a microfibbet at about a 45-degree angle horizontally at the bend of the hook and take one turn of thread over it to hold it in place, forming one half of the tail. Lay a second microfibbet at the opposite angle at the bend of the hook and take one turn of thread over it. Adjust the length of the tail by pulling on the two microfibbets. Take another turn

of thread over the microfibbets (not too tightly) to hold them in place and then another just forward of this turn even tighter. Trim off the butts of the microfibbets.

The above technique produces a very fine tail end to the body at the bend of the hook, but can be a little tricky to master. An alternate method is to just use a few hackle fibers to form a tail much like you would for a standard Catskill-type pattern. Another alternate method is to dub in just a small ball of dubbing right at the bend of the hook before tying in the microfibbet tail. This will help them to keep the 45-degree flare in both directions, but makes for a slightly fatter tail end to the body. Yet another alternate method is to not use a tail on the Comparadun. Use whatever method works best for you. One of the best fishermen that I know claims that you don't really need a tail on this fly at all.

10 Dub the body forward forming a tapered body. You do not stop when you get to the wing. The body continues all the way beyond the wing to just behind the eye of the hook. When you get to the wing, however, you will need to do a little more tugging and pulling on the deer hair to keep the wing flared the way that you want. Use the winds of dubbing immediately behind and in front of the wing as further support for the position of the wing. Whip finish.

Fishing the Fly

The Comparadun is a great fly for slower water where a more realistic presentation is essential. It can be difficult to see in the faster water of mountain streams. The uncluttered silhouette that it presents to the fish is ideal for conditions present when fishing for trout on many of our Southeastern tailwaters and spring creeks.

Other Comparadun Patterns

The March Brown

Hook: Mustad 94840 #12-20
Thread: Orange or brown
Wing: Light to medium color deer hair fibers
Tail: 2 ginger microfibbets or ginger hackle fibers
Body: "March Brown" dry fly dubbing (tannish-brown with a hint of red)

The Mr. Rapidan

Hook: Mustad 94840 #12-20
Thread: Tan
Wing: Light deer hair fibers
Tail: 2 dark moose hairs or dark microfibbets
Body: A blend of fine dubbing (50% Quill Gordon, 50% March Brown)

The Adams

Hook: Mustad 94840 #12-20
Thread: Black
Wing: Medium to dark deer hair fibers
Tail: 2 brown or gray microfibbets or brown and grizzly hackle fibers
Body: Muskrat dubbing

The Blue Winged Olive (BWO)

Hook: Mustad 94840 or TMC 100 #16-20
Thread: Olive
Wing: Medium to dark deer hair fibers
Tail: 2 olive or gray microfibbets or ginger to brown hackle fibers
Body: Olive, olive-brown, or olive-gray dubbing

The Light Cahill

Hook: Mustad 94840 #12-20
Thread: Pale yellow cream
Wing: Light deer hair fibers
Tail: 2 dark cream microfibbets or dark cream hackle fibers
Body: Creamy, yellow fine dubbing

Catskill-Style Flies

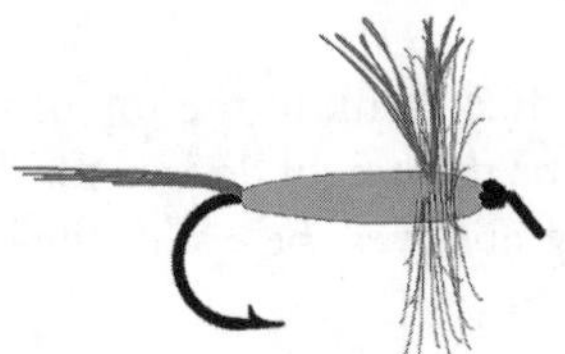

This style of fly tying originated in the Catskill area of New York with such famous fly tyers as the Dette family and others. It has since spread to become what is probably the single most popular approach to tying dry flies throughout the United States. I've often wondered why, since while these flies are appropriate for the Catskill streams, those same sort of conditions do not prevail in the rest of the country. For whatever reason, when you walk into almost any fly shop in the Southeast or elsewhere and ask to see their "dry flies," these are usually the style of fly with which you will be presented. Quite frankly, I've found the Parachute or Comparadun styles to be much more effective on our tailwaters or when dealing with selective fish and the Wulff style or Humpys to float better on our mountain streams. When you tie this

The Light Cahill

Hook: Mustad 94840, TMC 100 #14-18
Thread: Pale yellow cream
Wing: Wood duck flank fibers tied upright and divided
Tail: Dark cream hackle fibers
Body: Creamy, yellow fine dubbing
Hackle: Dark cream

style of fly I strongly recommend that they be tied as sparse as possible. Most of the examples that you buy in fly shops are tied with very heavy hackles and tails. There is an old saying in the mountains of the Southeast: "Heavy flies catch fishermen, sparse flies catch fish."

Tying Instructions

1 Start the thread just behind the eye of the hook and wind it back to about $\frac{1}{3}$ hook shank length behind the eye. Then wind it forward to about $\frac{1}{16}$ inch to $\frac{1}{8}$ inch behind the eye.

2 Lash a clump of wood duck flank to the top of the hook, at this point measured so that it will be the height desired for the wing when upright. Tips should be pointing out over the eye of the hook, butts toward the bend.

3 Grasp the fibers by their tips and pull them upright. Take a number of windings of thread around the hook shank at the base of the clump to support it in this upright position.

4 Bring your thread through the middle of and behind the clump dividing it into two sections. Take one turn of thread around the hook behind the fibers. Then further divide and separate the two sections of fibers by taking a modified figure eight loop around both of the sections. To do this the thread goes around the base of the far section and then back through the middle. Then it goes around the base of the near section and back through the middle, ending up behind the wing on the far side of the hook. Take another turn around the hook behind the wing to hold it all in place.

5 Trim the butts of the wood duck to form a taper toward the bend of the hook and lash this all in place by winding the thread to the bend of the hook.

6 Secure the tail in place with a couple of turns of thread and trim the butts.

7 Dub the body forward to just behind the wing, forming a trim tapered body.

8 (* See Glossary on Preparing Hackle) Tie in the hackle by the butt just in front of the wing with the tip facing backward. Wind the hackle

around the hook taking one turn behind the wing and then two turns in front. Secure and trim the hackle as you are finished with it.

9 Whip finish just behind the eye of the hook.

Other Catskill Patterns

The Adams

Hook: Mustad 94840, TMC 100 #16-18
Thread: Black
Wing: Mallard flank fibers tied upright and divided
Tail: Mixed brown and grizzly hackle fibers
Body: Muskrat dubbing
Hackle: One brown and one grizzly hackle tied sparse
Note: The Adams was originally tied with wings made from grizzly hackle tips rather than the Mallard flank called for here.

The Light Hendrickson

Hook: Mustad 94840, TMC 100 #12-18
Thread: Gray
Wing: Lemon wood duck flank fibers upright and divided
Tail: Medium bronze dun hackle fibers
Body: Pinkish tan dubbing
Note: Originally this pattern called for fur from a Vixen's belly that had been bleached slightly by her urine
Hackle: Medium bronze dun

The Dark Hendrickson

Hook: Mustad 94840, TMC 100 #12-18
Thread: Gray
Wing: Lemon wood duck flank fibers upright and divided
Tail: Medium bronze dun hackle fibers
Body: Muskrat dubbing
Hackle: Medium bronze dun

The March Brown

Hook: Mustad 94840, TMC 100 #12-18
Thread: Orange or brown
Wing: Wood duck flank fibers tied upright and divided
Tail: Ginger hackle fibers
Body: "March Brown" dry fly dubbing (tannish-brown with a hint of red)
Hackle: One ginger, one grizzly hackle tied sparse

The Sulphur

Hook: Mustad 94840, TMC 100 #14-18
Thread: Pale yellow
Wing: Mallard flank fibers tied upright and divided
Tail: Wood duck flank fibers
Body: Pale yellow to dirty orange dubbing
Hackle: Cream or light ginger hackle tied sparse

The Blue Winged Olive

Hook: Mustad 94840, TMC 100 #16-18
Thread: Olive
Wing: Mallard flank fibers tied upright and divided
Tail: Dun hackle fibers
Body: Olive, olive-brown, or olive-gray dubbing
Hackle: Medium to dark dun hackle tied sparse

The Gray Fox

Hook: Mustad 94840, TMC 100 #12-18
Thread: Yellow
Wing: Mallard flank fibers upright and divided
Tail: Golden ginger hackle fibers
Body: Fawn/beige dubbing
Hackle: Light grizzly and golden ginger mixed

The Mr. Rapidan & Wulff-Style Flies

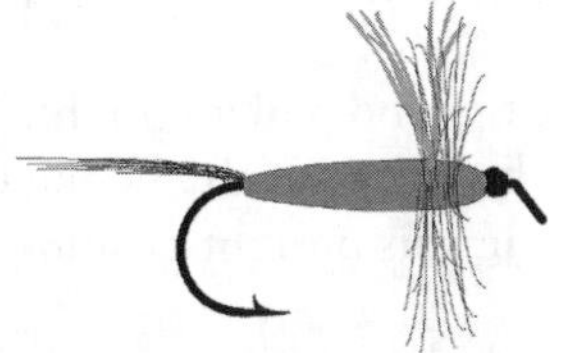

Harry Murray has been fly fishing, teaching and writing about it out of his combination pharmacy, fly shop and lunch counter in Edinburg, VA, for what seems like a much longer time than it really is. If you're fishing the Shenandoah Valley area of Virginia, be sure to drop by Harry's for the latest advice and a friendly face. Harry is also a fly tyer with a number of flies that have proved to be more than just useful locally—such as the Mr. Rapidan. This is the Adams of Virginia dry fly patterns. The Mr. Rapidan as it was originally tied by Harry using calf tail for the wing is also

Hook:	Mustad 94840, TMC 100 #12-18
Thread:	Tan
Wing:	Yellow calftail or poly yarn upright and divided
Tail:	Stiff, dark moose or elk hair
Body:	A blend of fine dubbing (50% Quill Gordon, 50% March Brown)
Hackle:	One brown, one grizzly tied sparse

an example of what is known as a hairwing or Wulff-style fly—named after Lee Wulff. The basic technique for tying Wulff-type flies described below can also be used to create a number of other variations as well.

Tying Instructions

1 Start the thread just behind the eye of the hook, and wind it back to about $\frac{1}{3}$ hook shank length behind the eye. Then wind it forward to about $\frac{1}{16}$ inch to $\frac{1}{8}$ inch behind the eye.

2 Lash a clump of calf tail to the top of the hook at this point, measured so that it will be the height desired for the wing when upright. Tips pointing out over the eye of the hook, butts toward the bend.

3 Grasp the calf tail by its tips and pull it upright. Take a number of windings of thread around the shank of the hook at the base of the clump of calf tail to support it in this upright position.

4 Bring your thread through the middle of and behind the calf tail, dividing it into two sections. Take one turn of thread around the hook behind the calf tail. Then further divide and separate the two sections of calf tail by taking a modified figure eight loop around both of the sections. To do this the thread goes around the base of the far section two or three times and then back through the middle. Then it goes around the base of the near section two or three times and back through the middle, ending up behind the wing on the far side of the hook. This is similar to the method used with an upright divided wood duck flank wing, but with the addition of a couple of loops around each section of calf tail. The extra turns around the calf tail help keep this material separated and divided. Take another turn around the hook behind the wing to hold it all in place.

5 Trim the butts of the calf tail to form a taper toward the bend of the hook and lash this all in place by winding the thread to the bend of the hook.

6 Secure the tail in place with a couple of turns of thread and trim the butts.

7 Dub the body forward to just behind the wing, forming a tapered body.

8 (* See Glossary on Preparing Hackle) Tie in the hackle just in front of the wing with the tips facing backward. One at a time wind the hackle

around the hook, taking one turn behind the wing and then two turns in front securing and trimming each hackle as you are finished with it.

9 Whip finish just behind the eye of the hook.

Fishing the Fly

Wulff style flies with their calftail wing enjoy much better flotation than flies with many other styles of wing, such as the traditional or Catskill-style flies. These are excellent flies for fishing for trout in our mountain streams.

Other Wulff-Style Patterns

The Royal Wulff

Hook: Mustad 94840, TMC 100 #12-18
Thread: Black
Wing: White calf tail tied upright and divided
Tail: Brown calf tail fibers tied sparse
Body: A band of peacock herl wrapped just in front of the tail, followed by a wider band of red floss, followed by another band of peacock herl wrapped just behind the wing
Hackle: Brown hackle tied sparse

The March Brown Wulff

Hook: Mustad 94840, TMC 100 #12-18
Thread: Orange or brown
Wing: White or cream calf tail tied upright and divided
Tail: Ginger calf tail fibers tied sparse
Body: "March Brown" dry fly dubbing (tannish-brown with a hint of red)
Hackle: One ginger, one grizzly hackle tied sparse

The Sulphur Wulff

Hook: Mustad 94840, TMC 100 #12-18

Thread: Pale yellow
Wing: White or dun calf tail tied upright and divided
Tail: Pale yellow or cream calf tail fibers tied sparse
Body: Pale yellow to dirty orange dubbing
Hackle: Cream hackle tied sparse

The Blue Winged Olive Wulff (BWO)

Hook: Mustad 94840, TMC 100 #16-18
Thread: Olive
Wing: Dun calf tail tied upright and divided
Tail: Dun calf tail fibers tied sparse
Body: Olive, olive-brown, or olive-gray dubbing
Hackle: Medium to dark dun hackle tied sparse

The Humpy

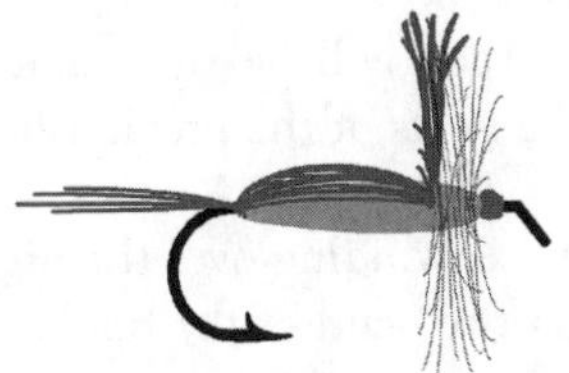

The Humpy is a great fast water pattern. It is almost impossible to sink and very easy to see. Unfortunately many people consider it a rather difficult fly to tie. The greatest problem seems to be in getting the proportions correct so that the wing comes out looking just right, rather than too long or too short. Be sure that you measure the length of the deer hair for the hump and the wing very carefully and then do your tie offs on these parts in just the right place and you will find that you can tie a quite good-looking Humpy. This fly has been attributed to Jack Horner and was originally called Horner's Deer Hair. I'm giving you the yellow version here, but it can be tied in almost any color that you would like. Yellow, olive, black and red seem to be the most popular colors.

Hook:	Mustad 94840, TMC 100 #12-18
Thread:	Yellow
Tail:	Fine deer, elk or moose hair in a light color
Body:	Fine deer or elk hair in light color pulled forward to form the hump and later wing
Under Body:	Yellow floss or fine yellow dubbing
Wing:	Tips of the hair used to form the hump
Hackle:	1 brown and 1 grizzly hackle

Tying Instructions

1 Tie in the tail, hook shank in length. The butts of the tail should be trimmed and lashed in at the center of the hook shank. Finish with your tying thread at the exact center of the hook shank.

2 Cut a clump of deer hair to form the body, hump and wing. For a #12 hook this should be about the diameter of a wooden kitchen match. Brush off the fuzz and stack in a hair stacker.
Align the clump of deer hair on top of the hook so that the tips of the stacked hair are exactly ½ hook shank length past the tips of the tail. Trim the butts so that they will be right at the center of the hook shank—aligned with the butts of the previously tied in tail.

3 Lash the deer hair in place, winding over the previously tied-in tail and finish with the thread at the bend of the hook.

4 Tie in a piece of yellow floss and then wind your thread back to just in front of the lashed-in deer hair body. You can also use dubbing here in place of floss if you prefer. Wind your floss forward to the thread, secure it in place and trim the excess floss. Be sure that your thread is just in front of the deer hair body and tail that you have tied down.

5 Grab the tips of the deer hair body extending back past the tail and bring them forward to form a hump over the top of the body that you have just formed with the floss or dubbing. Pulling the deer hair tightly forward, take several tight turns of thread to secure it in place.

6 Now bring the tips of the deer hair up to a vertical position and take several turns of thread in front of them to hold them in this upright position.

7 Bring the thread up and through the middle of the clump of deer hair to divide it in half. Go around the hook behind the hair wing and then take several figure eight turns and reverse figure eight turns around the two sections of the hair wings to form the two sections and hold them in place. Finish with the thread in front of the deer hair wing.

8 (* See Glossary on Preparing Hackle) Tie in the brown and grizzly hackles. Then take one turn behind the wing and two turns in front of it with each of them. Secure each in place as you finish the turns.

9 Whip finish.

Variations

As I indicated earlier, the Humpy can be tied with almost any color of floss that you would care to use. In addition to the yellow indicated above, orange and red are very effective Southeastern colors. If you'd like something a little more subdued, try olive, gray, or tan. The Humpy also works well if tied with a dubbing substituted for floss.

This pattern is usually tied with the commonly available acetate or rayon floss, but it becomes even more effective when it is tyed with silk floss which takes on more of a translucency when wet.

Some folks have also been experimenting with a simplified version of the Humpy that uses a closed cell foam hump in place of the deer hair. The tying procedure is modified thusly: Tie in a deer hair tail. Lash a small strip of closed cell foam tightly to the top of the hook with the excess hanging over the tail (about $^{1}/_{8}$" wide and $^{1}/_{16}$" thick for hooks #14-18 and a little larger for hooks #10-12). Apply the floss or dubbing body to about $^{2}/_{3}$ of the way forward on the hook. Bring the foam forward over the top of the body and secure it in place immediately in front of the body. Trim off the excess foam. Tie in one brown and one grizzly hackle by their butts just in front of the body. Wind the two hackles forward to just behind the eye of the hook one at a time. Secure each in place after they have been wound forward. Trim off the excess. Whip finish just behind the eye of the hook.

Fishing the Fly

The Humpy is another of those flies that it is almost impossible to sink. When dealing with the fast waters of a Southeastern mountain Trout stream, this is always a pattern to have handy. I've always found that the Yellow Humpy is the most effective color for our mountain Trout, but you might also want to have some other more subtle colors available as well if the fish start getting a little picky. Gray is a very good second choice. When the Smallies are hitting the surface I've also found that the Humpy works just as well on them as it does on Trout. It's not a bad panfish fly, either.

The Quill-Bodied Flies

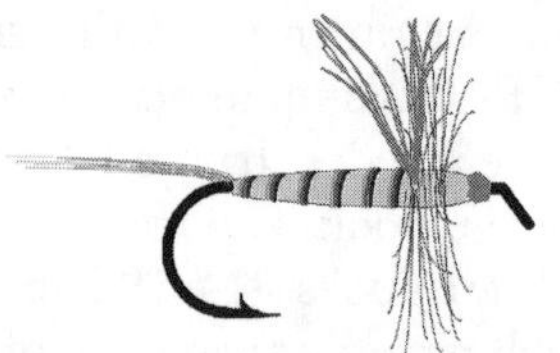

The Quill Gordon, the Red Quill and the Variants are flies popular in the Southeast that are tied in a very similar manner. The winging technique is the same on the Quill Gordon and Red Quill while the Variants use no wing. They use slightly different tailing and hackle as well as different quills to form the bodies. Preparing quills for tying can vary considerably. While they all use stripped quills as their body material, the quills are not the same and must be prepared in different ways. The Quill Gordon, for example, uses the stripped quill of the eye of peacock herl. The Red Quill uses the stripped quill of a reddish-brown hackle feather. To strip a hackle feather for the Red Quill or any of the Variants simply soak it in a 50% solution of clorox and water then rinse it off when the barbules have burnt away. Hackles are tougher feathers than peacock eye herl and this does not have to be a carefully watched technique. With the eye of peacock herl for the Quill Gordon, however, you are dealing with a much more delicate feather. If you use the clorox technique then it has to be watched very carefully or the clorox can dissolve the entire herl, quill and all. Many people prefer to strip the quill of the peacock herl by using a pencil eraser or just by running it carefully between the thumb and forefinger of one hand. Experiment until you find what technique works best for you. The tying instructions given below will apply equally well to either the Quill Gordon or the Red Quill. Simply omit the wing for the Variants and use a feather for the hackle that is 2-3 sizes larger than what is normal for that hook size.

Quill Gordon

Hook:	Mustad 94840, TMC 100 #12-16
Thread:	Gray
Wing:	Wood duck flank fibers tied upright and divided
Tail:	Dun hackle fibers
Body:	Stripped eye of peacock herl
Hackle:	Dun hackle

Red Quill

Hook:	Mustad 94840, TMC 100 #12-16
Thread:	Gray
Wing:	Wood duck flank fibers tied upright and divided
Tail:	Reddish-brown hackle fibers
Body:	Stripped quill of reddish-brown hackle feather
Hackle:	Reddish-brown hackle

Tying Instructions

1 Start the thread just behind the eye of the hook and wind it back to about $1/3$ hook shank length behind the eye. Then wind it forward to about $1/16$ inch to $1/8$ inch behind the eye.

2 Lash a clump of wood duck flank to the top of the hook at this point, measured so that it will be the height desired for the wing when upright. Tips pointing out over the eye of the hook, butts toward the bend.

3 Grasp the fibers by their tips and pull them upright. Take a number of windings of thread around the hook shank at the base of the clump to support it in this upright position.

4 Bring your thread through the middle of and behind the clump dividing it into two sections. Take one turn of thread around the hook behind the fibers. Then further divide and separate the two sections of fibers by taking a modified figure eight loop around both of the sections. To do this the thread goes around the base of the far section and then back through the middle. Then it goes around the base of the near section and back through the middle, ending up behind the wing on the far side

of the hook. Take another turn around the hook behind the wing to hold it all in place.

5 Trim the butts of the wood duck to form a taper toward the bend of the hook and lash this all in place by winding the thread to the bend of the hook.

6 Secure the tail in place with a couple of turns of thread and trim the butts. Use your thread to form a tapered underbody between the tail and the wing. Finish with your thread just above the base of the tail.

7 Secure the narrow end of the quill in place just above the tail and then wind your thread forward to just behind the wing. Wrap the quill forward to the thread and then take a couple of turns to secure the forward end of it in place and trim off any excess.

8 (* See Glossary on Preparing Hackle) Tie in the hackle just in front of the wing with the tips facing backward. Wind the hackle around the hook taking one turn behind the wing and then two turns in front securing and trimming it as you are finished.

9 Whip finish just behind the eye of the hook.

Fishing the Fly

The mountain Trout streams of the Southeast are where the insects that the Quill Flies imitate exist and, for the most part, these are the streams where these flies are at their best as well. For the same reason, Spring is the time of the year when these flies are usually their most productive. The Quill Gordon and Red Quill are most easily fished in the pools and tailouts of mountain streams, while the Variants can be highly effective in the faster stretches.

The Variants

The three following patterns are all quill-bodied flies that employ oversize hackle and no wing to create what Art Flick, the originator of these patterns, referred to as a "Variant." You can follow the previous tying instructions, just omit the steps dealing with the wing.

Dun Variant

Hook: Mustad 94840, TMC 100 #12-16
Thread: Olive

Wing: None
Tail: Dark dun hackle fibers
Body: Stripped quill of a brown hackle feather
Hackle: Dark dun (use hackle 2-3 sizes larger than the hook. e.g., for a #16 hook you would use a #10-12 size hackle)

Cream Variant

Hook: Mustad 94840, TMC 100 #14-16
Thread: Cream
Wing: None
Tail: Dark cream hackle fibers
Body: Stripped quill of a dark cream hackle feather
Hackle: Dark cream (use hackle 2-3 sizes larger than the hook. e.g., for a #16 hook you would use a #10-12 size hackle)

Gray Fox Variant

Hook: Mustad 94840, TMC 100 #12-16
Thread: Yellow
Wing: None
Tail: Golden ginger hackle fibers
Body: Stripped quill of a dark cream hackle feather
Hackle: Golden ginger, dark ginger and grizzly mixed (use hackle 2-3 sizes larger than the hook. e.g., for a #16 hook you would use a #10-12 size hackle)

The Quill-Winged Flies

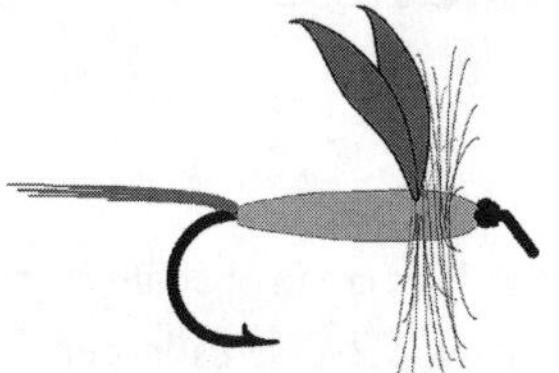

The last group of flies together with this group point out one of the unfortunate areas of terminology in fly tying similar to the English language in general where the use of the same word with two different meanings can be a basis for confusion. Quill has several meanings to the fly tyer. In the last group of flies it referred to the center section of a feather that had been stripped of all of its barbules. Here it is used to refer to a primary or flight feather from which sections of barbules are taken to create the wing of a fly. Forming the wings of flies from sections of barbules cut from the quill or primary flight feather of Mallards and other water birds is a practice that dates back in fly tying to some of the first wet flies ever recorded. It is not as common among contemporary dry flies to see such wings being used. There are, however, a number of lovely old dries: the Blue Dun, the Blue Quill and the Royal Coachman that use such a wing and are useful in the Southeast, particularly when certain insects such as the Blue Quill are hatching or in the case of the Royal Coachman as an all-around attractor pattern. Setting these wings is not the easiest task facing a fly tyer which may also explain why such flies have diminished in popularity over the years. The Blue Quill uses a body formed from stripped peacock herl. Please refer to the previous section on Quill-Bodied Flies for details on stripping peacock herl and using that stripped herl for forming the body of the fly. The tying instructions below are for the Blue Dun. Winging the Blue Quill is identical in procedure to that for the Blue Dun. The body of the Royal Coachman is formed by first tying in a band of peacock herl just in front of the tail, then tying in a band of floss, and then another band of peacock herl just behind the wing.

The Blue Dun

Hook: Mustad 94840, TMC 100 #12-18
Thread: Gray
Wing: Mallard wing quill sections
Tail: Medium blue dun hackle fibers
Body: Muskrat dubbing
Hackle: Medium blue dun

The Blue Quill

Hook: Mustad 94840, TMC 100 #12-18
Thread: Gray
Wing: Mallard wing quill sections
Tail: Medium blue dun hackle fibers
Body: Stripped peacock herl
Hackle: Medium blue dun

The Royal Coachman

Hook: Mustad 94840, TMC 100 #10-18
Thread: Black
Wing: White duck wing quill sections
Tail: Golden pheasant tippet fibers
Body: Two bands of peacock herl, divided by a wider band of red floss
Hackle: Brown to dark brown

Tying Instructions

1 Start the thread right behind the eye of the hook and wrap the thread to a point approximately $^1/_3$ of the way back toward the bend.

2 Prepare the Mallard quill wing sections for use.

a. Begin with a matched pair of Mallard wing quills or primary flight feathers. You will be cutting a section of barbules from each feather that match, creating a right and a left wing that are a mirror image of one another. Before you do this though, take a good look at the pair of feathers. First you should notice that the inside of the feather is lighter in color than the outside. This is the same way that your wing sections should line up with the inside of the feather on the inside and the outside of the feather on the outside. The next thing to notice is that a short distance away from the center shaft of the feather there is a line running parallel to the shaft. This line marks a point where each individual barbule changes from a hard texture closer to the shaft to a softer texture farther away from the shaft. You always want to cut a quill section that is long enough so that when you bring the thread across the pair of sections to attach the wing it will be coming across the softer part of the barbules.

b. Cut a section of barbules from the left wing quill that is approximately 1/4" wide for a #16 hook. Cut a section smaller or larger for smaller or larger hooks. Cut another section the same size from the same part of the right wing quill. You now have a matched pair of quill wings.

c. Place the left quill section on the tip of your index finger with the inside facing up and the tips extending out from the tip of your finger. Using a pair of tweezers, place the right quill section on top of the left quill section being careful to align them with one another.

d. Now grasp both quill sections together with your thumb and index finger. Lay the pair of quill sections along the top of the hook with the tips extending forward over the top of the eye. Line up the quill sections with the thread that you have positioned on the hook so that the length extending forward from the thread is approximately twice the hook gap width. Take two turns of thread over the top of the quill sections and around the bottom of the hook.

e. Next take several turns of thread in front of the quill sections to force them into an upright position. It will help if you hold the sections in this position while you are taking the turns of thread.

f. Then take the thread behind where the wing sections are attached and take a turn of thread around the shank of the hook without going around the quill sections. Bring the thread between the two wing sections from back to front and take one turn of thread around the hook in front of the wing. Bring the thread between the two wing sections from front to back and then take one turn of thread around the hook shank only behind the wing. You should now have a pair of wings that have been formed from the two matched quill sections and are upright and divided from one another.

g. Cut off the butts of the wing sections at the bend of the hook.

3 Wind your thread from just behind the wing to the bend of the hook, securing the butt sections of the wing down and forming a tapered underbody.

4 Attach a clump of hackle fibers to form the tail of the fly.

5 Dub a tapered body forward to right behind the wing of the fly.

6 Take a turn of thread in front of the wing. (* See Glossary on Preparing Hackle) Attach the butt of the hackle feather in front of the wing with a couple of wraps of thread. Then take a wrap of thread over the hackle feather behind the wing and wind your thread forward to just behind the eye of the hook.

7 Wind one turn of the hackle feather behind the wing and two to four turns in front of the wing, finishing with the feather just behind the thread. Take two turns of thread over the top of the hackle feather to hold it in place and trim off the excess feather.

8 Whip finish.

Fishing the Fly

Quill-winged flies can be used in a variety of ways for fishing the mountain Trout streams of the Southeast, but they all share one peculiarity in common. Because of the way that their wings are formed from Mallard wing feathers, they simply will not float as long or as well as some of the other dry flies in this section of the book, such as Wulff-style flies or Parachutes. This does not mean, however, that as soon as the wing has gotten soaked and the fly begins to sink that you need to stop fishing with it. On the contrary, this is the time to remember that there are many other ways to catch fish rather than just with dry flies. A soaked quill-winged fly makes an excellent wet fly and can be fished that way just as long as you would like. A highly productive tactic for fishing these flies is to fish a stretch of mountain stream with them first as a dry and then cover the same water fishing the same fly as a wet. You will be amazed how many fish you missed the first time through that you will turn up on the second.

The American Express

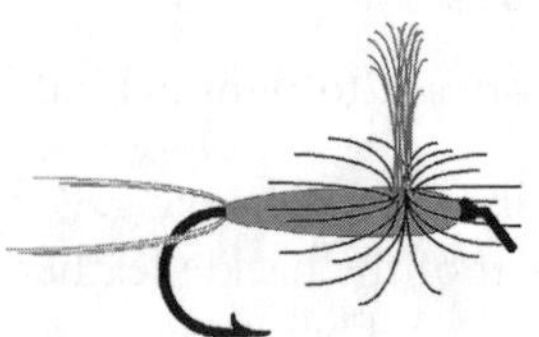

This pattern originated with Wayne Clodfelter of North Carolina. Wayne is editor of *TroutNC,* both in print and on the Internet. If you want to know what is happening with trout fishing in North Carolina, try subscribing to Wayne's *TroutNC.* Wayne is also a fine fly fisher, fly tyer and the only man I know who wades Alaska wet. The pattern and tying instructions below are Wayne's and reprinted with his permission.

Hook:	Tiemco 9230 or 900BL, size 14 or 12
Thread:	Uni-thread, 6/0, Tan
Wing:	Polypropylene yarn, Tan, posted for parachute hackle
Tail:	Brown hackle fibers, tied split
Body:	Spectrablend dubbing, medium Tan
Hackle:	Brown rooster neck, oversized, tied parachute style

Tying Instructions

Place hook in vise. Start thread about 10% behind eye and wrap tightly to approximately 40% position (this lays a thread base for tying in the wing). Cut poly yarn approximately to length, and divide strands with dubbing needle in half or thirds (depending on thickness of strands) to achieve proportional density. Extend poly yarn over eye of hook and tie it at 30% position. Post wing by wrapping thread horizontally around base of the wing up to a distance of approximately 1 inch.

Wrap thread back to bend of hook and wrap a very small ball of dubbing around hook to aid in splitting tail fibers. Select 8 to 10 hackle fibers for tail and hold in position, so that tail extends beyond bend of hook approximately the length of the hook shank. Take two or three wraps around tail fibers in front of ball of yarn. Apply pressure with finger on top of wraps and divide tail fibers in half with other hand. Position near-side half of tail fibers and take two or three tight turns of thread to secure tail in position. Repeat for far-side half of tail.

Twist dubbing onto thread and wrap forward to eye of hook and back to front of wing, forming a slightly full (rather than thin) tapered body.

Select a rooster neck hackle with hackle fibers roughly the same length as the hook shank. Tie in, shiny side up, and wrap parachute style around base of wing. Be sure to make succeeding wraps under previous wraps. Tie off hackle. Wrap thread forward to eye of hook, forming thread head, whip finish and clip thread.

With scissors, clip wing to height approximately equal to, or slightly less than body length. I make two cuts, the one in front angling upwards at about 20 degrees, and another overlapping cut angling downward toward the rear at the same angle. This gives the wing a slightly angular, or rounded, silhouette.

Note: After hackle is tied in, and just before wrapping hackle, I usually apply some head cement to the posted base of the hackle. This may be considered poor technique, but I find that it helps to keep the parachute hackle from climbing up the wing after catching numerous trout. Another method is to apply a spot of cement to the posted wing just where it protrudes from the hackle after the fly is completed.

Fishing the Fly

This fly is Wayne Clodfelter's version of the Parachute and, as such, can be used wherever a Parachute fly might be used. Great for tailwaters and spring creeks, it also is useful in mountain streams as well. The poly post wing makes this fly an excellent floater that keeps it going in rougher water. The realistic silhouette helps with the pickier Trout. Wayne's color combinations seem to strike some kind of a chord with Southeastern trout as well, because this fly is a consistent producer.

Other Color Combinations

Hackle/Tail	Body	Wing
Brown	Med. Tan	Yellow
Brown	Med. Tan	Sparkle Wing
White or Lemon	White or Lemon	Cream
Brown	Orange	Tan
Ginger	Pale Yellow	Cream
Ginger	Med. Tan	Tan
Cream	Pale Yellow	Cream
Cream	Fluor. Green	Cream

Note: Change thread color to match body color

The Green Drake (Parachute-Extended Body)

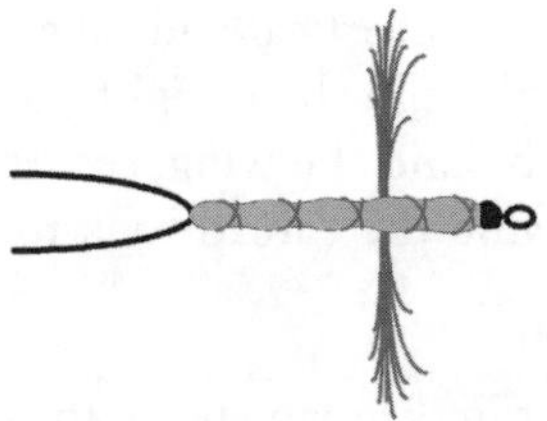

While the Green Drakes down in the Southeast don't get as big as some of the ones up in the Northeast, we still get them down here as well. Like elsewhere they are a very seasonal hatch that you will be lucky to find, but also like elsewhere they can be a great experience when these large mayflies are coming off. This particular pattern I developed while I was fishing Tim Pond up in Maine, but it works just as well for the Southeast. Having never fished a Green Drake hatch before I had tied up what I thought were some pretty darn big flies (#6–8), but when I saw the size of the ones on Tim Pond I found that the flies I had tied were just too small. So I developed

Hook:	Mustad 94840, TMC 100 #4-12
Thread:	Olive
Wing:	Yellow poly yarn
Body:	Olive dyed deer hair tyed in forward and pulled back, overwrapped and trimmed
Tail:	2-3 of the Olive deer hair tied long
Hackle:	Grizzly dyed yellow

this extended body pattern since the largest hook that I had with me was a #6 and the flies were about a #0. When the Green Drakes are coming off in the Southeast, they can produce some of the largest Brown Trout catches around. I've taken a 29½" Brown with this pattern on a Virginia spring creek.

Tying Instructions

1. Start the thread just behind the eye of the hook and wrap the hook all the way to the bend and then back to ⅓ hook length behind the eye.

2. Tie on a clump of Poly Yarn about 1" long with several turns of thread. The base of the clump should be pointing toward the back of the fly and the tips of the clump should be extended well over the eye of the hook. Then pick it up so that it is vertical and take several wraps of thread right in front of it to hold it in the upright position. Trim the base of the clump into a taper behind the wing, secure the taper to the hook with thread and then wind the thread back to just behind the eye of the hook.

3. Cut a clump of deer hair in the diameter of the body desired. For a #12 hook this would usually be about twice the diameter of a wooden match. Brush the fuzz from the hair and stack it in a hair stacker. Align the stacked hair with the top of the hook so that the tips would be in the position of the ends of the tail. Trim the butts of the hair so that they will fall just behind the eye of the hook.

4. Lay the clump of hair flat on top of the hook. Hold it by the butts and position it so that half of the clump flares to one side of the wing and half to the other. The idea is to have the wing coming up out of the center of the clump of hair that forms the body. Secure the butts of the clump of hair to the hook just behind the eye with a couple of wraps of thread.

5. Start lashing the hair to the hook by working the thread back to the bend in an open spiral. When you get to the bend of the hook, grasp the tips of the hair clump and work the thread off of the hook and around the hair in an open spiral until you get to where you want the extended body to end and the tail to begin. Take a couple of wraps of thread around the hair at this point and work your way back to the hook wrapping in the opposite direction from what you wound on the way out. Note that there will still be a length of hair sticking out from the end of the extended body. Most of these hairs will be trimmed away leaving 2-3 hairs to form the tail of the fly.

6 When you get back to the hook with the thread continue the wrapping process until you reach a point on the body of the fly just in front of the wing.

7 (* See Glossary on Preparing Hackle) Tie in a piece of hackle and lash it to the body by its butt with a couple of wraps of thread.

8 Take the hackle and wrap it a couple of times around the post wing to form the parachute hackle and then tie off the end to the body and trim off the excess. Wind the thread to just behind the eye of the hook and whip finish.

9 Trim off most of the hair sticking out of the back of the body leaving only two to three hairs to form the tail of the fly. Trim the post wing sticking out of the top of the body to the height desired.

10 Use some head cement to glue the hair together where the tail protrudes from the extended body and a bit more just behind the whip finish.

Variations

Green drakes vary quite considerably in color from one location to another. You can use a variety of colors of deer hair, poly yarn posts and hackle to better match your particular coloration. Colors can vary from olive to bright green to yellow.

The spinner of this fly (often known as a Coffin Fly) is usually white or cream. To imitate the spinner version use white deer hair, dun poly yarn, and grizzly hackle along with a couple of moose hairs to form the black tail. You can also tie a downwing version of the Coffin Fly by tying a single piece of poly yarn across the body to imitate the spent wing and use no hackle. This, incidentally, was the version of this fly that took the aforementioned huge Brown.

Fishing the Fly

The Green Drake is one of those flies that you may never use more than once or twice in your life, but then when you do need it, you are awfully glad that it's in your fly box. This fly has one purpose, and that is to give you an imitation of the insect for those times when you actually find yourself in the middle of a Green Drake hatch.

The Thorax Fly

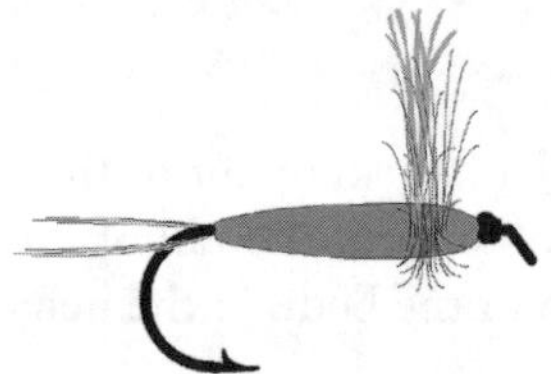

This is another of Wayne Clodfelter's patterns from *TroutNC.* Based on the thorax flies of Dr. Edgar Burke and Vince Marinaro, this is an updated version in the materials and colors that Wayne uses for his American Express pattern also featured here. Once again the tying instructions are Wayne's.

Hook:	Tiemco 5230 size 14 or 16
Thread:	Uni-Thread, 6/0, waxed, Tan
Wing:	Polypropylene yarn, Tan, posted
Tail:	Brown hackle fibers, tied split
Body:	Spectrablend dubbing (Orvis), Medium Tan
Hackle:	Brown rooster neck

Tying Instructions

Place hook in vise. Start thread about 10% behind eye and wrap tightly to approximately 45% position (this lays a thread base for tying in the wing). Cut poly yarn slightly longer than hook shank, and divide strands with dubbing needle in half or thirds (depending on thickness of the strand) to achieve desired density. Extend poly yarn over eye of hook and tie it at 40% position.

Post wing by wrapping thread a few times horizontally around the base of the poly yarn.

Wrap thread back to bend of hook and wrap a very small ball of dubbing around hook to aid in splitting tail fibers. Select 6 to 10 hackle fibers for tail and hold in position so that tail extends beyond bend of hook approximately the length of the hook shank. Take two or three wraps around tail fibers in front of ball of dubbing. Apply pressure with finger on top of wraps holding tail fibers. This pressure will separate the fibers to the left and right of the small ball of dubbing. Use other hand to help position both sides of split tail while moving the finger pressing on the wraps slightly to force more fibers to left or right to evenly divide tail fibers. Position near-side half of tail fibers and take two or three tight turns of thread to secure tail in position. Repeat for far-side half of tail.

Twist dubbing onto thread and wrap forward almost to eye of hook and back to front of wing, forming a thin body. Wrap thread back behind wing roughly to 50% position for tying in hackle. Select a rooster neck hackle with hackle fibers roughly one and one-half times the width of the hook bend. Tie in by the butt, shiny side forward, at approximately the 50% position. Wrap thread forward to 10% position. Wrap hackle forward, past wing, to 10% position and tie off. Wrap thread forward of dubbing and form small thread head and tie off with whip finish. Clip thread (I do not use head cement with whip finish).

With scissors, clip wing to height approximately equal to, or slightly less than body length. I make two cuts, the one in front angling up to the middle of the wing post, and an overlapping cut angling downward. This gives a slightly angular or rounded appearance to the wing from the side. Finish the fly by clipping a 60-degree wedge out of the bottom of the hackle. This facilitates the fly riding lower in the surface film. This feature is enhanced by dressing the fly with floatant (I use Gehrke's Gink) and stroking downward-angled hackle fibers up to the 180-degree position.

Fishing the Fly

Wayne's Thorax Fly is another of those flies designed for slower waters, still water, and picky trout. This fly presents a highly realistic silhouette to the fish and can really help out when they are being fanatically careful about what they are taking. It is not, however, a fly that floats well in fast mountain streams.

The Black Fly

In the early spring on many Southeastern tailwaters you get a massive hatch of what are referred to locally as "black flies." While similar in appearance, these luckily for us do not seem to share their Yankee cousins' thirst for human blood. These hatches are most commonly fished with a midge pupa imitation or a Chironomid, however, if you'd like to try using a dry fly the following pattern is simple to tie and works just fine. A small black EHC will also do the job.

Hook:	Mustad 98459, TMC 100 #18-20
Thread:	Black, 8/0 to 12/0
Body:	Black poly or antron dubbing
Wing:	Gray poly yarn tied in like an EHC or Trude wing

Tying Instructions

1. Start the thread at the bend of the hook.
2. Dub the body forward in a cylinder-like shape.

3 Tie in a tuft of gray poly yarn just behind the eye of the hook in a wing like that of an EHC or Trude.

4 Whip finish.

Fishing the Fly

The Black Fly is another of those flies for a limited time of year. The Black Fly hatch in the Southeast only occurs in some areas and only at certain times. The rest of the time this fly doesn't do you a whole lot of good. But, when you are in the middle of a Black Fly hatch, this fly can be deadly. Black Fly hatches can be extremely heavy and trigger very selective feeding on the part of the Trout. When you run into that, this is a very handy fly to have.

The Trico (Dun and Spinner)

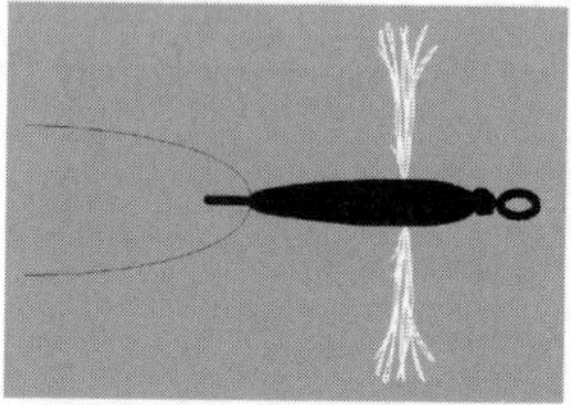

The Trico is not a fly that is widely distributed throughout the Southeast, but there are enough pockets around to make it worth having some of these when you do encounter a hatch. For the small fly addict Tricos can be very exciting. Fishing these tiny flies is both frustrating and habit forming. They usually require very delicate presentations, careful attention to matching size, noticing whether the fish are going for the duns or the spinners, and a lot of luck as well.

Tying Instructions

1 Start the thread just behind the eye of the hook and wind it to the bend.

2 Lay in one of the microfibbets at about a 45-degree angle to the hook and take a turn over the top of it. Pull on the butt or tip of the microfibbet to adjust the length to about 1½ times shank length.

3 Lay the second microfibbet at about a 45-degree angle to the hook but on the opposite side from the first and take a turn of thread over the top of it. Pull on the butt or tip of the microfibbet to adjust the length to about 1½ times shank length. (See the tying instructions under the Parachute for more details on this tailing technique.)

Dun

Hook: Mustad 98459, TMC 100 #22-24
Thread: Black, 8/0 to 12/0
Tail: 2 black microfibbets tied forked
Wing: Upright tuft of gray poly yarn
Body: Black

Spinner

Hook: Mustad 98459, TMC 100 #22-24
Thread: Black, 8/0 to 12/0
Tail: 2 black microfibbets tied forked
Wing: 2 tufts of white poly yarn tied spent
Body: Black

4 Take a couple more turns of thread up the hook shank to secure the microfibbets in place and trim off the excess butts. Wind the thread up to a point about $1/3$ of the hook shank behind the eye.

5 Tie in the poly yarn for the wing, either one piece upright for the dun or two pieces to the sides for the spinner. Secure each tuft in place with several turns of thread with the tuft falling forward over the eye or to the sides of the eye. Then take several turns of thread in front of the tuft(s) to force it upright or out to the sides of the body. Trim the butts of the tuft(s) into a taper and then return the thread to just above the tail.

6 Dub the body of the fly all the way to just behind the eye of the hook and then whip finish. Work the thread carefully around the wing(s) to further support the position of the wing(s). Trim the wing(s) to the length desired.

Fishing the Fly

The Trico is another fly with a limited distribution throughout the Southeast, but absolutely essential when you run into a hatch. If you think that you might encounter Tricos, I strongly recommend that you have both duns and spinners tied up and ready. Our Southeast Trout can get very picky when they're feeding on Tricos and may turn up their noses at either one or the other.

The Poly Wing Midge

After the last terrestrial has scurried away to hide for the winter and before the first of the spring hatches, the dry fly addict has very few options available except for the frustrating but reliable midge. Even in the dead of winter a sunny day will often bring out swarms of these tiny little beasts along with trout dappling the surface after them. When it comes to dealing with the #20 and smaller hooks that midge patterns are tied on, however, many fly tyers shy away. Those tiny little hooks can be daunting if you haven't tied on them before, but here are a few tips that may help you get started along with an easily tied pattern and some variations on it.

Midge Tips

Start with one of the larger hooks such as #20 rather than jumping right in to something like an almost invisible #26. Begin with a simple pattern that is easy to tie. Be sure that you have a very good light and if possible a magnifier. There are a number of light/magnifier combinations specifically designed for fly tying available, but if you can't swing the price then drop by your local office supply store and check around. There are usually a couple of styles of light/magnifier combinations available at much more reasonable prices. A magnifier with a built-in fluorescent light will usually run you around \$60-70 and with a little bit of searching you can find a magnifier with a built-in incandescent light for somewhere in the \$15-30 range. All of this will help if you haven't tackled one of those little bitty hooks before. Remember too that tying midges is much like tying larger flies. At first it seems difficult, but with practice it all gets easier.

To help you along, here is a midge pattern and a number of variations on it that are easy to tie and for those of you like myself whose vision isn't what it used to be, easier to see on the water as well. It employs techniques with which many of you are already familiar on larger flies and even if the first few ties aren't as pretty as you might want, it will still catch fish. I call it The Poly Wing Midge.

Hook:	Dry fly hook #20-26 (for those of you who have trouble attaching these to your tippet you might want to try one of the "big-eye" hooks)
Thread:	Black 8/0 to 12/0 (you need a good quality fine, but still strong thread)
Body:	Stripped herl from the eye of a peacock tail feather
Wing:	Poly Yarn—available wound on cards at your local fly shop in a variety of colors—white, yellow, gray, black, etc.

Tying Instructions

1 Start thread just behind the eye of the hook and wrap about 1/3 of the way toward the bend.

2 Take a herl from the eye of a peacock tail feather and using a pencil eraser carefully strip it almost to the quill. Leave just a little of the fibers on the quill. This is an easy technique that was first shown to me by Rick Murphree. Just "erase" the fibers off of the quill on a hard, flat surface. You will end up with a quill that has no fibers on one edge and just a few on the other. The fiberless edge will be lighter in color and the edge with a few fibers will be darker in color. When wound around the hook as a body this will give you a nicely striped and "segmented" looking body.

3 Place the quill alongside the hook shank with most of the quill sticking out behind the hook. Wind the thread the remainder of the way to the bend of the hook, securing the quill to the side of the hook as you go. Note that the edge of the quill w/o fibers and lighter in color should be facing up. Also note that as you erase the fibers off of the quill there will be a portion of it that is very thin and weak and should be clipped off. It may take a try or two until you can determine the portion of the quill that is strong enough to use.

4 Wrap the thread back to just behind the eye of the hook and let it hang.

5 Wrap the quill in a tight spiral forward to the thread. It may help to grasp the end of the quill with a pair of hackle pliers as you wrap. Note that the side of the quill w/o the fibers and lighter in color should be facing forward as you wrap. This will create the striped "segmented" body with the few remaining fibers sticking out from the sides of the hook.

6 Take a couple of turns of thread to secure the quill in place just behind the eye of the hook and clip off the excess quill. Often there is enough left over to make a second body.

7 Wrap the thread slightly back from the eye of the hook—usually about ⅛ hook shank length.

8 Take an appropriate sized group of Poly Yarn fibers for the wing about ½" long. Depending upon the size of the hook this will be a group of fibers from ¼ to 1/16 of the thickness of the Poly Yarn strand.

9 Lay this along the top of the hook with just a little bit sticking out over the eye of the hook and with most of the length running along the top of the hook and extending out the back. Secure it in place with a couple of wraps of thread. Note that the wing of the P.Y. Midge is applied in much the same manner as the wing of an EHC. Trim the front yarn close to the thread.

10 Whip finish and trim off the excess thread.

11 Trim the back of the P.Y. wing to desired length—usually about hook length.

Body Variations

1 Use colored thread for the body with clear Nylon Thread or mono wrapped in one layer over it.

a. Start thread just behind the eye of the hook.

b. Lay a piece of clear Nylon Thread or mono on top of the hook and wrap the colored thread over it and the hook all the way to the bend.

c. Trim Nylon Thread or mono sticking out the front of the hook.

d. Wrap colored thread back to just behind the eye of the hook.

e. Wrap Nylon Thread or mono forward to the colored thread.

f. Take a couple of turns of colored thread to secure the Nylon or mono in place.

g. Trim off the excess Nylon Thread or mono.

h. Attach the wing and finish the fly.

i. Note that clear Nylon Thread is available prewound on spools and can be used with a bobbin just like regular thread, making the whole process a little easier than working with just a piece of monofilament.

2 Use colored thread for the body with a little bit of dubbing and clear Nylon Thread or mono spiraled forward as ribbing.

a. Start thread just behind the eye of the hook.

b. Lay a piece of clear Nylon Thread or mono on top of the hook and wrap the colored thread over it and the hook all the way to the bend.

c. Trim Nylon Thread or mono sticking out the front of the hook.

d. Apply a little bit of dubbing to the thread and wrap forward to just behind the eye of the hook.

e. Spiral the Nylon or mono forward to just behind the hook eye as ribbing.

f. Take a couple of turns of colored thread over the Nylon Thread or mono to secure it in place.

g. Trim off the excess Nylon Thread or mono.

h. Attach wing and finish fly.

i. Note that it doesn't take much dubbing with this method. You do not want a fat Caddis-like body, but just a little bit of fuzz sticking out between the ribbing. An artificial dubbing such as Scintilla works well for this. The color of the thread and the dubbing can be used to imitate whatever color midge you desire: olive, gray, tan, black, etc.

3 Use colored thread for the body with a bit of clear or colored plastic tubing such as Larva Lace slipped over the top. The thread is then wound

back from the bend of the hook over the top of the thread as ribbing and the wing is attached as usual.

This basic winging technique and the variations on the body technique will allow you to easily imitate many different types of midges. The wing is easy to tie and can be done using a variety of colors. White or yellow wings for those of us who have trouble seeing the fly and gray, brown or black wings for those who demand a more realistic look. The variations on the body technique can also provide different colors for different situations and flies that will ride higher or lower in the water. The Nylon Thread or mono wrapped over colored thread will give you a colored body that will ride lower in the film, while the dubbing technique will give you a body that will ride high on top.

Fishing the Fly

Midges are so ubiquitous throughout the Southeast year-round that this is a fly the fly fisher should always have handy. It is absolutely essential, however, in the late fall, winter and early spring. Fishing for midges on the surface can be an extremely tricky proposition, however. Midge fishing is some of the trickiest and most delicate fishing around. One of the nice things about this pattern is that it can easily be adapted to the specific midges that you will encounter. Pay attention to how the midges are sitting in the water and which ones the fish are taking. Applying your floatant judiciously will also help determine just how high your fly will sit. Floatant applied just to the wing will keep the body sitting lower in the water, while floatant applied to the body as well as the wing will make it ride higher.

The Quigley Emerger

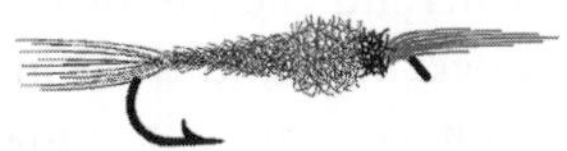

On a recent trip up to Vermont I got a lot of great help from Keith Blake at Fly Tier's Heaven in Essex Junction. If you're ever in that part of Vermont and looking for some good advice about where to fish and what to use be sure and drop by. One of the interesting items that I picked up there was the following pattern. It is an emerger that is tied with deer or elk hair for a "wing" that is not upright, but flares out over the eye of the hook sort of like a flat comparadun. The tail, abdomen and thorax of the fly are formed from a few strands of marabou which stick down into the water and make for enticing movement. Then just below the "wing" is a couple of wraps

Hook:	Tiemco 5262 (2X Nymph) or equivalent, # 10-20
Thread:	Black
Wing:	Elk or deer hair tied in as a flared clump (a lá Comparadun), but with the tips sticking out over the eye of the hook rather than standing upright
Tail, Abdomen and Thorax:	A few strands of Marabou tied in as a short tail and then wound up the hook to form the body
Collar:	A couple of wraps of Peacock Herl to form a collar just above the body and below the "wing"

of peacock herl. When properly tied and fished the "wing" sticks up above the surface of the water and the body and tail hangs down into it creating an emerger pattern that is easier to see than many others. A simple idea for an emerger pattern, but very effective.

This is an emerger pattern that I have found to be extremely useful on Southeastern tailwaters during a heavy hatch. When the fish are being highly selective about what they are slurping in out of the hatch the little bit of movement imparted by the marabou can sometimes be just the trigger that is needed to induce a strike.

Tying Instructions

1. Start the thread just behind the eye of the hook. Then take a small clump of elk or fine deer hair and tie it in with the tips sticking out over the eye of the hook. As you tie it in make it flare as you would for a comparadun wing.

2. Trim the butts of the hair so that it can form a tapered body from the wing to the bend of the hook and then wrap the butts with thread all the way down to the hook bend.

3. Take a few strands of Marabou in the color desired and tie the tips in as short tail ($1\frac{1}{2}$ times gap width). Wrap the thread up to just behind the wing leaving the butts hanging free.

4. Grasp the butts of the Marabou and wrap them up the hook to the thread forming the abdomen and thorax. Secure them in place with the thread and cut off the excess butts.

5. Tie in a strand of Peacock Herl just behind the wing and take a couple of wraps with it forming a collar just above the body and behind the wing.

6. Tie off the Peacock Herl and trim off the excess.

7. Whip finish.

Variations

Use different colored Marabou for different flies. Yellow or orange works well for a Sulphur hatch, olive for a BWO hatch, etc.

Use Krystal Flash or metallic threads as ribbing on the body.

Fishing the Fly

This fly is fished as you would a dry fly with a nice drag-free drift. If you are using floatant be careful that you just apply it to the hair and do not get any on the Marabou. The idea of the fly is that the hair will stick up above the surface (so you can see where the fly is) and the marabou tail will be below the surface wiggling and enticing the fish. In fishing the fly it may actually help to wet the tail and body of the fly before you cast the first time in order to achieve the proper presentation.

The Klinkhammer Special

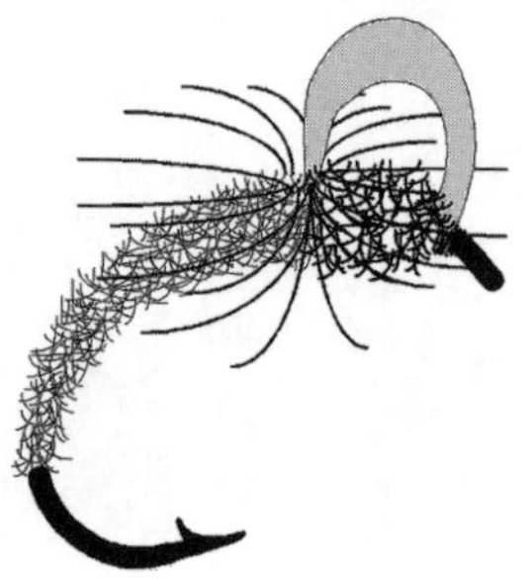

Since first being devised some twenty years or so ago by Hans van Klinken the Klinkhammer Special has been recognized in Europe as one of the premier emerger patterns for trout and grayling. While it isn't as well known in the United States, the variation given here has proven to be an extremely effective fly for both warm water and cold water fish in the Southeast. It was originally tied on the Partridge K12ST hook, but that is a hook that can be difficult to find in many parts of the United States, though now there are some equivalents by other manufacturers. David Allerton's version given here adapts it to the more readily available Mustad 94840 hook, utilizes colors that work well in the Southeast and employs foam for better flotation and visibility. You'll find both versions below and I encourage you to adapt the colors and materials to your own preferences for your particular area. For whatever variation that you would like to try, it is important to remember that the fundamental of the fly is that the abdomen of the fly float underneath the surface of the water to attract the fish and improve hookups while the parachute hackle and foam or wing be on or above the surface of the water for visibility and floatation. Keep that in mind in tying and fishing the fly and you can't go far wrong.

The Klinkhammer Special (Southeast Version)

Hook: Mustad 94840 #10-18 with the front end bent downwards slightly and the gap opened a bit to accomodate the bend.

Thread: Black or olive

Rib: (Optional) Gold wire

Abdomen: Olive hare's ear dubbing

Foam Hump or Covert: Yellow or white flat foam cut into a strip ⅛" wide.

Hackle: Yellow dyed grizzly wrapped as a parachute around the foam tie in point between the abdomen and thorax

Thorax: Olive hare's ear dubbing mixed with yellow hare's ear dubbing and/or antron dubbing. This should be a very coarse dubbing and in the larger versions may need to be applied with a dubbing loop

Tying Instructions

1 The first part of tying this fly is preparing the hook. Take a Mustad 94840 hook and bend the front end slightly downward at a point about ¼ shank length behind the eye of the hook. On larger hooks you don't need to position the bend point as far backwards as you do on smaller hooks. Then open the gap of the hook slightly so that you don't decrease your hooking power.

2 Start your thread at the point where you bent the hook and wrap it backwards to the hook bend. If you are going to rib the fly you should tie in your ribbing material by one end as you do this.

3 Dub the abdomen forward to the bend that you put in the hook. The abdomen should have a taper to it with the thinnest point being at the back of the hook.

4 Cut a piece of flat foam into a strip about ⅛" wide. Tie it in by one end at the front of the abdomen.

5 Tie in a piece of grizzly saddle hackle by its tip and then wrap it a couple of times around the base of the foam piece that you have just tied in. Secure it to the hook with a couple of turns of thread and cut off the

excess. You are forming what will be a parachute-style hackle around the base of the foam, but still leaving the free end of the foam unsecured at this point.

6 Dub the thorax of the fly thicker than the forward end of the abdomen. Finish dubbing slightly behind the eye of the hook leaving room to tie in the free end of the foam.

7 Pull the free end of the foam forward forming a hump over the top of the thorax. Take a couple of turns of thread to secure it in place just behind the eye of the hook. Trim off the excess foam. Lash down the foam a little more and then whip finish.

The Klinkhammer Special (Traditional Version)

Hook:	Partridge K12ST or other long shank curved hook #12-22. Bend the hook slightly downward at the middle of the hook shank.
Thread:	Black
Wing:	White or colored poly yarn
Abdomen:	Tan poly dubbing
Thorax:	Peacock herl
Hackle:	Brown or dun hackle tied in parachute style at the base of the wing

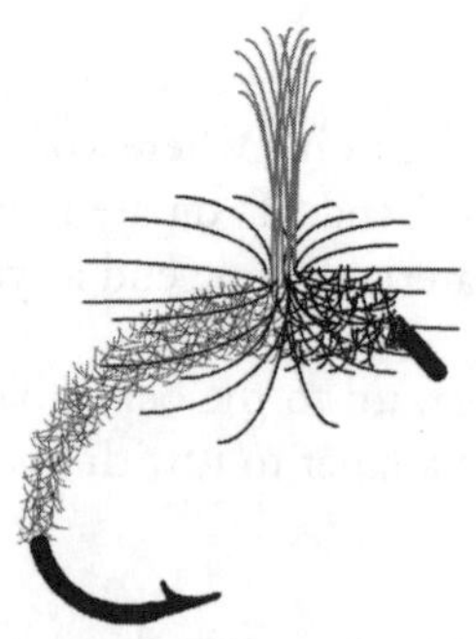

Tying Instructions

1 First prepare the hook. Bend the hook downward slightly just at the middle of the hook shank.

2 Start your thread just behind the eye of the hook and wind to a point about 1/8 to 1/4 inch behind the eye of the hook. This distance will be shorter on larger hooks and longer proportionally on smaller hooks.

3 Take a piece of poly yarn about twice hook shank in length that you have thinned to the thickness that you desire for the post wing. Lay it at the thread point with about half in front and half in back. Take a couple of turns of thread to secure it in place.

4 Trim the back half of the "wing" material to form an underbody for the abdomen/thorax of the fly. This should be no longer than where you want the tip of the abdomen to begin at the back of the fly and should taper from thin near the back of the fly to fatter near the front of the fly.

5 Take your thread and wind it over the top of this poly yarn underbody to a point approx. 3/4 of the way from the eye of the hook to the point of the hook.
This will be the tail end of the abdomen of the fly. If you have any stray pieces of the poly material sticking out the back, trim them off.

6 Dub an abdomen forward to a point about 2/3 of the way from the tail end of the fly to the eye of the hook. This should form a taper from thinner at the tail end of the fly to fatter at the front end.

7 Tie in 1, 2 or 3 pieces of peacock herl by one end (depending upon the size of the fly) at this point and trim off the excess butts.

8 Wrap the thread forward to just in front and underneath of where the poly wing material is emerging from the previous thread wraps. Pick up the wing material by its end and hold it upright perpendicular to an imaginary line that runs from the eye of the hook to this point. Take several wraps of thread in front of the winging material to make it stand upright at this point.

9 Take the ends of the peacock herl and wrap them around the hook forward until they are just behind the now upright post wing. Take a couple of turns of thread to secure them in place and let the ends dangle. You will need them later.

10 Take a piece of dry fly hackle that you have previously prepared as for a dry fly (*see Glossary on Preparing Hackle). Lash the butt of the

hackle to the hook shank in front of the post wing. Move the thread to just behind the eye of the hook.

11 Holding the hackle out of the way, wrap the peacock herl forward to just behind the eye of the hook. Take a couple of turns of thread to secure it in place. Trim off the excess herl.

12 Take a couple of turns of hackle around the base of the post wing to create a parachute-style hackle. End with the hackle tip forward over the eye of the hook. Take a couple of turns of thread to secure the hackle in place and then trim off the excess. Whip finish or finish with several half hitches if you have trouble getting the whip finish under the parachute.

13 Cut the top of the post wing to the length desired—usually about ½ hook shank length.

Variations

Vary your dubbing material as desired. The original Klinkhammer was designed as a Caddis or Sedge imitation, hence the peacock herl thorax. If you are doing a Mayfly emerger then continue the dubbing in place of the peacock herl and use a finer dubbing than you would for a Caddis imitation.

Use a different color dubbing as desired.

Use a different color hackle as desired.

Fishing the Fly

For this fly to be presented properly it is important that the back portion of the abdomen be below the surface of the water, while the parachute hackle and wing or foam rests on the surface or is on top. This may mean applying any floatant very carefully so that it is only on the wing/foam and parachute hackle. No floatant should be applied to the part of the fly that is to stick down into the water. It can actually be very helpful to prewet the rear portion of the fly to get a proper presentation. Then fish it as you would any dry fly.

Wet Flies

Wet Flies: A Neglected Heritage

The first flies used by fly fishermen were wet flies. They were the first flies used in England, the first used in the United States. Once upon a time they were the first flies used by most fishermen when they began fly fishing and the first flies tied by beginning fly tyers. Simple to tie and fish, these flies are often today neglected in favor of the more "sophisticated" dry flies, emergers and nymphs.

One of the first books printed on the subject of fly fishing, *A Treatyse Of Fysshynge With An Angle,* usually attributed to Dame Juliana Berners, dealt with the subject of wet flies. Early in this century most of the classic works in fly tying such as *Favorite Flies and Their Histories* by Mary Orvis Marbury devoted long sections if not their entire contents to the wets. Even after the popularity of dries began to dominate the flytying texts, there have still been a few tyers devoted to the wet fly. *The Art of Tying the Wet Fly* by James Leisenring and Pete Hidy in the 1940's, Sylvester Nemes series on the soft hackle wet and most recently Dave Hughes' *Wet Flies* all have periodically revived interest in this area of fly tying.

In spite of a solid history, plenty of currently available material, and the fact that wet flies catch fish (often when others won't), it is still unusual today to see someone tying on a wet when astream. They have been so neglected recently that many fishermen today just don't know how to tie or fish them anymore. Fishing the wets can be the simplest thing in fly fishing such as an easy down and across drift or a slow retrieve, but many more sophisticated techniques have been developed as well. If you'd like to repair this area of your flyfishing knowledge I'd strongly recommend Dave Hughes' book *Wet Flies.* He covers all of the wet flyfishing techniques in a great deal of depth.

So here are some patterns that span three of the basic types of wet flies: the classic winged wet, the soft hackle wet and the modern lifelike wet. If you can tie these three patterns, you should be able to handle most wet flies that are out there.

The Leadwing Coachman

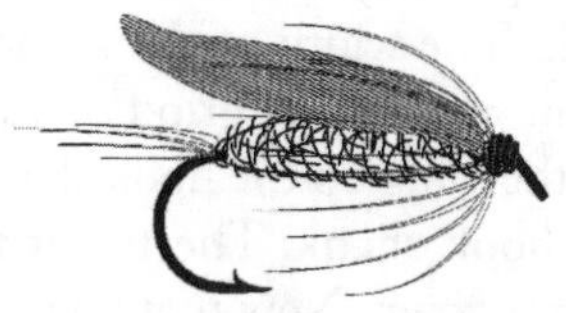

One of the classic winged wets. This fly has been catching fish longer than you or I have been alive and it still works today.

Hook:	Mustad 3906, 3906B or other wet fly hook, #10-16
Thread:	Black
Body:	Peacock Herl
Hackle:	Brown
Wing:	Mallard Duck Quill

Tying Instructions

1 Start your tying thread just behind the eye of the hook and wrap it back to the bend.

2 Take 2-4 peacock herls and bind the butts to the shank of the hook then wrap your thread to about $^{1}/_{16}$ inch behind the eye. Spiral the peacock

herl forward on the hook to the thread and then take a couple of wraps of thread to secure it in place. Trim off the excess peacock herl.

3 Pick a brown hackle with barbules that will reach from the thread to about the point of the hook. Tie in the hackle by its tip at the front of the peacock herl body and then trim off the excess tip hanging over the eye. Wrap the hackle 4-6 times around the hook with the tips of the barbules pointing generally toward the back of the fly. It may take a little practice to get this just right. Secure the hackle in place with a couple of turns of thread and trim off the excess butt.

4 (See the section on Quill Winged Flies, p. 38.) Snip a right and left section of duck Mallard primary quills about ⅛ in. wide from a matched pair of mallard quills. The width of the section varies with the size of the hook. With a pair of tweezers grip the duck quill section that is to form the far side of the wing on the hook shank. Hold and measure the section against the hook shank. The tip of the quill should flare up where the bend curves down. Now that you know where the quill is to go, you can hold the quill between your left thumb and forefinger and release it from the tweezers. Allow the quill to slide slightly down the side of the hook shank so that it covers the upper portion of the body. Tie it down by taking a turn of thread over, down the far side, under and straight up. Take one more turn in the same area to secure the section.

5 Pick up the other duck quill section with your tweezers, and measure it against the first one. Cover the upper portion of the body with the second duck quill while aligning the top edges of both quills. Tie it in. Note that the concave sides of the quills face each other.

6 Secure the area with thread and clip the excess butts.

7 Whip finish.

Fishing the Fly

Although most often thought of as Trout flies for use in mountain streams, the wet flies are actually among the most versatile of the flies in where they can be fished, how they can be fished, and for what species. Yes, these are great flies for our mountain Trout streams, but they are equally effective on our tailwaters. They will also catch numerous other species besides Trout, being great panfish flies.

The Soft Hackle Wet

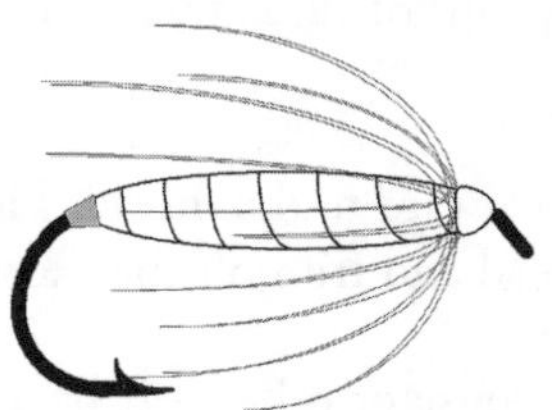

Soft hackle wets are very versatile flies that can produce for you in a wide variety of situations. During a sulphur hatch, for example, a yellow soft hackle wet will often produce fish that have rejected repeated offerings of dry flies. Try an olive one during a BWO hatch. They also can be deadly flies just retrieved slowly on still water.

Hook:	Mustad 3906, 3906B or other wet fly hook #10-16
Thread:	Color of body floss
Tag:	Gold or Silver Mylar or Tinsel
Ribbing:	Fine Gold, Silver or Copper Wire
Body:	Floss (Olive, Yellow, Orange, or other color)
Hackle:	Partridge, Grouse or other soft feather

Tying Instructions

1 Start your thread near the back of the hook and tie in the mylar or tinsel for the tag. Take a couple of wraps of the tag material just behind where the bend of the hook starts and secure it in place with a couple of wraps of thread. Trim off the excess material.

2 Cut a piece of ribbing material about 2-3 inches long. Secure one end of it to the top of the hook shank in front of the tag and let the excess hang over the back of the hook.

3 Cut a piece of floss about 8-10" long. Secure one end of it to the top of the hook shank and wind the thread forward to about 1/16" behind the eye. Note: It is easier to handle floss if it is wet. Keep the floss and your fingers wet while working with the floss. Carefully wrap the floss forward on the hook to the thread forming a tapered cigar shaped body. Take a couple of wraps of thread to secure the floss in place and trim off the excess floss.

4 Spiral the ribbing forward to the thread. Tie off the ribbing with a couple of turns of thread and trim off the excess.

5 Pick a partridge, grouse or other soft hackle feather that has barbules that will reach about from the thread to the bend of the hook. Hold the feather by its tip with a pair of hackle pliers and strip the barbules off of one side of the feather A FEW AT A TIME. Lay the butt of the feather just in front of the body and secure it in place with the thread as you wrap the thread forward to just behind the eye of the hook. Trim off the excess butt that is hanging over the eye of the hook. Wrap the feather around the hook 2-4 times depending upon the size and fullness of the feather. The stripped side of the feather should be toward the hook shank and the feather should be worked forward in a slight spiral. With a little practice you will be able to work it so that the tips of the barbules point generally toward the back of the hook.

6 Take a couple of turns of thread to secure the feather in place just behind the eye of the hook and trim off the excess feather.

7 Whip finish.

Variations

Most tyers use acetate floss for this fly, but you will get even more depth to the body by using Tying Silk, available as Pearsall's Gossamer at some stores in the U.S. and Canada. You might also find some silk threads and flosses available at embroidery and knitting stores as well. If you do find some silk to use, remember that it will go translucent when wet. The shank of the hook should be painted white before tying or covered first with pearlescent, silver or white mylar to keep the brass of the hook from muddying the color of the silk.

A favorite Southeastern variation on the fly uses a dubbed body instead of floss. One of the translucent dubbings is preferred and a version using an Orange body is known as The Tennessee Volunteer.

Fishing the Fly

Of all the wet flies, the Soft Hackle Wet is one of the most versatile. This is a great fly for the mountain streams of the Southeast fishing for Trout, but is is equally effective on the tailwaters as well. My experience with it on our tailwaters has been that it is especially useful in fishing for Brown Trout, taking a much higher proportion of Browns than any other fly that I've tried. It is useful in both still water and fast, on Trout, Panfish, Smallmouth, Bass, and even small Stripers. It doesn't matter what I'm fishing for, this is a great fly to have along.

The Gold Ribbed Hare's Ear Wet Fly

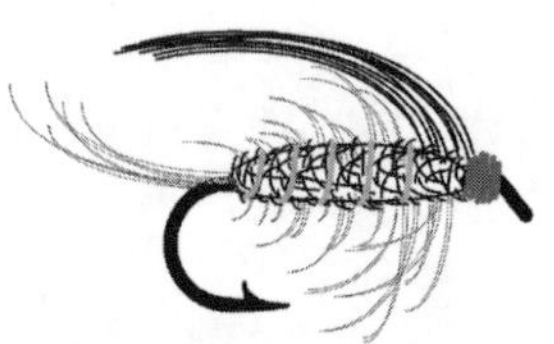

This is one of Dave Hughes' patterns for a rougher looking, more lifelike wet fly.

Hook:	Mustad 3906, 3906B or other wet fly hook #10-16
Thread:	Red
Hackle:	Furnace Hen
Tail:	Furnace Hen
Rib:	Narrow gold tinsel
Body:	Hare's Mask Fur
Wing:	Grouse-wing quill sections or a clump of furnace hen-hackle barbs

Tying Instructions

1 Choose a hackle with barbules that are slightly longer than the hook shank. Tie in the hackle by the butt about 1/16" behind the eye of the hook.

2 Wind the thread back to the bend. Tie in and cock slightly upward a tail of hackle fibers about hook shank in length.

3 Tie in the tinsel rib and let it hang over the back of the hook.

4 Make a dubbing loop with your thread. Apply fur to the dubbing loop and twist to make a shaggy rope. Wind the body forward to just behind where the hackle is tied in.

5 Spiral the ribbing forward to just behind where the hackle is tied in. Take a couple of turns of thread to secure the ribbing and trim off the excess.

6 Spiral the thread back through the body to the middle.

7 Wind the hackle backwards through the thorax to the thread. Take a turn or two of thread to secure the hackle in place and trim off the excess.

8 Spiral the thread forward to just in front of the body.

9 Prepare two matching wing slips from a grouse wing quill or just take a clump of barbs from the furnace hen hackle. The tips should reach the midpoint of the tail. Grouse-wing slips should be mounted like the instructions for the wings on the winged wet fly above. A hackle wing is simply bound in place on top of the hook.

10 Whip finish.

Fishing the Fly

This version of the Gold Ribbed Hare's Ear Wet is one of the new breed of shaggier, more realistic looking wet flies championed by Dave Hughes. It is an extremely effective fly when fishing for Trout on both the mountain streams and tailwaters of the Southeast. I have found it to be most productive when fished with some kind of motion to call attention to itself. Its very shagginess moves well and seems to be attractive to fish.

Tying Silks

If you have ever leafed through some of the older flytying books or for that matter any number of even recent English tying books you will undoubtedly have seen references to silk, tying silk, or silk floss. You may have assumed that what was being referred to was a material that is no longer available or has been superseded by more modern materials and if you did tie up the pattern you probably substituted modern tying thread and floss for the "silk." For most fly tyers in the United States today, using tying thread and rayon or acetate floss is something that is taken for granted. This was certainly not always the case, nor should it necessarily be so for all circumstances. Although they are difficult to find, silk thread and silk floss are still available and for certain flies the "modern" substitutes really do not create the same feeling to the fly.

Silk thread, unlike most current tying threads, has practically no stretch to it. Many old time tyers feel that this gives you much better control over certain flytying techniques from spinning deer hair to securing upright divided wings with a figure eight. It is, however, not as strong as most synthetics. Unbeknownst to many, it is still being manufactured in black and white and a variety of sizes. I recently came across some over in Linville, North Carolina in an old-time country store/fly shop and grabbed several spools at a bargain price. Except for an occasional find such as this though, you are going to have trouble finding it in fly shops in this country at any price. Mail order locations are rather limited as well. *Fly and Field* and *English Angling Trappings* are the sort of companies here in the U.S. where you might be lucky enough to locate some. If you have any English connections, silk threads are still widely available "across the pond."

Silk floss or tying silk is for many applications a much more desirable material than the more readily available rayon or acetate flosses. Rayon and acetate flosses are opaque. Silk floss and tying silk are translucent when wet. This translucency gives them a visual depth when used in fly tying that is just not duplicable with the artificials. Soft Hackle Wets take on a whole new feeling when tied with silk floss rather than artificial floss. Floss bodies on nymphs have a lifelike appearance rather than just being opaque blobs. The bodies on Humpys and Henryville Specials similarly have a three dimensionality to them that they did not have before. Silk floss or tying silk are a material for which experienced fly tyers can find numerous uses.

The very translucency of silk floss that makes it desirable, however, also calls for certain precautions when tying with it. The translucency means that one can also actually see the color of the hook through the floss. In the case of brass or black hooks, the hook color will tend to turn the silk floss into a drab approximation of itself. To forestall this happening, one should either paint the hook shank white before tying, or lay in an undercoat of thread beneath the floss. Then when the floss becomes wet the translucency will create a more lifelike color with a great deal of depth.

Silk floss like the more common acetate or rayon flosses also requires some care in handling. Most tyers prefer to apply the floss while it is wet—either from a small bowl of water kept at hand or from the wetting agent we all have available in our own mouths. Since silk floss comes on small spools it can also be helpful to have a bobbin that is capable of handling spools that average about ½ inch from top to bottom. Such bobbins are available, but can also take a little diligent searching on the tyer's part.

Locating silk floss can be the most difficult and sometimes expensive part of putting it to use though. There are a few mail order houses such as the two mentioned above that have a selection of colors available, but at a fairly steep price. I was lucky enough lately to acquire a very nice collection of *Pearsall's Gossamer* when my wife made a stop by Farlow's in London on a trip to England. Later I discovered a yarn store in Damariscotta, ME on the World Wide Web that was offering "bobbins" of silk floss in a wide variety of colors very inexpensively. Craft, yarn and embroidery stores are certainly worth checking out as a possible source. All of these difficulties locating silk floss are well worth the effort when you see the results of using them in tying. You may finally begin to understand why Soft Hackle Wets were once such a popular fly and why Henryville Specials were originally tied with silk floss. The rayon and acetate flosses are a pale imitation of the real thing.

The following is a simple pattern that makes use of the translucent properties of tying silk.

The Silk Midge Larva

Hook:	Mustad 94840 or TMC 101 #20-24, Mustad 80250 or TMC 2487 #18- 22. (Paint the hook shank white where it will be covered by the silk, or cover it with thread in that area.)
Ribbing:	Fine gold wire (or other color to provide a contrast to the floss)
Body:	Silk floss in yellow, orange, olive, claret or other color desired

Tying Instructions

1 Either paint the shank of the hook white where it will be covered with the floss or wrap in one layer of thread in that area. You can use either white thread or thread in the color of the floss.

2 Take a piece of fine gold wire about 2" long and lay it on top of the hook with the end sticking out the back.

3 Start the floss just behind the eye of the hook and wrap to the bend. Then wrap the floss forward building up a tapered body. Finish with the floss just behind the eye of the hook.

4. Finish the fly with a couple of half hitches or a whip finish that uses only a couple of turns with the floss. Trim off the excess.

Fishing the Fly

This fly is one that is usually fished under a strike indicator. It can also be highly effective tied onto a dry fly as a trailer or dropper converting the dry fly into some double duty as a strike indicator as well. I expected the drabber colors such as olive, gray, etc. to work well with this fly, but the big surprise that I got when I first started experimenting with it was just how well the bright colors such as yellow, orange, and claret worked. It's great on Trout in any kind of water where there are midges, which, in the Southeast, is almost any kind of water at all.

The Belle Watling

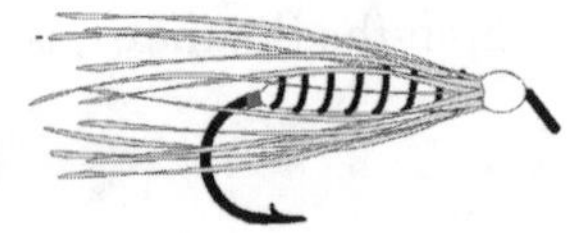

This phlaming phlorescent phloosey, the hottest thing to come out of the South since Sherman's March to the Sea, began life as a staid and stolid New England maiden. Years of puritanical privation, however, festered under her stiff, starched skirts. Decades of diligent down and across dunking as the former Parmachene Belle finally found fruition in the balmy breezes of Dixie and emerging from her encased enclosure she enthusiastically embraced her new nomenclature now known as The Belle Watling! Some say she's a serpent and siren, but she has ripped the restraints of retrograde respectability reveling in her recently repressed but now fervent and unfettered freedom. Scatter boys, she's hot cargo!

Slipping her stiffly starched strictures, she first presented her passionate percolating possibilities on the Clinch River in East Tennessee. This seemingly mild-mannered tailwater meanders through secret sites in Oak Ridge, Tennessee (The Atomic City), releasing radioactive rainbows and bruising bionic browns. Fish that glow in the dark were fuming at fogyish flies and fairly floundered on the Belle's fluid, fluttering and flaming feathers.

Her second succulent success came at SEC-I on that simmering section of stream below Moomaw Dam in Virginia where the previous purveyors of illegal lighting turned landowners were locked in legal flagellation with intrepid trespassers upon their traditional territories. The waters fairly boiled with controversy and into this churning caldron clambered The Belle to come forth as champion catcher of colossal char-like critters.

With the trout types trembling timidly at her toes, she trekked on to weave her wiles in yet wider worlds. Bluegill, smallmouth and hunkering hawgs hung on her hotly highlighted hems. Ladies and gentlemen, I give you:

The Flaming Flash, The Phluorescent Phenomena, The Fabulous Floozy:

!!! The Belle Watling !!!

Hook:	Mustad 3906 or equivalent #10-14
Thread:	Orange, yellow or other color
Tag:	Gold Mylar
Ribbing:	Fine Gold Wire wrapped in an open spiral
Body:	Floss—fluorescent orange, orange, yellow or other color, tapered so that it is narrower at both ends and fatter in the middle
Collar:	Rainbow Krystal Flash tied in just behind head 1½ times hook length

Tying Instructions

1 Start thread near the bend of the hook and tie in a tag of gold mylar just behind the bend. Tie in about 1½" to 2" of fine gold wire in front of the tag and let it hang to later be used as ribbing over the body.

2 Tie in 3-4" of floss and wrap the thread to just behind the eye of the hook. Wrap the floss to form a tapered body that is narrower at both ends and fatter in the middle. Secure the floss about ⅛ hook length behind the eye of the hook with a couple of wraps of thread and trim the excess floss.

3 Wrap the gold wire forward in an open spiral as ribbing to where you tied off the floss. Take a couple of turns of thread to secure it in place and trim off the excess.

4 Form a collar of 8-12 strands of Rainbow Krystal Flash each about 2-3" long and secure in place with several wraps of thread. The ends of the Krystal Flash should extend well beyond the back of the hook. These will later be trimmed to length. The butts of the Krystal Flash will probably extend over the head of the fly and need to be trimmed to just behind the eye. Then take several more wraps of thread over the butts of the Krystal Flash behind the eye to form a neat "head" on the fly and

whip finish. Coat this head with a little epoxy or gloss acrylic lure finish. Trim the ends of the Krystal Flash behind the back of the hook to about $1\frac{1}{2}$ times hook length.

5 *Note:* The tricky part of tying this fly is getting the Krystal Flash to be evenly distributed around the entire body of the fly like a collar. After securing it loosely in place with one or two wraps of thread you will need to grasp the Krystal Flash just behind the thread and twist it around the body until it is relatively evenly distributed on all sides. This takes a little bit of practice, but can quickly be mastered. After you are happy with the distribution of the Krystal Flash then take a couple more tight wraps of thread to secure it in place before trimming the butts just behind the eye of the hook. After trimming the butts of the Krystal Flash then use the thread to form a neatly tapered "head" on the fly much like on a streamer.

Fishing The Fly

The Belle Watling (named after Rhett Butler's favorite madam) is best fished with a little action to get the Krystal Flash moving. She likes to wiggle her hips. In moving water she can be fished like a wet fly, but often your hits will come at the end of the swing as you start a slow retrieve back. In slow or still water your best bet is usually a slow, erratic retrieve. Initially designed for trout, she has also proved deadly on a variety of other fish. Bluegills and smallmouth love her and big lunker hawgs go wild when she swivels her hips. She has a wide variety of flashy costumes that she can change into as the conditions require. Just vary the color of the floss body as you desire.

The Red Assed Pheasant Tail Wet

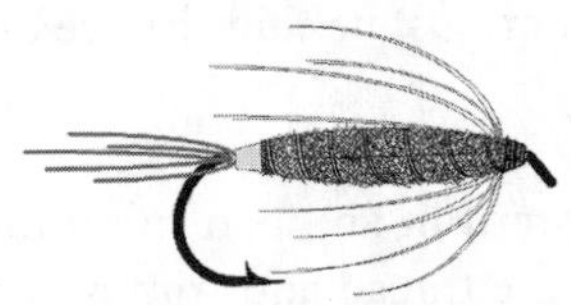

This is a wet fly pattern that is greatly loved in the Southeast, but has found its way to other parts of the country as well. This particular pattern was adapted from one by R.A. Skehan (a Yankee, by gum).

Hook:	Mustad 3906, TMC 3976 #10-16
Thread:	Black
Tag:	Red or fire orange thread
Tail:	A few short pheasant tail fibers (optional)
Rib:	Fine gold or copper wire
Body:	Several pheasant tail barbules
Hackle:	Grizzly hen hackle or partridge tied as a wet fly collar

Tying Instructions

1 Start the thread just behind the eye of the hook and wind it to the bend. Cut off a piece of red thread for the tag and secure it in place at the bend

with the tying thread. Wrap the tag just behind the bend of the hook, then secure the other end with the tying thread and trim off the excess.

2 Take several barbules from a pheasant tail and tie them in by the tips just above the tag with a couple of wraps of thread. The tips of the barbules will form the tail of the fly if you desire a tail. Let the butts of the barbules hang out of the way.

3 Tie in the ribbing and let it hang out of the way.

4 Form a tapered underbody using the thread. Finish with the thread just behind the eye of the hook.

5 Wrap the butts of the pheasant tail barbules forward forming the body of the fly and tie them off just behind the eye of the hook. Trim off the excess.

6 Wrap the ribbing forward in an open spiral to just behind the eye of the hook, secure with the thread and trim off the excess. I recommend that you wrap the ribbing in the opposite direction from the one that you used to wrap the barbules. This will make for a sturdier fly.

7 Tie in the hen hackle or partridge and take a couple of turns just behind the hook eye as a wet fly collar. Trim off the excess and whip finish.

Fishing the Fly

This is one of those general purpose wet flies that can be used in almost any circumstances and on any kind of fish. While it was originally developed for use on mountain Trout, it works equally well on their tailwater cousins and for a wide variety of other species as well. This is a great panfish fly, for example, and has been known to produce a number of Smallmouth very effectively.

The Arkansas Red Butt

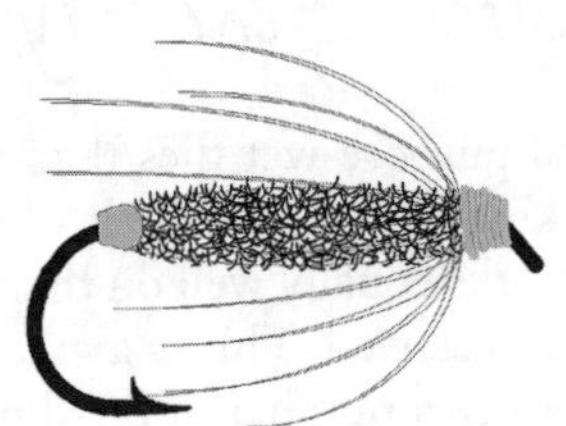

Peacock herl flies have always been good producers on the mountain streams of the Southeast and this one is no exception. This pattern is from Jerry Cobb. He's had great success with it on the streams in the higher elevations in the Smokies as well as on Northern Arkansas trout streams.

Hook:	Mustad 3906, TMC 3976 #8-16
Thread:	Red
Tag:	Red thread
Body:	Peacock herl
Hackle:	Partridge tied as a wet fly collar
Head:	Red thread built up fairly heavy

Tying Instructions

1 Start the thread just behind the eye of the hook and wind it well beyond the bend to form the tag. Wind it back to the bend of the hook.

2 Tie in several peacock herls and then wind the thread to just behind the eye of the hook.

3 Wrap the peacock herls forward to slightly short of the eye and tie off. Trim off the excess.

4 Tie in a partridge hackle and take a couple of wraps to make a wet fly collar. Tie off and trim the excess.

5 Use the thread to build up a red head and whip finish.

Fishing the Fly

This is one of those general purpose wet flies that can be used in almost any circumstances and on any kind of fish. While it was originally developed for use on mountain Trout, it works equally well on their tailwater cousins and for a wide variety of other species as well. This is a great panfish fly, for example, and has been known to produce a number of Smallmouth very effectively.

The Hard-Bodied Ant Wet Fly

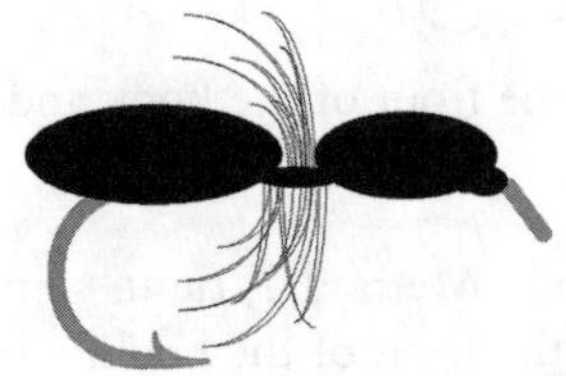

When good friend David Allerton was going through one of the first rough copies of this book he insisted that it was absolutely necessary for any book on Southeastern Flies to include a pattern for The Hard Bodied Ant Wet in spite of the fact that there were already a couple of ant patterns in here. I've fished enough with David to know that when it comes to flies that work in the Southeast I'd better listen to him. If you're in one of those situations where you haven't got the least idea about what you should be tying on, this is one of the best flies that you can choose. It's simple to tie and extremely effective.

This fly has been around for quite some time now and precisely who is responsible for which tying method can be a subject for some debate. Most often it is attributed originally to Keith McCafferty from Pennsylvania. Schwiebert mentions his version of this fly in *Trout* which uses a lacquered body over a thread base. The acetone method of tying the fly is covered by Dean in an article in *Field & Stream.* The epoxy method is used by Rod Yerges and is covered extensively in Harrison Steeves' and Ed Koch's *Terrestrials.* Whichever method you decide to use, this is a fly that is a mainstay on trout waters of the Southeast.

Hook:	Mustad 3906, 3906B or other wet fly hook, #12-16
Thread:	Black, red or cinnamon (depending upon the color ant that you want)
Body (Method 1):	Acetate floss in black, red or cinnamon wound on in two lumps and then dipped in acetone
Body (Method 2):	Your tying thread wound into two lumps and then Epoxied
Hackle:	Black, red or brown hackle wound around the hook a couple of times

Tying Instructions

1 Start the thread at the front of the hook and wind it all the way to the bend.

2 If you are using Body Method 1, tie in some Acetate Floss and then wind the thread to the front of the hook.

a. Wind the floss around the hook forming two lumps. These imitate the segmented body of the ant with a larger lump near the back of the hook and a slightly smaller lump near the front.

b. Tie off the floss with the thread and then do a quick whip finish behind the eye of the hook and trim off the excess thread and floss.

c. Dip the hook in Acetone. This will soften the Acetate Floss and cause it to dry into a shiny, hard body. Exercise extreme caution when using Acetone. It is highly volatile and should only be used in areas with excellent ventilation. It should also never be used around any kind of heat source or open flame.

3 If you are using Body Method 2:

a. Use your tying thread to form the two lumps of the ant body with a larger lump in the rear and a smaller one in front.

b. Whip finish and trim off the excess thread.

c. Cover the lumps with clear Epoxy and let dry.

4 Restart your thread and tie on a couple of turns of hackle. Trim off the excess hackle and whip finish. Remember that this is supposed to be a

wet fly. This is a good place to use up some softer hackle instead of your good dry fly hackle. The hackle can be tied on either between the lumps or in front of them. Your call.

5 With either Body Method 1 or 2, it is best to tie up a bunch of bodies at one time and then either dip in Acetone or coat with Epoxy all at once. Let them all dry and then tie on the hackle.

Fishing the Fly

Remember when fishing this fly that ants are not aquatic insects and the hard-bodied ant represents an ant that has drowned. So while it is fished like a wet fly, it is usually best when presented at as close to a dead drift as possible. What this fly really tries to achieve is a fly that will float in the meniscus rather than on top of it like most dry flies. If you notice dead ants in the water, this is where you will find them.

The Improved McGinty

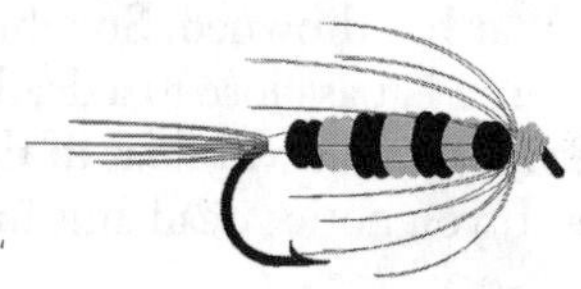

Although in the Southeast this fly is usually thought of as a panfish fly, it can also be deadly on trout—especially during the terrestrial season. Simple to tie, easy to fish and guaranteed to bring you home a mess of bluegills for supper.

Hook:	Mustad 3906B, TMC 3796 #10-16
Thread:	Yellow
Tag:	Flat gold tinsel
Tail:	Red hackle fibers
Body:	Alternating bands of yellow and black chenille
Hackle:	Partridge tied in as a wet fly collar

Tying Instructions

1 Start the thread at the bend of the hook and tie in a tag of flat gold tinsel just behind the bend.

2 Tie in the tail about gap width long.

3. Tie in a piece of yellow chenille and take a couple of turns to make a band. Secure the end of the chenille with a turn of thread and let the rest of the piece lie on the top of the hook pointing forward.

4. Tie in a piece of black chenille and take a couple of turns to make a band. Secure the end of the black chenille with a turn of thread and let the rest of the piece lie on the top of the hook pointing forward. Note that you tie in the black chenille over the top of the remainder of the piece of yellow chenille and then form the black band over the tail of the yellow piece. The next band will be yellow so you can then pick up the yellow chenille and wind it over the tail of the black piece and so forth to create alternating bands of black and yellow chenille without having to restart the chenille after each band. In each case though you do have to work the thread forward to secure each piece of chenille in place in turn.

5. Using this method, create at least two bands of yellow chenille and two of black chenille. Depending upon the size of the hook and the width of the bands of chenille, you may be able to create more.

6. Just behind the eye of the hook tie off both pieces of chenille and trim off the excess.

7. Tie in the partridge feather and take a couple of turns to form a wet fly collar. Tie it off and trim the excess. Whip finish.

Fishing the Fly

Although the coloration of this fly makes one think of a terrestrial, such as a yellow jacket, I have found that this fly really isn't at its most effective when it is presented as a terrestrial, but rather when is is presented as a wet fly. Both Panfish and Trout seem to like it best when it is presented with some movement. A down and across swing with the current is effective, but I've had even better luck with a slow, erratic retrieve.

Nymphs and Other Subsurface Patterns

Using Nymphs and other flies that seek to imitate the subsurface stages of insect life does not have the heavy handed traditions associated with it that has sometimes plagued new developments in dry flies. It was the scientific types that through aquatic studies proved that the vast majority of the food taken by Trout is subsurface in nature and thus it is usually with at least a passing nod to science and imitation that most nymph and other subsurface patterns were developed. This has been both boon and bane to the fly fisherman. Quite frankly, it has meant that until recently most nymph patterns are pretty dull affairs with little of the dash, color, and splashes of creativity and originality that often appear in dry flies, wet flies, and certainly in streamers. In recent years, though, more creative types have also descended upon nymph fishing with the result being a greatly increased variety of forms available to the fly fisher. The use of beads in nymph tying, as just one example, has stimulated an entirely new approach to the look and feel of these formerly merely dull and drab flies.

While often looked upon by the dry fly purist as something akin to "bait chucking," the major thing that nymph fishing has going for it is very simple. It catches fish. It catches fish regularly. It catches fish when dry flies don't work. It catches fish when streamers don't work. It even sometimes catches fish when bait doesn't work. It catches fish. This is a hard recommendation to overlook.

The techniques of nymph fishing can also be as simple or as complex as a fly fisherman desires or the situation demands. Most first time nymph fishermen will simply tie on a strike indicator with the nymph some distance beneath it. This is a technique that is often productive and certainly is simple, but there can be a good deal more to nymph fishing technique than just that. It would be well worth your effort to explore a variety of other techniques as well. Following this introduction, for example, is an article on a form of nymph fishing that has developed directly from some of the earliest fly fishing done in the Smokies. It would also be productive for you to understand the principles involved in such time honored techniques as "high sticking," the "Leisenring Lift," and the "hand twisted retrieve." All of these are methods of presenting nymphs that are often ignored by many modern fishermen, but that have been proven effective time and again over the years. Exploring the techniques of nymph fishing in more depth will result in both more productive and more enjoyable fishing.

Gettin' Down: Alternate Nymphing Techniques

While the dry fly purist may view the use of nymphs in any form whatsoever as heresy, most fly fishers have long realized, as Sawyer did originally, that most of a trout's diet consists of life forms that are found underneath the water rather than on the surface. With this in mind, a wise fly fisher should pursue the development of their nymphing techniques with as much interest as their dry fly presentations. Most nymphing today though seems to consist solely of drifting a fly along underneath a strike indicator. There are many situations where this is certainly the best approach. You can achieve greatly extended drifts on tailwaters and larger streams, for example, with the proper use of strike indicators.

In the mountain streams of the Southeast, however, the strike indicator is often not the most productive method of fishing the nymph. The quickly varying depths that one encounters in short stretches of water make changing the depth of the nymph below the indicator both tedious and time consuming. Also, when one comes upon the occasional really deep pool, it is impossible to get the fly all the way to the bottom of these pools in the short run that it has to sink. These deep pools in the mountains often hold the largest trout.

Hearkening back to the beginnings of fly fishing in the Southeast and a reminder of some of the early "primitive" techniques used might be helpful to some of the supposedly more "sophisticated" fly fishers of today. In the article on the origins of Smoky Mountain Patterns, I wrote briefly about the "cane pole" technique of many of the early fishers. This was actually similar in many respects to the nymphing techniques developed by Frank Sawyer and others in England and the United States. Long before anyone ever heard of strike indicators, nymphing often consisted of what is generally known as "short line" nymphing or "high sticking." The fisher uses very little line out of the end of the rod and by raising and lowering the tip of the rod and controlling the amount of line played out they are able to control the depth of the nymph in the water. In this technique often there is no line at all in the water, only leader and tippet. This method is easiest to employ when working cross stream. You toss the nymph upstream, then as it flows downstream raise the tip of the rod to control the depth of the fly. The tip of the rod is at its highest point as the fly is directly in front of you. Then as the nymph floats past you, start lowering the tip of the rod to play out more line. This technique not only allows you to control the depth of the nymph in the water, but also keeps you in close touch with the nymph as it bounces along the bottom and makes "feeling" a strike easier because of a minimum amount of slack in the line. It is also possible to use "short line" nymphing as an upstream and a downstream presentation, but considerably more difficult. In both of these latter cases one has to be able to work both the tip of the rod with the right hand and the line with the left hand simultaneously. By raising and lowering the tip of the rod and letting out or bringing in line at the same time, you are able to achieve the same effect that I described in the cross stream version. Needless to say, all of this takes considerable more coordination and practice than just letting the nymph float downstream under a strike indicator. For mountain streams the advantage is in being able to very quickly vary the depth of the nymph as the depth of the stream changes. With the short pockets, pools and runs of mountain streams, this can be a serious advantage. Nowadays with fish becoming wise to and wary of strike indicators, returning to the "short line" nymphing of yesterday can often fool fish that may run and hide at the first sign of a little circular piece of foam floating on the water.

There is another nymphing technique that is found in the mountains of the Southeast that can be extremely useful when dealing with the runoffs of spring or when you encounter those really deep pools where the big ones are hanging out on the bottom. When the water is fast, high or deep you may have trouble just getting the nymph down quickly enough to do you any good. The length of the pool is still short and the nymph may not have time to drop all the way to the bottom fast enough. This technique is often known in the Southeast as the "all mono" system. There is also a variation on it that is practiced on the Steelhead streams of the Midwest where it is often referred to as "chuck and duck." It's not pretty fishing, but it has taken some mighty large fish. I got the largest fish that I've ever taken out of the Oconoluftee during spring runoff using the "all mono" system.

This system gets its name from the fact that it doesn't even use a fly line, but substitutes instead a length of monofilament line in its place. The preferred monofilament to use is one that is highly visible. Berkley used to make a godawful-looking fluorescent green mono that was perfect for this. You want monofilament line that you can see so that you can tell what is happening with your line. Since very little if any of the line is actually going to be in the water, it doesn't matter whether the fish can see it or not. I keep an old reel spooled up with highly visible mono in my tackle box for when I want to bring it into use. Tied to the tip of the line is about a 5' length of clear monofilament or tippet material with the fly on the end of that. For deep or murky water situations, the fly of choice is usually a weighted nymph in a large size. A big stonefly, yallerhammer, muskrat nymph, Pat's nymph or Miller nymph is perfect for this. Often a second fly is tied on as a dropper. In addition to the weighted nymph, it is usually necessary to add some weight to the tippet about 6-8" above the top fly as well.

Which fly rod to use is not a matter of line weight, but length and flexibility. You are not "casting" this rig like you would a fly line. A short rod that is very flexible is what is preferred, but almost any fly rod will do the job. I've got a really cheap rod that I once picked up on a trip when I hadn't been planning on fishing that is a fiberglass composite that I've found to be ideal. It's so soft that it feels like a spinning rod.

The next step is learning how to cast this combination. The important thing to remember is that you are not casting the line like you would with a fly rod, but casting the weight on the end of the line as you would with a spinning rod. Adjust the line coming from the tip of the rod so that there are only a few inches of mono line above where the tippet is tied on hanging down from your tiptop. Grasp the mono just above the reel with one finger of your rod hand to hold the above in position. In your other hand you are holding several large open loops of line carefully so that they do not get tangled. Take the tip of the rod back slowly and stop. Then bring the rod forward as you would in casting a spinning rod. At the end of the forward motion, release the line with the finger of the rod hand and simultaneously release the loop of line with the other hand. If you have done all of this properly, the weight on the end of the tippet will pull the line out of the tiptop of the rod and it will strike the water where you have aimed. It does take a little practice to get this technique down. You will also find that you may have to adjust the amount of weight on the tippet to get it to work properly. Once you have everything adjusted, you will find that you can place the nymph extremely accurately with this technique and because you don't have a back cast to worry about, you can also work very closely to bushes, trees, etc.

Ideally you want to be working cross stream while you are casting. Aim for an upstream position that will start the nymph drifting downstream in the lane that you want. After completing the cast, immediately grasp the line that has not gone out the rod with the hand that is not holding the rod. By raising and lowering the tip of the rod and pulling in and letting out line you achieve a version of "short line" nymphing much like what I described above that will get you farther down into deep pools than is possible by using a fly line. Even the fastest sinking fly line will not sink as fast as mono with weight on the end. The highly visible mono will allow you to track the drift of the line as it moves downstream and adjust your depth accordingly. Pull in line and raise the tip of the rod as the fly moves toward you and then let out line and lower the tip of the rod as the fly moves past you and away. With a little bit of practice you will be able to get a nice long "drift" down the complete length of a deep pool with this technique. If you are doing it properly without too much line out you will also be able to feel the strike as well as use the mono line as an indicator. Raise the tip of the rod and pull on the mono with your free hand to set the hook. Then you need to get onto your reel as quickly as possible. The larger the fish the faster this is necessary. Do not try playing a big fish with the mono line. You could end up with a very nasty cut.

The Midwest version of this technique known as "chuck and duck" is similar, but larger in scale. Remember, they are using it for 5-20 lb. Steelhead. Seven to ten wt. rods are used to help fight the fish. Fly line is used in place of monofilament (though the line does not even have to be matched to the weight of the rod) and a section of red amnesia is added between the end of the line and the leader/tippet to help serve as a drift/strike indicator. Weight is added or subtracted from the end of the line by using a mesh "baggie" that can have split shot placed inside and there are usually two nymphs or a nymph and an egg pattern on the tippet both as droppers. Heavier weights are necessary to pull the fly line out of the rod as opposed to the "all-mono" system. The larger scale and heavier weights necessary make up the "duck" part of the system. If you've ever fished the Pere Marquette or a number of other Midwest Steelhead streams, you have probably seen this technique in use.

Remember I warned you at the start of this section that this wasn't a pretty technique. It certainly bears little resemblance to "classic" fly casting, and dry fly purists will be appalled. There is no denying, however, its effectiveness in certain situations where "classic" fly casting just will not get the job done. The heavy flows of spring runoffs will keep any nymph from getting down to the fish without lots of extra weight and trying to "cast" that much weight with anything smaller than about a 10 wt. rod is even more dangerous than the "chuck and duck" technique described above. In the tight circumstances of mountain fishing with rhododendrons overhanging the streams on both sides, there is often no way to even get a roll cast going with that much weight on the end. Up in the Midwest they have a similar situation with alders that makes getting casting room difficult to impossible. The "all mono" system of the Southern Appalachians and the "chuck and duck" technique of the Midwest both are similar responses to a set of unusual circumstances. Neither are techniques that I would recommend for general fly fishing, but when the necessity arises they can be extremely useful weapons to have in your arsenal.

The Bead Head Pheasant Tail

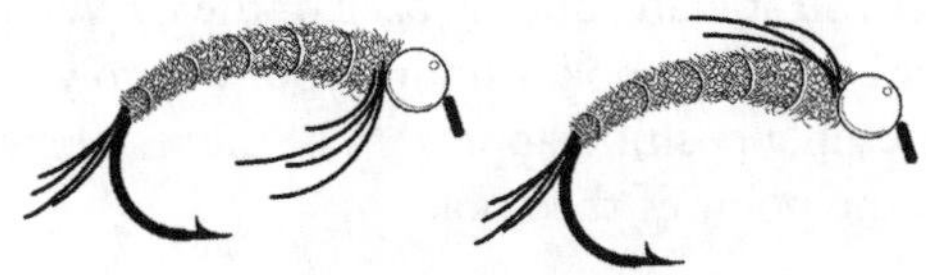

Since first being developed by Frank Sawyer, the Pheasant Tail Nymph has been one of the most enduring and effective flies in the fisherman's arsenal. It is simple to tie, uses very few materials and catches trout in a wide variety of situations. Anytime that fishermen start compiling lists of their favorite nymphs, the Pheasant Tail is sure to number among them. With the introduction of the bead head it was to be expected that one of the first nymphs to be given a bead head variation would be the Pheasant Tail. I was first introduced to the Bead Head Pheasant Tail by H.B. McCowan and have developed the versions that are listed here from his variation and several years of

Hook:	Tiemco 2487 or equivalent, #12-20
Bead:	Copper Bead in size appropriate to hook size
Thread:	Black
Ribbing:	Copper Wire
Tail, Abdomen, Thorax, etc.:	Ring Neck Pheasant Tail Fibers

fishing the fly. It has proven effective in East Tennessee on the Clinch, the Hiwassee, the Watauga and in the Smokies on both Rainbows and Browns—taking among other fish: a 23" Brown on the Watauga, a 18" Brown on the Hiwassee and +20" Bows on the Clinch.

Tying Instructions

1 Slip bead over the end of hook and slide it around to just behind the eye. Position hook in vise so that eye is slightly down. This will hold bead in position just behind the eye and keep it from slipping back on you while you are tying.

2 Start thread just behind the bead and take a couple of wraps. Cut a 3" piece of copper wire and position one end of it at the thread on the hook with the other end sticking out the back of the fly. Wrap the thread over the copper wire and the hook, working your way toward the back of the fly until you reach a position approx. $^2/_3$ of the way between the back of the bead and the point of the hook.

3 Continue wrapping the thread forward and then backwards on the hook to form a tapered body with the thread. The taper should be slightly smaller than the bead at the front of the hook and only a thread or two thick at the back. Complete the taper with the thread at the back of the hook.

4 Take 3-6 Ring Neck Pheasant Tail Fibers (depending upon the size of the hook) and with two turns of thread attach them so that the tips form the tail of the fly (approx. hook gap in length). The butts should point toward the head of the fly. Spiral the thread forward to just behind the bead leaving the butts outside these winds of thread.

5 Grasp the butts of the Pheasant Tail Fibers and spiral them forward to just behind the bead. Note: You may find it useful to use hackle pliers to grasp the fibers. Take a couple of wraps of thread to secure the fibers in position behind the bead.

6 Spiral the copper wire forward in an open spiral to just behind the bead. It is best to wrap the copper wire in the opposite direction from the direction that you used to wrap the fibers forward. This will provide extra strength to the fly. Five to six turns is usually about right. Take a couple of turns of thread to secure the copper wire and cut off the excess.

7 The butts of the Pheasant Tail Fibers should now be used to form a collar just behind the bead using turns of thread to hold them in position. Trim the excess butts so that the collar is about $^1/_3$ body length.

8 Whip finish behind the bead and cut the thread.

Variations

1 There are several different ways that you can use the butts of the Pheasant Tail Fibers to form variations on this fly:

a. Position the excess butts on the underside of the fly and trim to gap width to form legs. This gives you a fly that is similar to a scud.

b. Position the excess butts on the top side of the fly and trim to about ½ body length to form a wing case.

2 Substitute red copper wire for natural copper wire.

3 Pheasant tail is available dyed in a variety of colors. Using dyed pheasant tail in combination with different colored wire can provide for a number of variations on this fly.

4 Beads are available in copper, gold, silver, black and other colors. These can make for even more variations on this fly.

Fishing the Fly

The combination of bead head and copper wire make this a heavy fly. It is most effective in moving water, however, it does not have to be fast water. It is usually fished with a strike indicator just above or bouncing along the bottom. In the smaller sizes (#16-20) it also makes a good midge pupa imitation and can be fished shallower. The best all-around size that I have found is #14.

This is a great fly to fish in high winds. Its weight makes it very easy to punch through wind even with a 5 wt. line. It is also a fly that is durable and still works just as well after being well chewed by a number of fish. One of my best days with the Bead Head Pheasant Tail was on the Hiwassee in 20+ mph winds. The fly that I started fishing with in the morning over a dozen fish later was pretty scruffy looking but still caught an 18" Brown in the afternoon.

The Pheasant Tail Nymph— Original Patterns

Since first being developed by Frank Sawyer in the 1930's The Pheasant Tail Nymph has become one of the most popular patterns throughout the world when fishing for trout. Sawyer, who worked as the river keeper on the Wiltshire Avon in England, designed this nymph to imitate several species of Baetis nymphs, but it has proven itself in a wide variety of situations and circumstances. Sawyer's pattern, however, has been so heavily adapted that most of the Pheasant Tail patterns out there now bear little relationship to the original. He had zeroed in on key elements of the nymph that he tried to capture in his pattern in the simplest and most elegant way possi-

The Pheasant Tail Nymph

So without much further ado, let's move to the pattern as it was intended to be:

Hook: #12-#24, 2XL Round or Perfect bend

Thread/weight: fine dark colored (enameled) copper wire

Tail/abdomen/thorax/wingcase: Red/brown fibers from a cock pheasant tail feather, matching the copper wire in color

Note: A good supply of enameled copper wire may be found taking apart old power supplies, dynamos, etc. To tie the nymphs on #18 hooks, use copper wire with a diameter of 0.06mm (0.0025") This wire will tie down to #28, should you be into 'wee' nymphs. The largest diameter I would use (for #12 hooks) would be 0.15mm (0.006")

ble. His pattern utilized only two simple materials: fine, dark colored copper wire and fibers from the pheasant tail. It did not even use thread.

Recently I have been corresponding with Hans Weilenmann of Holland who still has several of the original nymphs that were tied by Frank Sawyer himself. Hans sent me the following pattern that is closely based upon Sawyer's method of tying the nymph with comments on Sawyer's technique and his own. Hans has graciously granted me permission to reprint his pattern and comments in this article. With all of the numerous variations on the Pheasant Tail Nymph that exist in pattern books today, I thought that you might appreciate seeing how the first of these very popular nymphs were actually tied.

—L.J.

Tying Instructions

(by Hans Weilenmann, with comments on Sawyer's Original)
(These instructions assume a right-handed tyer)

I will describe how I tie this nymph, explaining also where I deviate from Sawyer's method and why. The final result of either method is very close. Use whichever you prefer.

1 Take a piece of copper wire, about 12 inches in length. Attach near the eye like you would do with thread. Build up a slight thorax covering one-third of the hook shank, then wrap the wire to the start of the bend.

2 Even the tips of four fibers of the tail feather, clip close to stem. At the back of the hook shank tie in the pheasant fibers near the tips, forming a short tail, with two or three turns of wire.

3 Keeping the wire tight, wrap the fiber butts toward the eye in a (counter) wrap, i.e., if you normally wrap materials over the shank and away from you (as most of us do) then you wrap the fibers over the shank toward you. Trap each successive turn with the tip of your left index finger to stop the fibers unwinding. Your final wrap should leave the butts sticking straight up, right behind the eye. Please note that the wire is not wound with the fibers, but left behind until step 4.

4 In open turns, spiral the copper wire toward the eye. These turns will "cross" the wrapped pheasant fibers, reinforcing the body and preventing the whole nymph coming undone when chewed upon by the fish.

5 After you have tied down the butts behind the eye, fold them back and make a few wraps of wire between the eye and the pheasant fibers. Next

take the wire in one open turn over the shank to just behind the thorax. Fold the butts back over the thorax and tie down with one or two wraps of wire, followed by a three-turn whip-finish (preferred) or a couple of half hitches. Clip butts, apply a very small amount of (thin) head cement and the P.T. nymph is complete.

Instead of the two-step approach I described, Frank Sawyer would wrap the pheasant fibers around the wire to form a rope and wrap toward the eye. There he would separate the fibers and the wire, tie down the fibers, move the wire behind the thorax, lap fibers back, wire back to front, lap fibers toward the eye again and tie off.

My objections to this setup are that:

a. The rope method results in a fatter, somewhat uneven, abdomen. Especially in smaller sizes I like to get a very slender silhouette.

b. Folding the wingcase forward again leaves a weak spot at the thorax/abdomen point. In my experience the fibers will break at this point after one or two fish and the nymph will lose definition. (And I like my flies to last.)

Cheers,
Hans

The Pheasant and Peacock

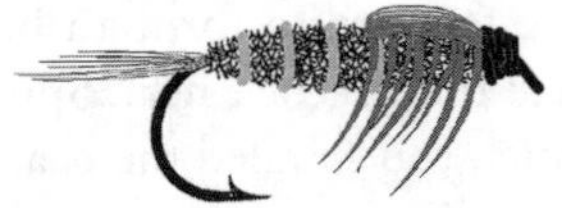

Two materials that seem to reappear again and again in Southeast mountain trout flies are Pheasant Tail and Peacock Herl. Here's a simple nymph that combines these two materials in one fly and is extremely effective on mountain trout. On my last trip to Abrams Creek in the Smokies after running through a number of different patterns with indifferent results, this turned out to be the fly that saved the day.

Hook:	Mustad 9671 or TMC 5262 (2X Nymph) #8-16
Thread:	Black
Tail:	3-4 Pheasant Tail fibers
Ribbing:	Copper Wire
Abdomen & Thorax:	2-4 Strands Peacock Herl
Wing Case:	4-8 Pheasant Tail fibers
Legs:	Partridge feather

Tying Instructions

1 Start the thread just behind the eye of the hook and wind to the bend.

2 Take 3-4 Pheasant Tail fibers depending upon the size of the hook and tie them in as a tail approx. 1½ times gap width in length.

3 Tie in a piece of copper wire about 2-3" long at the bend of the hook and let hang.

4 Tie in 2-4 strands of Peacock Herl at the bend of the hook and then wind the thread forward to the middle of the hook shank. Wrap the Peacock Herl forward to form the abdomen of the fly about ½ hook shank length. Tie off and let the excess herl hang in place. You will use this later to also form the thorax of the fly.

5 Spiral the copper wire forward to form a ribbing on the abdomen of the fly and to reinforce the peacock herl. Spiral the wire in the opposite direction from which you spiraled the peacock herl. If you wrapped the herl in a clockwise direction, for example, wrap the copper wire counterclockwise. When you reach the end of the abdomen, then start wrapping the copper wire in a tight spiral under what will be the thorax of the fly. This will serve to help weight the fly and give a little more bulk to the thorax. When you get to about ⅛" behind the eye of the hook, stop wrapping the wire and trim off the excess. Crisscross several turns of thread over the copper wire under the thorax to hold it in place. Finish with your thread at the front end of the abdomen.

6 Tie in 4-8 more pheasant tail fibers and let their ends hang toward the back of the fly. This will later form the wing case.

7 Take a partridge feather and tie it in by its tip. This will form the legs of the fly. It will be pulled forward over the thorax before the wing case is pulled forward. Selecting the proper size partridge feather for the hook is an important part of the process. Try to pick one that will give you legs hanging out the side of the wing case that are approx. hook gap in length. It may take a little practice to choose the right size feather. It is also usually best to tie in the tip of the partridge feather with the underside up so that when it is pulled forward the darker (top) side will be up. Let the butt of the partridge feather hang toward the back of the fly over the top of the pheasant tail fibers that you have tied in for the wing case. After tying both the pheasant tail fibers and the partridge feather in, the thread should be returned to the front of the abdomen of the fly, securing both of these items well in place and then it should be wrapped forward to just behind the eye of the hook.

8 Wrap the peacock herl forward to form the thorax of the fly. It should be wrapped over the top of the copper wire, the ends of the pheasant tail

that have been tied in and over the tip of the partridge feather. Secure the peacock herl with a couple of wraps of thread just behind the eye of the hook. Trim off the excess peacock herl.

9. Pull the partridge feather forward over the top of the thorax to form the legs and secure it in place behind the eye of the hook with a couple of wraps of thread. Trim off the excess hanging over the eye of the hook.

10. Pull the pheasant tail fibers that have been tied in over the top of the thorax and the partridge feather and secure it in place behind the eye of the hook with a couple of wraps of thread. This forms the wing case. Trim off the excess fibers hanging over the top of the eye of the hook.

11. Whip finish and add a little head cement if desired.

Fishing the Fly

This is among the most effective mountain Trout stream nymphs that there are. It has consistently produced Trout throughout the Southeast under all kinds of conditions. It can be weighted heavily enough to get down into the deepest mountain pools or tied lighter for shallower situations.

The Olive Bead Head

This fly was first developed while I was working on my variation of the Bead Head Pheasant Tail. I wanted something similar in feel, but in an olive color. It uses a synthetic dubbing such as Ligas or Spectrablend with a good deal of sparkle to it and closely resembles the Bead Head Pheasant Tail in shape and effect. All that I've said earlier about the Bead Head Pheasant Tail applies to this fly as well.

Hook:	Tiemco 2487 or equivalent, #12-20
Bead:	Gold bead in size appropriate to hook
Thread:	Olive
Ribbing:	Gold wire
Tail:	Wood duck flank
Body:	Olive, olive-brown or olive-gray artificial dubbing
Legs:	Wood duck flank fibers tied in on each side behind the head

Tying Instructions

1 Slip bead over end of hook and slide it around to just behind the eye. Position hook in vise so that eye is slightly down. This will hold bead

in position just behind the eye and keep it from slipping back on you while you are tying.

2 Start thread just behind the bead and take a couple of wraps. Cut a 3" piece of gold wire and position one end of it at the thread on the hook with the other end sticking out the back of the fly. Wrap the thread over the wire and the hook working your way toward the back of the fly until you reach a position approx. ⅔ of the way between the back of the bead and the point of the hook.

3 Take 3-6 Wood Duck Flank Fibers (depending upon the size of the hook) and with two turns of thread attach them so that the tips form the tail of the fly (approx. hook gap in length). The butts should point toward the head of the fly. Trim off the excess.

4 Dub the body forward in a taper with the body being quite small at the tail, working its way gradually to just slightly smaller than the bead at the front end.

5 Spiral the wire forward in an open spiral to just behind the bead. Five to six turns is usually about right. Take a couple of turns of thread to secure the wire and cut off the excess.

6 Take 3-6 Wood Duck Flank Fibers and attach them on each side of the fly right behind the bead as wing-like legs. These should be about hook gap in length and flare out from the side of the fly. Trim off the excess butts.

7 Whip finish behind the bead and cut the thread.

Fishing the Fly

The combination of scud hook and bead head make this a fly that is versatile enough to be used in a wide variety of situations throughout the Southeast. Effective on both mountain Trout streams and tailwaters, it is just a great all-around nymph.

Variations

This fly can be created in a wide variety of colors by varying the color of the dubbing, the bead, the wire, and using materials other than wood duck flank such as pheasant tail or mallard flank.

The Prince Nymph

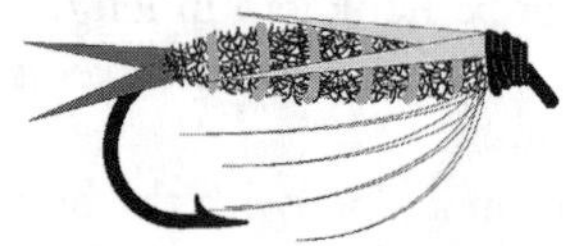

The Prince Nymph, also known as the Black or Brown Forked Tail, has been a staple of Southeastern fly fishers since it was first introduced by Doug Prince. This is another of those general purpose nymphs that are effective on both the tailwaters and the mountain streams of the Southeast. Weighted, this is a great fly for fishing the fast water conditions of spring runoff. The largest rainbow that I've ever taken out of the Oconoluftee (16") was on a Prince.

Hook:	Mustad 9671 or TMC 5262, (2X Nymph) #8-16
Thread:	Black
Tail:	2 brown or black goose biots tied forked about 1½ gap width
Rib:	Silver or gold tinsel
Body:	Peacock herl
Hackle:	Black or brown hen hackle tied in as a collar
Wing:	2 white goose biots tied in like a V to the bend of the hook

Tying Instructions

1 Start the thread at the bend of the hook.

2 Tie in two brown or black goose biots as a forked tail about 1½ times hook gap in length.

3 Tie in gold or silver tinsel for ribbing and let it hang.

4 Tie in several strands of peacock herl to form the body. Wind the thread forward to a point about ¼ shank length behind the eye of the hook.

5 Wrap the peacock herl forward to the thread. Tie off and trim the excess herl.

6 Spiral the tinsel forward to the thread. Tie off and trim the excess tinsel.

7 Tie in soft hackle and take a couple of turns to form a collar. Tie off and trim the excess hackle.

8 Tie in two white goose biots over the top of the body as a wing. These should form a V over the body top with the point of the V right behind the eye of the hook and the two tips of the V reaching to the bend of the hook.

9 Whip finish.

Fishing the Fly

The Prince Nymph is another of those all-purpose nymphs that are useful in both the mountain Trout streams of the Southeast and on its tailwaters. On the mountain streams I usually prefer the weighted version of this fly to help get it down to the bottom of pools where the big ones are hiding out.

The Gold-Ribbed Hare's Ear Nymph

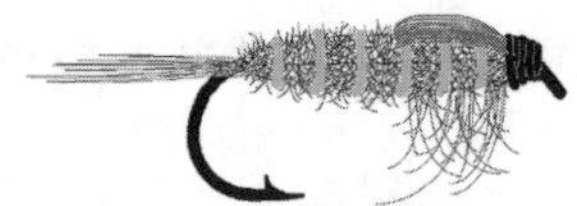

The Gold Ribbed Hare's Ear Nymph is one more of those flies that you should always have in your box in a variety of sizes. If you are unsure of what nymph to use then the GRHE can usually be a very good bet. In the Southeast it is useful in both the tailwaters and the mountain streams and can even be used to pick up a panfish when you're in the mood for a nice mess of bluegills.

Hook:	Mustad 9671 or TMC 5262, (2X Nymph) #8-16
Thread:	Brown
Tail:	Brown hackle fibers or brown partridge ($1\frac{1}{2}$ times gap width)
Rib:	Fine gold tinsel or wire palmered up to thorax
Abdomen:	Hare's mask and ear dubbing blend
Wing Case:	Gray duck or goose quill section
Thorax:	Hare's mask and ear dubbing blend
Legs:	Thorax picked out

Tying Instructions

1 Start your thread just behind the eye of the hook and wind it to the bend.

2. Tie in the tailing material and trim the butts of the tail.
3. Tie in the ribbing just above the tail and return the thread to the bend of the hook.
4. Dub the abdomen of the fly in a taper to a point about ½ way up the hook.
5. Spiral the ribbing to the top of the abdomen and tie it off.
6. Tie in the wing case material and let the other end hang toward the back of the fly.
7. Dub the thorax of the fly with the same material as the abdomen, only slightly fatter.
8. Pull the wing case material over the top of the thorax and secure it in place just behind the eye of the hook. Trim off the excess.
9. Whip finish.
10. Pick out the "legs" from the bottom of the thorax dubbing.

Fishing the Fly

The Gold Ribbed Hare's Ear nymph, after the Pheasant Tail nymph, is probably the second-most successful nymph ever created. This is another of those all-purpose flies, fish it anywhere and for anything nymphs that you have got to always have handy. I'm fond of using a heavily weighted version in the mountains and a bead head version that is tied on a scud hook for the tailwaters.

Variations

1. The fly can be tied weighted or unweighted.
2. It can be tied with or w/o a bead head.
3. It can be tied in a variety of colors. Use light or dark hare's ear and mask dubbing or dubbing that has been dyed olive.
4. In addition to being tied on a standard nymph hook, it can also be tied on a scud hook.

The Red Fox Squirrel Nymph

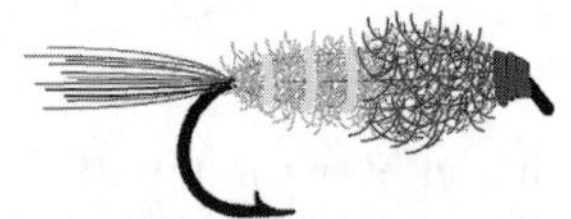

Hardly any flytying book today would be complete without at least one pattern by Dave Whitlock in it. This one is certainly among Dave's best. It's a general purpose nymph that can be used throughout the mountains of the Southeast to represent many different forms of subsurface insect life: caddis pupa, mayfly nymphs, stonefly nymphs, and even crawfish. Just look at the wide number of hook sizes upon which it can be tied and you'll get an idea of how varied and useful it can be.

Hook:	Mustad 9671, TMC 5262 #2-18
Thread:	Brown
Weight:	"Lead" wire wound around forward half of hook shank
Tail:	Body hairs from the back of a red fox squirrel (tied gap width past bend in length)
Rib:	Gold oval tinsel or gold wire depending upon the size of the hook
Abdomen:	Orange belly fur from a red fox squirrel blended about half and half with a synthetic dubbing close in color
Thorax:	Fur and guard hairs from the back of a red fox squirrel blended about half and half with a synthetic dubbing close in color

Tying Instructions

1. Start the thread just behind the eye of the hook and wrap it to the bend.

2. Take a piece of "lead" wire and wrap it tightly around the forward half of the hook shank. Wrap the thread forward over the top of the wire back and forth several times, securing it in place. Finish with the thread at the bend.

3. Tie in a tail of some body hairs from the back of a red fox squirrel. These should be about gap width long past the bend of the hook.

4. Tie in a piece of gold oval tinsel about 2-3 inches long just in front of the tail. This should hang loose over the back of the hook for later use as ribbing. In the smaller sizes, gold wire should be substituted for the larger diameter tinsel.

5. Dub a tapered abdomen forward to about the center of the hook shank.

6. Dub a thorax forward to just behind the eye of the hook. The thorax should be slightly larger in diameter than the thickest portion of the abdomen.

7. Whip finish just behind the eye of the hook.

Note that in the smaller sizes a slightly finer, but still coarse dubbing should be used. In the larger sizes a very coarse dubbing is necessary. With the very coarse dubbing used in the larger sizes, a dubbing loop will help produce the shaggy look desired in this fly. You can also use your bodkin to pick out the dubbing to give the fly its properly disheveled appearance.

Fishing the Fly

This is a nymph that I'd recommend for our mountain streams, but not necessarily just for Trout. It is also highly effective for Smallmouth and panfish. I most commonly fish it in the larger sizes because I feel that its shagginess comes off better on a bigger scale. A good all-around nymph.

Variations

Any very coarse dubbing in the correct color can be used for this fly. If you can't get red fox squirrel, then gray squirrel dyed orange can be substituted for the abdomen and straight gray squirrel for the thorax.

The Scud

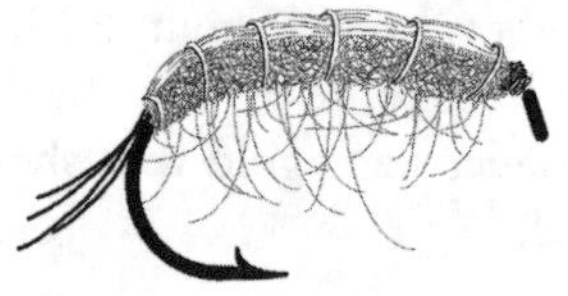

The scud is a freshwater crustacean common in tailwaters, ponds and streams which support heavy weed and algae growth. They come in a wide variety of colors and sizes. Where present they often form a major portion of the trout's diet. When fishing the tailwaters of the Southeast you should ALWAYS have some scuds along—usually in sizes 12-16.

Hook:	Mustad 3906B, TMC 3761 (1X Nymph) or TMC 2487, Mustad AC80250BR (Shrimp/Scud), #12-16
Thread:	Gray or Black 6/0 or 8/0
Weight:	(Optional) Medium lead wire
Tail:	Wood Duck Flank or Dyed Mallard
Rib:	Fine Silver or Gold Wire or Monofilament
Shellback:	Clear plastic strip cut from a poly bag about 1/8" wide
Body:	Coarse Gray, Olive or Olive Gray Dubbing
Legs:	Pick out fur on bottom of body

Tying Instructions

1 Start thread just behind hook eye and wrap back to bend.

2 Weight with lead wire wrapped around center of hook shank if desired. Wrap lead wire w/thread. Finish at bend of hook.

3 Tie in tail, about ½ shank length long.

4 Tie in ribbing and then shellback at bend of hook.

5 Wax thread well and twist on dubbing.

6 Wind dubbing forward making a smooth body to just behind eye.

7 Take a couple of wraps of thread to secure dubbing in place.

8 Pull shellback over top of dubbed body and secure in place with a couple of wraps of thread. Trim off excess plastic.

9 Wind rib over body and shellback, tie off and trim.

10 Whip finish and apply head cement.

11 Pick out dubbing on underside of body to form legs.

Variations

This fly can be tied weighted or unweighted. It can be tied with or without the mono eyes. Instead of picking out the legs try using a low-quality hackle feather w/barbules approx. hook gap in length. Tie this in by the tip after tying in the shellback at the back of the hook. Then, after dubbing the body, palmer (spiral) it forward to just behind the hook eye. Trim off the barbules on the top of the body, then pull over the shellback and the ribbing as above. The hackle feather forms the legs of the scud.

Experiment with different kinds of materials for the shellback: gold mylar, iridescent plastic, etc.

Scuds can be tied in many other colors besides those indicated in the pattern. Orange and pink are two other popular colors.

Fishing the Fly

This fly can be fished using a variety of nymphing techniques. It can be fished under a strike indicator, usually near the bottom. It can also be fished using short line nymphing technique—usually most effective in faster water. If sight fishing to a known location, try stopping the drift just short of the fish, causing the fly to rise. In still waters, imparting some movement to the fly will often induce a strike. If you can observe the natural movement of the scuds present, then try to imitate their actions at the depth at which the fish are feeding. The fly is very effective in tailwaters and ponds where scuds are plentiful. It can also be a deadly bluegill pattern.

The Sowbug (Cressbug, or Isopod)

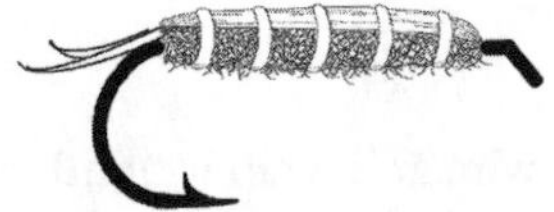

The Sowbug is a widely distributed crustacean from the order Isopoda. Found in most lakes, ponds and slow moving bodies of water, they are also prevalent in many tailwaters as well. Where they are present, they often form a substantial portion of the trout's diet. Characterized by a flat profile, a hard back, legs sticking out the sides of the body and two (or more) prominent antennae, they are not a difficult food form to imitate. The pattern given here was developed from a pattern brought back from the White River in Arkansas by Phil Brandt.

Hook:	Mustad 3906 #16 or equivalent
Thread:	Black
Antennae:	2 Natural Goose Biots
Ribbing:	5X Tippet
Back:	1/8" wide strip of scud back or clear iridescent plastic
Weight:	.015 dia. heavy soft wire (lead substitute)
Dubbing:	Gray Hareline Dubbing or Gray-Olive Nymph Dubbing

Tying Instructions

1 Start the thread at the front of hook and wind to the bend. Attach two goose biots approx. hook gap in length forming the antennae or what looks like a split tail.

2 Wind the thread to the front of the hook lashing one end of 3" of 5X tippet material or monofilament line to the side of the hook. The other end should stick out the back of the hook.

3 Wind the thread to the bend of the hook attaching one end of the ⅛" wide plastic or scud back to the top of the hook with enough sticking out the back of the hook to later be pulled forward to form the top shell of the sowbug. At this point you have the two biots, the ribbing and the shell material all sticking out the back of the hook with the thread at the bend.

4 Take about 2" of the wire and wrap it tightly around the center section of the hook forming a tight spiral from approx. 1/16" forward of the bend to 1/16" back of the eye. This usually takes about 8 wraps of wire. Trim off any excess wire.

5 Wrap the wire with thread in a criscross fashion. When finished the wire should be almost completely encased in the thread. Complete the wrapping process with the thread at the bend of the hook. Apply head cement to the thread encased wire and let it dry.

6 Using a non-serrated pliers or hemostat, flatten the wire to form the thin profile and wide back of the sowbug.

7 Apply the dubbing to the thread and wrap it around the flattened wire dubbing forward to just behind the eye of the hook.

8 Grasp the ⅛" plastic and pull it forward over the top of the dubbing. Secure it in place just behind the eye of the hook with a couple of turns of thread. Trim off the excess sticking out over the eye of the hook.

9 Spiral the tippet or mono ribbing forward in an open spiral over the top of the dubbing and plastic to just behind the eye of the hook. Secure it in place with a couple of turns of thread and trim off the excess.

10 Whip finish just behind the eye of the hook and cut the thread.

11 Pick out the dubbing just a little, only on the sides of the body. Trim any excess dubbing sticking out on the top or the bottom of the fly. This forms the characteristic legs sticking out the side of the body and also helps accentuate the thin profile and wide back and bottom.

Fishing the Fly

This is a slow water fly fished on a dead drift as close to the bottom as possible. It is usually fished with a strike indicator so that it drifts just above the bottom of a tailwater. When fished in a pond or lake it is often fished with a sinking line and then moved along slowly just above the bottom. It can also be fished in a pond or lake by allowing it the sink to the bottom and then using a series of slow, short retrieves, allowing it to again sink between each retrieve.

The Caddis Sparkle Pupa

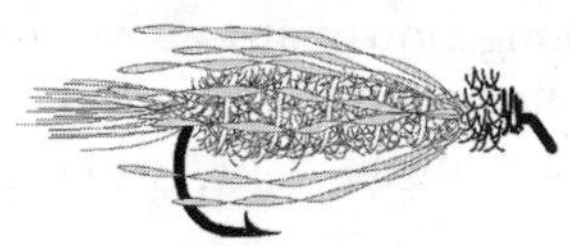

I was first introduced to this fly by Rick Murphree, a fly tyer and fisher from East Tennessee. This is a simple fly to tie that has proven to be effective on both the mountain streams and tailwaters of the Southeast. All of the materials used in tying this fly incorporate some kind of "sparkle" to them that helps make this a good attractor pattern even if there aren't any Caddis around.

Hook:	Mustad 9671 or TMC 5262, (2X Nymph) #8-16
Thread:	Black
Weight:	(Optional) Several wraps of "lead" wire
Tail:	A short strand of olive antron yarn
Rib:	Fine gold wire
Body:	Olive to olive-brown or olive-gray antron dubbing
Collar:	Rainbow Krystal Flash
Head:	Peacock herl

Tying Instructions

1. Start the thread behind the hook eye and wind to the bend of the hook.
2. Using "lead" wire wrap several turns of weight around the shank of the hook centering the turns on the shank.

3 Wrap the thread back and forth over the wire to secure it in place. Finish with the thread at the bend of the hook.

4 Tie in a short length of antron yarn as a tail (about gap width in length).

5 Tie in a piece of gold wire as ribbing and let hang.

6 Dub the body forward to about 1/4 hook length behind the eye. The body is usually tied in a reverse taper with the back a little fatter than the front.

7 Spiral the gold wire forward to the end of the dubbing and tie off and trim.

8 Cut 7-10 pieces of rainbow Krystal Flash and hold them distributed around the hook as a collar just in front of the body. Take a couple of turns to loosely hold them in place. Using your thumb and forefinger, distribute the flash around the hook shank as evenly as possible. You are trying to form a collar much like a wet fly collar. When you have them distributed well, take a couple more tight turns of thread to secure in place. Trim off any excess hanging over the eye of the hook.

9 Tie in a piece of peacock herl right where you have tied in the Krystal Flash. Take several turns to cover the butts of the Krystal Flash and form a head that ends up just behind the eye of the hook. Trim excess peacock herl and whip finish.

10 Trim the Krystal Flash hanging over the back of the hook so that in length it reaches to about the middle of the tail.

Fishing the Fly

The Caddis Sparkle Pupa is a nymph that is useful on both our mountain Trout streams and tailwaters. Even though the idea behind it was originally to imitate Caddis pupa it actually is useful for a good deal more than that. While usually fished as a nymph, this is a fly that can be fished as a wet fly as well. A versatile contender.

Variations

This fly can also be tied as a bead head. Colors can be varied by using different color antron yarn and dubbing.

The Glass Bead Bodied Nymph

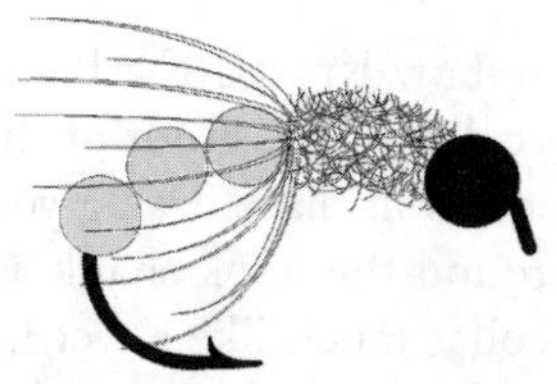

Recently there have started to appear already packaged for fly tyers a number of different kinds of glass beads. I've already mentioned in earlier articles utilizing these in place of the metal beads for bead head nymphs, but many fly tyers even before these beads were available in fly shops had already been experimenting with using them for the bodies of nymphs. Using beads for the body of the nymph builds a strong segmented feeling directly into the nymph while the glass of the beads give it a very attractive translucency. Claude Freaner, a fly tyer and friend from Virginia, has been doing this for a number of years. The following is an adaptation of one of Claude's early Bead Bodied Nymph patterns that is useful as both a Caddis pupa and a scud imitation.

If you have trouble finding the right size or color beads for what you would like to do in the fly shops then be sure and take a good look around your local craft store. They carry a wide variety of glass beads, many of which work just fine for this pattern. The color of the glass beads and the color of the dubbing in this pattern can be varied to whatever colors of each you desire. They can both be the same or the color of the dubbing can provide a contrast to the color of the bead. For a Caddis imitation, for example, you might want to use green beads with a brown or black dubbing. You could even use a different material in place of the dubbing such as peacock herl. For a scud imitation, on the other hand, you would probably want to use the same color in both the beads and the dubbing such as olive, gray, etc.

Hook:	Tiemco 2487, 2457 or Mustad 80250BR (Scud) Hook, #12-14
Beads:	1 black bead (glass or metal) for the "head" and 4 colored beads for the "body" size 11/0 for a #14 hook or size 10/0 for a #12 hook
Thread:	Black or to match color of dubbing
Hackle:	Partridge, grouse, sage hen or other soft hackle
Thorax:	Synthetic dubbing of color desired

Tying Instructions

1 Flatten the barb on the hook to help the beads slide on.

2 Slide the black bead onto the hook first followed by the 4 colored beads. *Hint:* it is very helpful to have something to hold the hook and something else to grasp the beads while you are doing this. The hook can be placed in your vise upside down secured near the eye or you can grasp it in a pair of hemostats. The beads can be grasped with a pair of tweezers or something else like an electrical test probe. If you use a black metal bead, this will give you a nymph that is more heavily weighted; a black glass bead will give you a nymph that is less heavily weighted.

3 After you have the beads on the hook, secure it in the vise in the usual manner. Slide the beads toward the head of the hook.

4 Tie on several windings of thread about ⅔ of the way from the eye of the hook to the point of the hook and whip finish in the same location. This thread serves as the stop to keep the glass beads from sliding off the point of the hook. It may take a time or two to get this thread "ball" just the right size to keep the beads from sliding off. The whole arrangement will also be more secure if you will put a little head cement on the thread "ball."

5 Move the colored beads away from the black "head" bead and back to the thread "stop" that you have just created. The black bead should be positioned just behind the eye of the hook. There should be a space between the colored beads and the black bead about ¼ hook length or

less. Depending upon the size of the beads that you are using, you may have to do a little adjusting of the location of the "stop" to get your proportions just right on the fly.

6 Tie on a soft hackle feather just in front of the colored beads. Take one turn around the hook with this hackle and tie it off. Trim off the excess.

7 Twist some dubbing onto your tying thread and dub a "thorax" forward to just behind the black bead. A synthetic "buggy" looking dubbing is usually best for this. This is also the location where you could wind in some peacock herl if you wanted to substitute that for the dubbing.

8 Whip finish directly behind the black bead.

Fishing the Fly

Claude's concoction is much easier to achieve variations for now than it was when he originally created it. You will find that glass beads are much more readily available in fly shops than they used to be and that the selection at crafts stores has greatly increased as well. The result is that it is a lot easier to suit this fly to your particular needs and conditions. Work with both the mountain stream and tailwater variations to create something that is perfect for your particular situation. This is a great nymph for difficult conditions where you are having trouble getting the fish to hit.

Midge Larva and Pupas

It's winter and the young fly fisherman's fancy turns to thoughts of midges (old one's too for that matter). Any day with just a little bit of warmth in the air brings out hatches of them even when there is nothing else around. Midge patterns are (except for the size) among the simplest of flies to tie. They usually require very few materials and the techniques involved are easy to master. Once you get over being intimidated by small hooks they are not difficult. These three patterns offer a variety of midge larva and pupa imitations and are adaptable to a wide range of conditions. One of the greatest joys of winter fishing is to tie into a large trout with a light rod, tippet and a small fly.

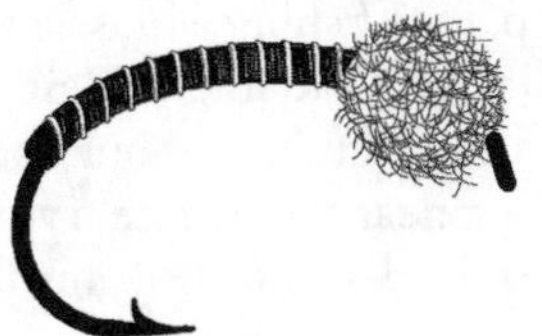

The Brassie

Hook:	Tiemco 2487 Scud #16-20
Thread:	Black, Brown, Olive or Tan
Ribbing:	Small Copper Wire
Thorax:	Hare's Ear Dubbing

Tying Instructions

1 Start the thread just behind the eye of the hook and wind it toward the back about 3-4 turns. Take about 2-3" of copper wire and lay one end

of it on top of the hook with the other end extending out the back. Wrap your thread over the copper wire attaching it to the hook. Wind the thread in tight turns to about the point on the hook where the bend is vertical.

2 Wind the thread back to about 1/3 to 1/4 of the way behind the eye. Spiral the wire up to the thread in an open spiral (about 5-8 turns depending upon the size of the hook). Take a couple of turns of thread over the wire at the point 1/3 to 1/4 of the way behind the eye and clip off the excess wire.

3 Dub your thread with a little bit of hare's ear or other coarse dubbing and wrap a thorax from this point up to the eye.

4 Whip finish and clip the thread. This is a slightly different version of the regular brassie. The more common brassie is usually tied with the winds of wire tight against one another rather than in an open spiral.

Fishing the Fly

Brassies can imitate either larva or pupa and are usually fished with a strike indicator. The most difficult part of fishing a brassie is determining what depth to set it below the strike indicator. Watch for bulging rise forms. If there are a lot of these, that tends to indicate that you should be setting your depth shallow. If there are few fish feeding near the surface try deeper. It often takes some experimentation to find the right depth to fish this fly.

Variations

Use different color thread and either natural or colored copper wire.

The WD-40

Hook:	Tiemco 2487 Scud # 16-20
Thread:	Body color for your midge: olive, brown, black, gray, etc.
Tail & Wing Case:	Wood duck flank fibers (hence the WD of the name)
Thorax:	Coarse dubbing like hare's ear

Tying Instructions

1 Start the thread behind the eye and wind it to the back of the hook. Tie in about 3-5 wood duck flank fibers as a tail about hook gap in length. Wind the thread over the wood duck fibers toward the eye of the hook so that the butts stick out over the eye. This forms the abdomen of the fly with the thread.

2 Pull the butt ends of the wood duck fibers back over the body so that they are now directed back toward the tail. Wrap the thread back toward the rear of the hook enough for the thorax, about $\frac{1}{4}$ to $\frac{1}{3}$ hook length.

3 Dub the thread with the hare's ear and wrap toward the eye forming the thorax and leaving enough room to tie off the head. Bring the wood duck fibers back over the top of the dubbed thorax toward the eye of the hook and tie them off to form a wing case. Cut off the butt ends of the wood duck fibers and whip finish the head of the fly.

Fishing the Fly

Fish the WD-40 dead drift near the bottom as a midge larva with a split shot and strike indicator. Let it swing at the end of the drift and rise up toward the surface as a natural would rise. Many of the strikes will come at this time. After the swing and rise, slowly bring the fly back in a hand twist retrieve and this will also bring an occasional strike. If the trout are on the surface feeding, take the weight off of the leader and fish as you would a dry fly. At the end of your drift also try a slow retrieve.

Variations

If you want to fish it exclusively as a midge pupa, try using a thin copper wire as ribbing on the abdomen. In a #14-16 hook size this also makes a fair to middling scud imitation. This is a fly that has been touted highly on FLYFISH@. My thanks to Henry Kanemoto for this variation.

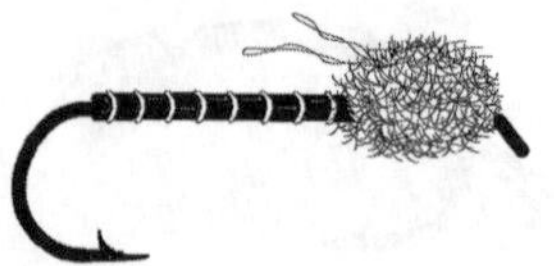

The Clinch River Midge

Hook: Mustad 9671 or equivalent 2X Nymph hook #18-22 or Tiemco 2487 (Scud hook) #16-20
Thread: Black
Ribbing: Fine Silver Wire
Thorax: Hare's Ear Dubbing
Wing Case: Two strands of Rainbow Krystal Flash

Tying Instructions

1 Start the thread behind the eye of the hook and take a couple of wraps. Place about 2-3" of fine silver wire on top of the hook with one end at the thread and the other end sticking out the back of the hook. Secure the wire in place with a couple of wraps of thread.

2 Wind the thread tightly to the bend of the hook and then forward to about 1/4 of the way behind the eye. This forms the abdomen of the fly with the thread.

3 Spiral the wire forward to the thread in open spirals. It usually takes about 4-6 turns depending upon the size of the hook. Secure the wire at this point with 2-3 turns of thread and clip the excess wire.

4 Dub your thread with Hare's Ear Dubbing and take 2-3 turns of thread and dubbing to begin forming the thorax of the fly.

5 Before the thorax is completely formed, take two strands of Rainbow Krystal Flash and lay them on top of the dubbing with excess sticking out in both directions. Finish wrapping the thorax with the dubbed thread completing your windings just behind the eye of the hook. This also secures the Krystal Flash in place.

6 Trim the excess Krystal Flash sticking out the front even with the dubbing and whip finish the fly. Then trim the excess Krystal Flash sticking out the back to about 1/2 the length of the abdomen.

Fishing the Fly

This is a midge pupa imitation and should be fished pretty much like the Brassie. The small amount of Krystal Flash and silver ribbing are a closer imitation of a midge pupa than the Brassie though. When you see bulging rise forms near the surface, this can be a more effective fly fished shallow than the Brassie. I got the idea for this fly from an old Kentucky fisherman who often fishes the Clinch. My variation on his fly was to add the silver ribbing and substitute Krystal Flash for two white feather fibers sticking out the back of the thorax.

The Pheasant Tail Midge

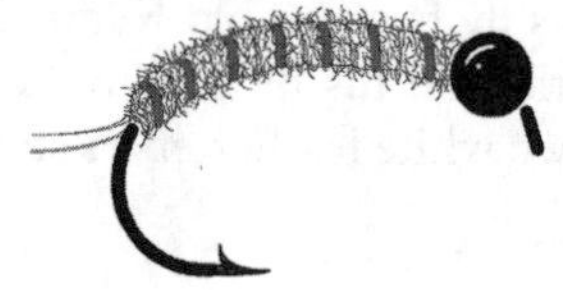

This fly was first developed as a variant on the Bead Head Pheasant Tail, but since has gone through so many changes that it has taken on a life of its own and deserves a new name. The inspiration for it came originally from the Bead Head Pheasant Tail as well as suggestions from H.B. McCowan and others. It was only after the recent introduction of very fine beads in a variety of colors that tying this fly in the small sizes necessary to imitate midge pupa has become possible. It has proven itself on numerous midge hatches and the variations make it highly versatile. The basic idea is to use a couple of feather barbules such as from a pheasant tail, turkey, dyed turkey, etc., to create the body of the fly. The mini barbules that stick out from the sides of the larger barbules have proven to give a nice combination of movement and lifelike appearance to the body of the fly. The copper or other color wire ribbing provides strength over the top of the feather barbules and the bead head can be varied in color to suit local preferences or needs.

Hook:	Tiemco 2487 (scud hook) or equivalent, #16-22
Bead:	Black (or other color) Bead in size appropriate to hook size
Thread:	Black (or color of feather barbule)
Ribbing:	Fine Copper (or other color) Wire
Tail & Body:	2 Ring Neck Pheasant Tail Fibers or Turkey Feather Barbules either natural or dyed

Tying Instructions

1 Slip bead over end of hook and slide it around to just behind the eye. Position hook in vise so that eye is slightly down. This will hold bead in position just behind the eye and keep it from slipping back on you while you are tying.

2 Start thread just behind the bead and take a couple of wraps. Cut a 2" piece of wire and position one end of it at the thread on the hook with the other end sticking out the back of the fly. Wrap the thread over the wire and the hook working your way toward the back of the fly until you reach a position approx. ⅔ of the way between the back of the bead and the point of the hook.

3 Take 2 Ring Neck Pheasant Tail Fibers or Turkey Barbules and with one turn of thread attach them so that the tips form the tail of the fly (very short). You can now gently pull on the butts of the fibers to get the tail to the desired length. When you have got the tail the length that you desire, take another tight turn over the first one. The butts should point toward the head of the fly. Spiral the thread forward to just behind the bead leaving the butts outside these winds of thread.

4 Grasp the butts of the Pheasant Tail Fibers and spiral them forward to just behind the bead. Note: You may find it useful to use hackle pliers to grasp the fibers. Take a couple of wraps of thread to secure the fibers in position behind the bead.

5 Spiral the wire forward in an open spiral to just behind the bead. Five to eight turns is usually about right depending upon the size of the hook. Take a couple of turns of thread to secure the copper wire and cut off the excess.

6 Whip finish behind the bead and cut the thread.

Variations

The variations on this fly are almost endless:

Use different color beads including glass beads in a variety of colors.

Use different kinds and colors of feather barbules: dyed and natural pheasant tail, dyed and natural turkey, etc.

Use different kinds and colors of wire: copper, gold, silver, red, green, etc.

Fishing the Fly

This is your basic midge pupa that needs to be fished just in the surface film or under the surface to the depth that the fish are feeding. You can use a strike indicator to vary the depth from just below the surface to all the way to the bottom. It can also be fished effectively on a dropper under a dry or wet fly and sight fished to highly selective fish using short line nymphing technique. The key to the success of the fly is the action of the mini-barbules that stick out from the sides of the feather barbules used to form the body of the fly. Barbules should be selected carefully to utilize this property.

The Muskrat Nymph

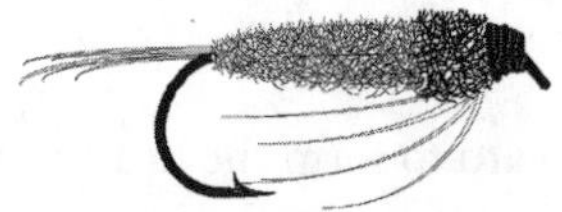

The Muskrat Nymph is one of the classic nymph patterns. As popular as the Pheasant Tail or Gold Ribbed Hare's Ear, like these patterns it does not seek to imitate a specific insect, but rather to be generic enough to resemble any number of them. Also like many of the other generic nymphs that have become classics over the years, it has developed dozens of variations. Practically any flytying book that you go to has some slight variation on the Muskrat Nymph. The original is usually attributed to Polly Rosborough.

Hook:	Mustad 9671 or TMC 5262, (2X Nymph) #8-16
Thread:	Black
Tail:	Muskrat fur
Body:	Muskrat dubbing fur
Head:	Peacock herl or black ostrich herl
Hackle:	Partridge body feather, tyed in beard style

Tying Instructions

1 Tie in thread at the hook eye and wind to the hook bend.

2 Weight with lead wire if desired and wrap thread over wire.

3 Tie in tail, about ½ shank length long.

4 Wax thread well and twist dubbing onto the thread.

5 Wind dubbing forward making a body with a smooth taper that stops about ¼ shank length behind the eye.

6 Take a couple of wraps to secure the dubbing.

7 Tie in peacock herl in front of dubbing and wrap thread forward to behind eye.

8 Wind peacock herl forward to form the head and take a couple of wraps to secure it in place. Trim off excess herl.

9 Tie in partridge fibers just behind the eye, beard style.

10 Whip finish and apply head cement.

Variations

The fly can be tied weighted or unweighted and with or without a tail.

Any number of different materials can be used for the body and the tail: Polly Rosborough's original pattern calls for a blend of muskrat belly, beaver belly and jackrabbit fur. Gary Borger's pattern calls for a complicated artificial fur mixture, silver ribbing and the tail and collar from a coot.

Fishing the Fly

The Muskrat Nymph is a highly effective nymph pattern in the mountains. The wide variety of insect life combined with a general sparseness of insect population means that generic patterns such as the Muskrat Nymph or, in dry flies, the Thunderhead are very productive.

The Stonefly Nymph

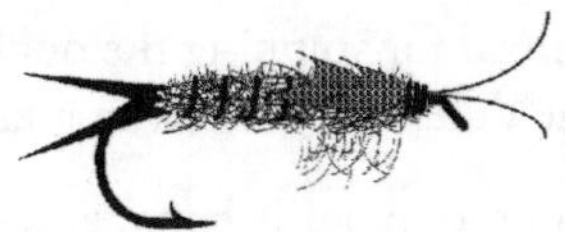

The large nymphs of these flies can be very productive in the spring and summer months. This particular pattern was first shown to me by Dave Cox, a great teacher of fly tying and generally delightful curmudgeon. This pattern can be varied in both size and color to imitate other stoneflies.

Hook:	Mustad 9672, TMC 5263 #4–8
Thread:	Black
Weight:	"Lead" wire
Tail:	2 brown goose biots tied forked about $1\frac{1}{2}$ times hook gap in length
Ribbing:	Black larva lace plastic tubing
Body:	Kaufmann's nymph blend, brown stone dubbing
Wing Pads:	2 ringneck pheasant "church window" feathers
Antennae:	2 moose hairs

Tying Instructions

1 Before placing the hook in the vise, bend it downward about 15 degrees at a point about $\frac{1}{3}$ shank length behind the eye.

2 Place the hook in the vise and start the thread just behind the eye. Wrap the thread to the bend of the hook.

3 Wrap about 9-10 turns of "lead" wire centered on the hook shank. Wrap the wire with thread to secure it in place. Return the thread to the bend.

4 Tie in a small ball of dubbing at the hook bend to help in positioning the tail.

5 Tie in two brown goose biots as a forked tail about 1½ times hook gap length.

6 Tie in a 3-4" piece of black larva lace tubing for later use as ribbing.

7 Wind the thread to about ⅓ of the hook shank behind the eye.

8 Make a loop of thread for spinning the dubbing. Spin in lots of dubbing and then wrap the dubbing forward in a taper to the thread.

9 Tie off the dubbing loop, let it hang, and spiral the tubing forward to this point as ribbing. Tie off the ribbing and trim off the excess ribbing.

10 Take two ring neck pheasant "church window" feathers and cut or burn them to shape as wing pads. You can cut them with a pair of scissors into a heart shape or use a wing burner to produce the characteristic stonefly wing pad shape. Tie in the first wing pad just in front of the abdomen that you have dubbed and ribbed.

11 Dub some more material in front of the first wing pad. This forms part of the thorax of the fly and should be slightly thicker than the front end of the abdomen that you have formed so far.

12 Tie in the second wing pad in front of this material.

13 Dub more material in front of the second wing pad to a point about ⅛" behind the eye of the hook. Tie off the dubbing loop and trim off the excess.

14 Tie in two moose hairs as antennae about an inch long, forking forward beyond the eye of the hook.

15 Build up a good "head" on the fly with the thread and whip finish.

Fishing the Fly

This is a fly that most folks think of as exclusively for mountain Trout, however, don't neglect the fact that it also works extremely well on our Southeastern Smallmouth streams. Many fishermen don't think of fishing for Smallies with nymphs, but it can be a very successful technique, and this is a great fly to use. A very versatile pattern that works well in a wide variety of colors and sizes.

The Hellgrammite/ Stonefly Nymph

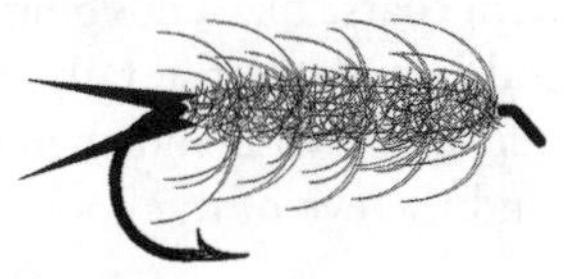

This fly was first brought to my attention by Creed Taylor who lives up around Blacksburg, VA, and has one of the nicest little streams running through his old family homestead there that you could ask for. I was lucky enough once to have Creed invite me over to fish for some of the monster smallmouth that inhabit the water just below the dam there. Many of you on the FLYFISH@ list know Creed as designer of the 1996 FF@ pin, but he is also a rabid smallmouth fisher after dark—"when the big ones come out." This is one of Creed's favorites for his home waters. This pattern was developed after a quick glance at his fly just at dark so I can't be too sure that this is how he ties it, but it does catch fish.

Hook:	Mustad 9672 or 3XL Nymph Hook #2-8
Thread:	Black
Weight:	"Lead" wire
Tail:	2 black goose biots tied in forked, 1½ times hook gap in length
Palmered Rib:	Soft black hackle or streamer feather
Dubbing:	Coarse black

Tying Instructions

1 Start the thread just behind the eye of the hook and wrap it to the bend.

2 Wind "lead" wire around the hook shank from a little behind the eye to about ½ the length of the hook. Wrap the wire with thread to secure it in place.

3 Tie in 2 goose biots to make a forked tail approximately 1½ times hook gap in length.

4 Tie in a soft black hackle by its tip at the bend of the hook.

5 Dub a body forward with coarse black dubbing. It should be formed into a taper with a thin end just above the tail, gradually getting fatter as you move to the center of the wire and then tapering slightly thinner as you get to just behind the eye of the hook.

6 Palmer the soft black hackle forward in an open spiral to just behind the eye of the hook. Tie off and trim the excess. Whip finish.

Variations

Create a wing case over the forward ⅓ of the body using turkey feather or other material.

Tie in a pair of long "feelers" at the front of the body using black rubber legging material or black moose hair.

Vary the color of the biots, dubbing and hackle.

Fishing the Fly

This baby is fished on the bottom. Use extra weight if you need to get it down and bounce it along the bottom with the current.

The Montana Nymph

This is another of those deceptively simple to tie, but highly effective flies that has proven itself a favorite throughout the Southeast as a stonefly nymph imitation. Usually tied weighted so that it can be fished on the bottom. A highly effective mountain trout pattern.

Hook:	Mustad 9672 or other 3X long nymph hook, #6-12
Thread:	Black
Tail:	Black hackle fibers ($1\frac{1}{2}$ times gap width)
Weight:	(Optional) "Lead wire" wrapped around the hook
Abdomen:	Black chenille
Legs:	Black hackle spiraled through the thorax
Thorax:	Yellow chenille
Wing Case:	Black chenille (note that this is the same piece of chenille used for the abdomen brought forward over the top of the thorax)

Tying Instructions

1. Secure the hook in the vise and start the thread just in front of the bend.

2. Take a clump of black hackle fibers and secure them in place at the bend of the hook as a tail that is about $1\frac{1}{2}$ times gap width in length.

3 Wrap the thread forward to just behind the eye of the hook. Take a piece of "lead" wire and wrap it around the hook 9-12 times in the general area that will form the thorax of the fly. Wrap the thread back and forth over the wire to secure it in place. Finish with the thread near the back of the hook.

4 Take a piece of black chenille about 3-4 inches in length and secure it near the bend of the hook. Wrap the thread forward to a point just slightly forward of the center of the hook shank. Wrap the chenille forward to the thread forming the abdomen of the fly. Secure the chenille in place with the thread and let the excess chenille hang down. This will later be used to form the wing case of the fly. At this point it may also be a good idea to secure the loose end of the chenille at the point where the thread is so that you can have a double strand of chenille that can be pulled forward over the top of the thorax. Whether to do this or not will depend upon the size of the hook and the size of the chenille being used.

5 Take a black hackle feather with barbs approximately gap width in length and secure it in place by its tip. Take a piece of yellow chenille about 2-3 inches in length and secure it in place.

6 Wrap the yellow chenille forward over the top of the weight to form the thorax of the fly. The thorax should be thicker than the abdomen. This may take several wraps of chenille to accomplish. Secure the yellow chenille slightly behind the eye of the hook and trim off the excess chenille.

7 Palmer the black hackle forward through the thorax and tie off just behind the eye of the hook. Trim off the excess hackle.

8 Using scissors, trim off the hackle barbules that are sticking up above the top of the thorax of the fly. Then pull the black chenille previously left hanging over the top of the thorax to form the wing case of the fly. Secure in place and trim off the excess chenille. Whip finish.

Variations

1 Variations on the size of the chenille used should be considered with the size of the hook. For smaller size hooks the micro chenilles or vernilles will make for a better proportioned fly.

2 Color: Black and yellow are the classic colors for this fly, but there are plenty of other variations possible. Black and Chartreuse is also popular, as is Brown and Orange.

3 Tailing Material: Try using two goose biots tied in forked as a tail instead of black hackle fibers. These also do not have to be black in color. Orange or Brown can make interesting variations here. Other material can also be used for a tail instead of black hackle fibers—muskrat guard hair, mink hair, etc.

4 Wing Case Material: Try using two goose biots tied in forked as a wing case (sort of like with a Prince Nymph). These can be black, brown, white or orange in color.

Fishing the Fly

This nymph is traditionally fished on the bottom. It is an excellent candidate for the short line nymphing or the all mono system described in detail earlier in this book, especially when heavily weighted. It is also a fly that works well during winter months, the runoffs of early spring, or whenever a stonefly hatch has been occurring.

The Woolly Worm

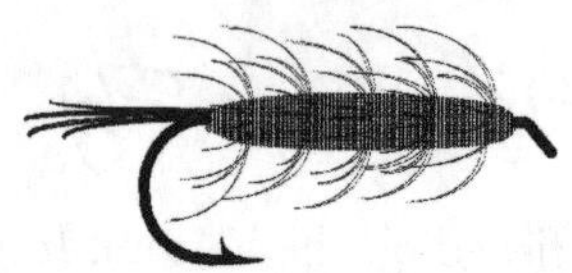

Although it looks a lot like a Woolly Bugger without the marabou tail, its fishing technique is actually closer to the Yallerhammer. This is a nymph that is usually tied weighted to get down into the deep holes in mountain streams. Like the Woolly Bugger, however, it can be tied in as many different colors as there are chenilles and saddle hackle. The pattern given here is for an olive, but it is also popular in brown, black, and can be tied using the variegated chenilles.

Hook:	Mustad 9671 or TMC 5262 # 4-16
Thread:	Olive
Weight:	"Lead" wire wrapped around hook as desired
Tail:	Red hackle fibers, gap width in length
Rib:	Olive saddle hackle, palmered through body
Body:	Olive chenille

Tying Instructions

1. Start the thread just behind the eye of the hook and wind it to the hook bend.

2. Wrap a number of turns of "lead" wire around the hook if desired. These should be centered on the hook.

3 Wrap the thread back and forth over the wire to hold it in place and finish with the thread at the bend of the hook.

4 Tie in several red hackle fibers as a tail, about gap width in length.

5 Take a nice long saddle hackle and grasp it by the tip. Stroke the barbules away from the tip so that they stand out from the quill. Tie in the saddle hackle by its tip right at the tail.

6 Secure the chenille to the hook right in front of the tail. Wrap the thread forward to just behind the eye of the hook. Then wrap the chenille around the hook to form the body of the fly. Finish wrapping just behind the eye of the hook and secure it in place with several turns of thread. Clip off the excess chenille.

7 Palmer the saddle hackle forward in an open spiral and tie it off with the thread just behind the eye of the hook. Trim off the excess saddle hackle and whip finish.

Fishing the Fly

This another of the bottom hugger mountain Trout flies that are so popular and useful throughout the Southeast. Use a heavily weighted version of this nymph to get down into the mountain pools where some of the big ones are hanging out.

The Zug Bug

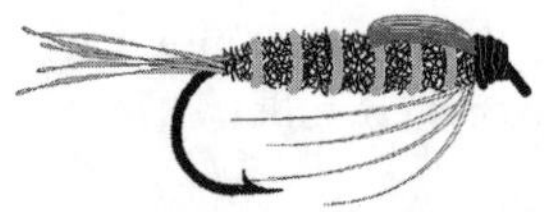

This is another of those general purpose nymph patterns that are useful in a wide variety of situations.

Hook:	Mustad 9671 or TMC 5262, (2X Nymph) #10-16
Thread:	Black
Tail:	Peacock sword fibers about gap width in length
Rib:	Silver tinsel
Body:	Peacock herl
Hackle:	Brown hen hackle tied in as a collar
Wing Pad:	A mallard flank feather tied in at the hackle by its butt and then cut square across at about 1/3 body length.

Tying Instructions

1. Start the thread at the bend of the hook.
2. Tie in several peacock sword fibers as a tail about hook gap in length.
3. Tie in silver tinsel for ribbing and let it hang.

4. Tie in several strands of peacock herl to form the body. Wind the thread forward to a point just slightly behind the eye of the hook.

5. Wrap the peacock herl forward to the thread. Tie off and trim the excess.

6. Spiral the tinsel forward to the thread. Tie off and trim the excess.

7. Tie in soft hackle and take a couple of turns to form a collar. Tie off and trim the excess.

8. Tie in a mallard flank feather by its base with the tip of the feather pointing toward the back of the hook. Trim the feather square across the body about ⅓ hook shank length back from where it is tied in.

9. Whip finish.

Fishing the Fly

A good general purpose nymph for both mountain Trout streams and tailwaters. It can be fished weighted or unweighted, depending upon your needs. If you are not sure about what fly to use, this can be a good one to try.

The Damsel Wiggle Nymph

This is my version of a pattern given to me by David Allerton, a friend and fine fresh and saltwater fly fisher from Florida. He was using it at the time to haul in one Smallmouth after another on the Shenandoah. I liked the pattern then and since have learned to love it even more. It has produced 24" Cutthroats out of Trout Lake in Yellowstone; Smallmouth, Bluegills, and Red-eye out of Lower Abrams Creek, Rainbows and Browns out of the Clinch, S. Holston and Watauga and Shad and Rainbows from the Saluda down in South Carolina. It's called a Damsel Wiggle Nymph, but I've found it a good producer whether there are any damsels present or not. It is definetly one of those flies that you always want to have along.

The origin of this fly is in the Marabou Damsel Nymph by Gary Borger which David and I adapted to our own preferences. The pattern given below is my version. David has several others that I've listed under Variations. This is a fly that readily adapts itself to different situations and can easily be tied to imitate very specifically a Damsel Fly nymph or tied as a more generic pattern. It is deadly in all of its variations.

Tying Instructions

1. Secure the hook in the vise and begin wrapping the thread at the front of the hook. Wrap the thread back to the bend.

2. Take about 8-10 strands of individual olive marabou fibers and about 3-4 strands of individual brown marabou fibers. Position them as the tail

Hook:	Mustad 9671, TMC 5262 or 2X Nymph hook (#8-12)
Thread:	Olive
Tail:	A few strands of olive and brown marabou
Abdomen:	Butts from the tail
Ribbing:	The olive tying thread
Wing Case:	4-5 strands of peacock herl
Thorax:	Olive hare's ear dubbing, picked out
Eyes:	Burnt monofilament

about hook length long. Take a couple of wraps of thread to secure the tail at the bend of the hook. Then, holding the tail in place, wrap the marabou forward around the hook to form the abdomen. Spiral the thread forward to secure the marabou in place.

3 Trim the excess marabou in the area of the thorax and wrap the thread back to the front of the abdomen (about ½ hook length).

4 Tie in 4-5 strands of peacock herl in front of the abdomen for the wing case.

5 Dub in olive hare's ear or other coarse dubbing for the thorax.

6 Pull the peacock herl over the top of the thorax and secure just behind the eye of the hook, leaving space for the mono eyes to be tied in.

7 Secure a pair of burnt monofilament eyes just behind the eye of the hook.

8 Whip finish.

9 Pick out the underside of the thorax to form "legs."

Variations

1 The fly can be tied weighted or unweighted.

2 Try a bead head version instead of with mono eyes.

3 Try other colors (orange, lime green, brown or black).

4 Instead of picked out legs try partridge or dyed grizzly saddle tied in as a beard or half collar.

5. Rib the abdomen of the fly with tinsel or wire.

6. Dub both the abdomen and the thorax using:
   a. Hare's Ear dubbing
   b. Hare's Ear dubbing mixed with antron
   c. Hare's Ear dubbing mixed with Aunt Lydia's Rug Yarn

7. For a buggier looking thorax, use a very coarse dubbing mix and a dubbing loop to apply it.

Fishing the Fly

The Damsel Wiggle Nymph can be fished in a variety of ways. The fly can be tied unweighted and fished with a small split shot about 6-8" up the tippet or it can be tied weighted. It can be fished much like a streamer or woolly bugger. In slow or still water it is usually best to give the fly a little time to sink before beginning the retrieve or you can use a sinking tip line depending upon the depth that you would like to achieve. It can be worked upstream, downstream or crosscurrent.

The fly can also be fished as a nymph—usually weighted using short line nymphing technique without a strike indicator. This can be especially effective in faster water.

The fly has proven effective on a wide variety of freshwater fish: trout, smallmouth, bluegill, red-eye, crappie and even largemouth. No matter what it is I'm fishing for, this is one of the flies that I want to have in my fly box.

Streamers and Woolly Buggers

Even though New England is usually thought of as the center of North American streamer development and fishing, these extremely effective flies are every bit as useful and popular in the Southeast. Two flies within this category, The Woolly Bugger and The Clouser Minnow, have probably accounted for more fish and more kinds of fish than any other two single flies used in the Southeast. The other great advantage of streamers is that in addition to attracting many different species of fish they also tend to attract large examples of those species as well. This can make streamer fishing extremely exciting when you suddenly find that your tackle and yourself are being pushed to their limits—and occasionally beyond.

Many fisherman think that streamer fishing is basically pretty boring. You just chuck it out there, pull it back in, and sooner or later, if you're lucky, something will hit it. Good streamer fishermen know that there can be considerably more to it than just that, however. Be sure to read the article in this section on "Controlling Density and Sink Rates of Fly Patterns," for example, to begin to grasp a better understanding of the often neglected vertical component of streamer fishing. Streamer fishing can take every bit as much observation, knowledge of conditions and fish habits, attention to proper presentation, and careful thought as the most demanding dry fly fishing.

Streamers are also the most versatile of fly patterns. While many of the dry fly patterns are used almost exclusively for Trout, it is an unusual streamer pattern indeed which can't be used for at least two to three very different species of fish. Clouser Minnows, for example, while originally being developed for Smallmouth, are also among the most popular and productive salt water patterns in the Southeast. They are great producers on Stripers and will even catch Trout as well. You can't ask for much more in the way of versatility than that.

The Woolly Bugger

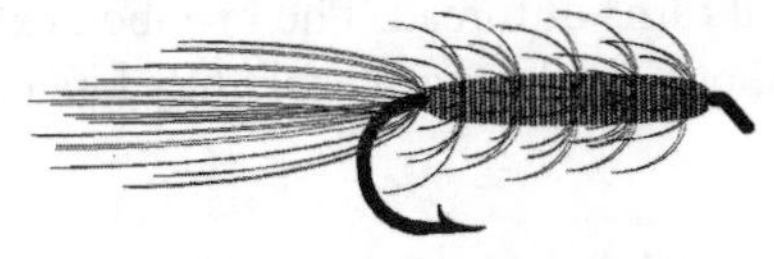

Since it was first devised by Russell Blessing, the Woolly Bugger has probably caught more fish and more kinds of fish than any other single fly pattern. In the Southeast it will catch just about any species for which you care to fish: trout, smallies, panfish, etc. Most of you probably already know the basic Woolly Bugger pattern given here, but I thought that I'd include a list of some of the many variations with which you may not be so familiar. The Woolly Bugger can be tied in as many different ways as there are types and colors of Marabou, Saddle Hackle, and Chenille.

Basic Olive Woolly Bugger

Hook: Mustad 79580 or TMC 9394 (3X to 4X Streamer Hook) # 4-16
Thread: Olive
Weight: "Lead" wire wrapped around hook as desired
Tail: Olive marabou
Rib: Olive saddle hackle, palmered through body
Body: Olive chenille

Tying Instructions

1 Start the thread just behind the eye of the hook and wind it to the hook bend.

2 Wrap a number of turns of "lead" wire around the hook if desired. These should be centered on the hook.

3 Wrap the thread back and forth over the wire to hold it in place and finish with the thread at the bend of the hook.

4 Take several pieces of marabou and secure it in place at the bend of the hook using several turns of thread. The marabou extending beyond the hook should be about shank length or slightly longer. Trim off the butts of the marabou.

5 Take a nice long saddle hackle and grasp it by the tip. Stroke the barbules away from the tip so that they stand out from the quill. Tie in the saddle hackle by its tip right at the butts of the marabou.

6 Secure the chenille to the hook right in front of the marabou. Wrap the thread forward to just behind the eye of the hook. Then wrap the chenille around the hook to form the body of the fly. Finish wrapping just behind the eye of the hook and secure it in place with several turns of thread. Clip off the excess chenille.

7 Palmer the saddle hackle forward in an open spiral and tie it off with the thread just behind the eye of the hook. Trim off the excess saddle hackle and whip finish.

Variations

There are so many variations on the Woolly Bugger that I would doubt that anyone knows all of them. Here are a few that I've found particularly useful:

Color: You name it, if marabou, saddle hackle and chenille comes in it, then someone has tied a Woolly Bugger with it. The most useful colors for trout are probably the olive given above and black, white, brown and grizzly. For other fish almost any color goes: Chartreuse is great for bass as are orange, yellow and red. I've even tied one up in cerise and found that it worked very well in low-light conditions. Remember too that you don't have to use the same color for the marabou, the saddle hackle and the chenille. One of my most effective variations on the olive Woolly Bugger uses peach or copper estaz (crystal chenille) for the body.

Chenille: You don't have to use regular chenille. Estaz or crystal chenille is also a very effective body material when you want a little more flash. Micro chenille and smaller versions of chenille are useful when tying the smaller sizes of the fly.

Bead Heads: Bead head Woolly Buggers help you get it down a little quicker and provide the extra little flash at the head of the fly that is just as effective with Woolly Buggers as with other flies.

Additions: A few strands of Krystal Flash or flashabou can also be effective additions to the Woolly Bugger. Usually tied in at the head of the fly and in a length slightly shorter than the distance from there to the tip of the tail.

Fishing the Fly

There are as many different ways to fish Woolly Buggers as there are ways to tie them. They can be fished as streamers, nymphs, or even wet flies. They can be used for Trout, Smallmouth, Panfish, Stripers, and just about any other gamefish that exists. I've even used them in salt water and they work just fine there also. To say that this is one of the most versatile flies ever invented is by no means an overstatement of the virtues of the Woolly Bugger.

The Worm Bugger

All right, all you purists out there had better stop reading right now. This is a fly that will make you cringe. The body of this fly is formed from one of those plastic worms that you buy by the dozen down at Hawg Heaven and are beloved of the 150-horsepower, glitter painted, flippin stick crowd. Yeeeehaw! For those of you with less delicate sensibilities, however, or those just interested in a great version of the Woolly Bugger that has a very lifelike feel to it and catches both trout and Hawgs, this is a great pattern.

Developed by Gerald Wilt down at Auburn, it can be fished just like a regular Woolly Bugger either weighted or unweighted. There is part of the technique of tying this fly that can be a little tricky the first time, but it really does not take too long to catch on to.

Hook:	Mustad 79580 or other 4X (or longer) streamer hook #6-8
Body:	Piece of transparent soft plastic worm in color desired
Thread:	Color of worm body
Ribbing:	Copper wire
Tail:	Marabou in desired color
Palmered Rib:	Saddle hackle in desired color
Weight (optional):	A pair of "lead" dumbbell eyes

Tying Instructions

1 Select a non-flavored, non-salted, transparent, soft, plastic worm about 6" in length in the color desired. The developer of the fly prefers "motor oil" (yup, that really is a color in these worms). From the tail section of the worm, cut a piece that is about 3/4 hook shank length. Carefully work this piece of worm onto the shank of the hook, centering it.

2 Place the hook in your vise. Start your thread behind the worm body and tie in one end of the copper wire for the ribbing. Whip finish the thread behind the worm body.

3 Carefully spiral the wire forward around the plastic worm body. You want it to be tight enough to slightly compress the plastic, but not cut into it. Wrap the end of the wire around the hook just in front of the worm body a couple of times to hold it in place.

4 Now comes the tricky part. You are going to soften the plastic so that it surrounds the wire. This is easiest if you use a rotary vise so that you can turn the body constantly while you are applying heat. If you don't have a rotary vise then take the hook out of your vise and hold it in a pair of hemostats so you can turn it easily. The best way to soften the plastic is to use a heat gun. This will let you control the temperature better and lessen the chances of catching the plastic on fire. If you don't have a heat gun then a cigarette lighter will do the job, but you will have to be more careful. When the plastic softens it will flow around the wire and form a round body. Let it cool completely and it will firm up again.

5 After the body has completely cooled, restart your thread behind the worm body. Attach a clump of marabou as a tail. Black or brown works well with the "motor oil" body. Then tie in the tip of the saddle hackle. Whip finish behind the body and trim off the thread. A dab of head cement or super glue is a good idea at this whip finish.

6 Restart the thread in front of the body. Spiral the saddle hackle forward around the plastic body between the spirals of the wire. If you used a transparent worm, you will be able to see the wire inside the body. Take a couple of wraps of thread to secure the saddle hackle in place in front of the body. Trim off the excess saddle hackle. Attach a pair of dumbbell eyes if desired. Whip finish. A drop of head cement or super glue on this whip finish is also a good idea.

Voila! You have a transparent, soft-bodied Woolly Bugger that is great for trout and bass.

Fishing the Fly

The Worm Bugger needs to be fished more like a streamer than many of the other versions of the Woolly Bugger. It doesn't work nearly as well on a drift as some Buggers do. Though it needs to be kept moving you don't have to necessarily keep it moving fast. It will work very well when retrieved at slow speeds as well as at quicker ones. Great for Bass and Smallmouth, I've also had a good deal of luck with it on Trout as well.

The Booby and Floating Woolly Buggers

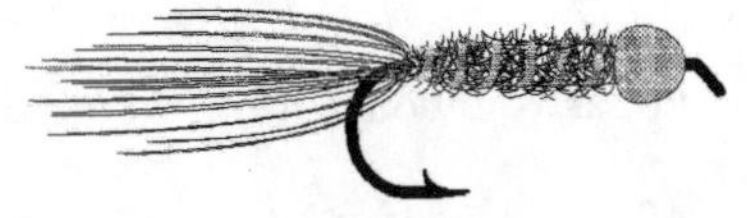

While those of us living in the Southeast have long had the advantage over our Northern cousins of a much greater number of days when we can fish because of the generally milder climate, there is an unfortunate opposite side to that climate. In addition to warmer winters we also have warmer summers as well. That means that there are also a number of days when the water temperature is high and the trout are just not very active. Finding an answer to the hotter days of summer has been a problem that has occupied Southern fly fishers for a number of years.

There's a fly that's been literally "floating" around England for some time now that might just provide you with an answer for those "dog days" of summer when the trout are lying on the bottom and don't seem to be interested in going for anything that you've been showing to them. The water temperatures are up and the trout just aren't very active. For the most part they're hugging the bottom in deep holes and trying to keep cool just like the rest of us when the temps get up in the 90s. To get them to hit anything, you're first going to have to get it down to where they are, second it's going to have to be something that pushes their buttons all the right ways and then finally it can't be moving too fast because their energy level isn't much better than ours in that kind of weather.

Well, English anglers have been using a fly called The Booby for quite a while to deal with these kinds of situations. First developed by Gordon Fraser, the Leicestershire nymph specialist, it is often referred to as a Booby Nymph. His pattern is as follows:

Hook:	Down eyed long shank hook #8-10
Thread:	Orange
Tail:	Orange marabou
Rib:	Gold or silver tinsel
Body:	Orange seal's fur or substitute
Head:	Two polystyrene beads

Tying Instructions

1 Tie on the marabou tail as you would for a Woolly Bugger.

2 Tie on the tinsel for later use as ribbing.

3 Dub a body forward of seal's fur or substitute and then spiral the ribbing forward through the body. Tie off the ribbing and trim the excess.

4 Cut out a small piece of white nylon stockings or tights and form a little bag into which the two polystyrene balls are placed. Tie the bag at the front of the hook. Use a figure eight to separate the two balls and whip finish.

Variations

If you ask two other English fly tyers how to tie one of the things, you're likely to get two entirely different answers. The Booby, you see, is not so much a pattern as it is a method of fishing a fly. The fly itself is a floating fly with lots of movement to it. But wait a minute, I thought you said that this fly was supposed to be fished down on the bottom? Bear with me. I also said that the way you fish the fly is just as important (if not more so) than the fly itself. As a matter of fact, if you have got a Woolly Bugger that floats, you've got another fly that can be fished exactly like the Booby. First though, you need to come up with a floating Woolly Bugger. There's lots of ways that you might do this that I'll be getting into shortly.

Other English Booby patterns use a great big hunk of foam tied onto the front of the hook. Sometimes it's tied on like a pair of huge distorted dumbbell eyes. Take a big piece of foam in whatever color you like and lash it perpendicular to the front end of the hook with figure eight crosses so it won't go anywhere. Another method of tying the Booby is to lash the foam on in line with the hook, maybe even trimming it to shape to provide a bullet-like head. The tail of the Booby is made out of some kind of material that moves well such as marabou or Arctic Fox. The body is often dubbed, usually with some kind of coarse dubbing. You may or may not want to lash on some strips of Krystal Flash or other flashy material and the colors can be anything from the drabbest olive to the brightest colors you can imagine.

With the idea of the Booby in mind, it doesn't take too much of a leap of the imagination to come up with a floating Woolly Bugger. You still usually want to stick with marabou for the tail just because there really isn't anything that moves as well and you do want movement to the fly. You do not, however, want to use chenille for the body. It soaks up too much water and sinks like a rock. Estaz or any of the plastic chenilles is a much better choice. Other choices for the body could be a piece of foam cylinder like you might use for a foam hopper body or one of those plastic worms that the Hawg fishermen buy by the dozen down at Wal-Mart. Elsewhere in this book you will find a pattern for The Worm Bugger that was developed by Gerald Wilt down at Auburn. A Worm Bugger without the lead dumbbell eyes to make it sink floats pretty dern well.

Saddle hackle for palmering along the body is moderately density neutral and you may not want to try to find a substitute for it at all. If, however, you really want to try a substitute for saddle that floats even better, then this could be your chance to experiment with Emu. You may have noticed that some of the flytying material catalogs lately have been carrying Emu feathers and wondered what in the heck the stuff was. If you have ever seen a piece of it you will notice that it looks a lot like a sort of slightly fluffy saddle hackle. The big difference between it and saddle, however, is that it floats. If you use Emu in place of saddle on your Woolly Bugger and don't use chenille for the body, you can tie a floating Woolly Bugger without having to resort to a huge foam head on the beast unless you decide that you particularly want one. Give the foam head a little bit of shaping and your Woolly Bugger turns into a fair to middling Sculpin imitation.

All of the above are some ideas about how you might go about tying a floating Woolly Bugger. Whether you decide to go with a great big foam head as in The Booby, a plastic worm body as in The Worm Bugger, Emu in place of saddle hackle, or whatever method you come up with to make your Woolly Bugger float, you've got the idea behind the fly.

Fishing the Fly

Now let's talk about how to fish this thing. You still need to get this floating fly down on the bottom. For most streams and rivers, a combination of sinking tip line and a hunk of weight on the tippet about 1 foot in front of the fly will do the job very nicely. For deep water and fast-moving streams, you might find that you need to go to a full sinking line or a lead head of some kind to get it down and keep it down. A little experimenting with the particular water in which you are fishing might be necessary to determine just how much weight you need in front of the fly to make it work. You want the fly to float just off the bottom as you drag the weight on the tippet along the stream or lake bed. So also remember to give the sinking tip line, lead head, etc., lots of time to really get all the way down to the bottom before you start pulling it back in.

The last thing to keep in mind as you are fishing this floating Woolly Bugger or the Booby is that it is fished with a SLOW retrieve, and I do mean SLOW! Too fast of a retrieve will cause both the weight and the fly to rise and get it too high off the bottom to be effective. INCH that sucker along the bottom so that you feel like it's barely moving. If you're in a little bit of current it may not even be necessary to move the fly at all. The current itself will provide all the movement that is needed. It is also sometimes possible to fish the fly cross current with the weight bouncing along the bottom. Anything other than perfect bottom conditions though will quickly snag or mire down the weight, your line and/or the fly and keep it from moving with the current. Usually your best option is a very slow upcurrent retrieve. Remember that the idea is to try to interest those trout that are hugging the bottom to escape the heat. They are not going to want to move very far or very fast even to get a tempting wiggling meal like you are presenting to them. This can also be a very effective technique on Smallmouth in streams or any bottom-hugging fish in a lake or pond. Granted that this technique is a far cry from casting to rising fish, but there are times when those fish just flat don't want to do anything but lethargically hang down there where it's cool. When that happens, then you're going to have to get down to where they are and make what you are showing them really interesting. That's exactly what this technique does.

The Muddler Minnow

Most of the streams and tailwaters of the Southeast abound with sculpins. This has made the Muddler Minnow one of the most popular streamer patterns around. The broad deer hair head gives it a close resemblance to this common forage fish. Although given here as the standard pattern as originated by Don Gapen, it can also be tied in a variety of colors and either weighted or unweighted. The weighted version is usually the one employed since the sculpin spends much of its time on the bottom. The Muddler is much more versatile though than just a sculpin imitation. Be sure

Hook:	Mustad 79580 or TMC 9394 (3X to 4X Streamer Hook) # 4-14
Thread:	Gray
Weight:	"Lead" wire wrapped around hook as desired
Tail:	Section of mottled turkey quill (gap width in length)
Body:	*Flat* gold tinsel
Under Wing:	Gray squirrel tail
Wing:	2 mottled turkey quill sections, tied to middle of tail
Head:	Spun deer hair trimmed to blunt head shape with some hair left untrimmed trailing behind the head

to take a look at the notes on Variations and Fishing the Fly underneath the tying instructions and check out David Allerton's article that follows on controlling density and sink rates of Muddlers.

Tying Instructions

1 Start the thread at the bend of the hook and tie in the tail section of turkey quill. Wind your thread to a point about ¼ shank length behind the eye.

2 If you want to weight the fly, wrap some "lead" wire from this point back on the fly. Then wrap over this wire with your thread to secure it in place. Try to smooth out the body as much as possible with the thread. Finish with the thread back at the front of the lead wire.

3 Tie in a long strand of gold tinsel. Wrap the tinsel to the bend of the hook and then back to the thread. Secure it in place with the thread.

4 Tie in a small clump of squirrel tail as an underwing. This should extend to about the center of the tail.

5 Tie in the far section of turkey quill wing section. This should also extend to about the center of the tail. Then tie in the near section of turkey quill wing section. These should both be tied in much like the quill wing of a wet fly. (See the section on Quill Winged Flies, p. 38.)

6 Wind the thread to just behind the eye of the hook and then back to the wing, filling in any uneven spaces.

7 Starting just in front of the wing spin several clumps of deer hair around the hook until you have filled in all the space between the wing and the eye of the hook. Whip finish just behind the eye of the hook.

8 Trim the deer hair to a broad wedge head shape, leaving a number of hair shafts trailing back alongside the body. There are a number of different shapes that can be used for the Muddler Minnow head. A somewhat flattened, broad wedge-shaped head seems to most closely imitate a sculpin.

Variations and Fishing the Fly

Color: The Muddler can be tied in a variety of colors to either imitate the local sculpins or some other beast entirely. Olive Muddlers, for example, make a pretty good dragonfly nymph imitation. Tan, yellow and/or green Muddlers work very well as a hopper. A black or dark brown Muddler can work as a cricket.

Weight: Muddlers can be tied weighted or unweighted, but just because you've got an unweighted Muddler doesn't mean that you can't fish it below the surface. Weight on the tippet in front of the Muddler will get it down to the bottom and can be a very effective way of fishing the fly. Read the section on "The Booby and Floating Woolly Buggers" elsewhere in this book for some ideas on fishing an unweighted Muddler deep. You can also fish a Muddler with weight on the tippet like a jig with an up and down motion by using a retrieve/pause technique.

Unweighted Muddlers can be fished on the surface when well lubricated with floatant. This technique can be very effective around vegetation and snags (it would be a good idea to tie one up with a weed guard for this approach).

Don't just think of the Muddler as a sculpin imitation. It's a very versatile fly that can be fished in a wide variety of different ways. Use your imagination in both tying and fishing the fly.

David Allerton's easy variation on the Muddler: Tie in a marabou tail like you would for a Woolly Bugger. Tie on a zonker or cross-cut rabbit strip just in front of the tail. Weight the shank with "lead" wire to the point where the deer hair head would begin. Cover the "lead" with pliobond or goop and let dry to tacky. Then wind the zonker strip forward to where the deer hair head would begin. Tie off and trim the excess. Spin a deer hair head. Whip finish. Trim the head to shape. Presto, you've got an easy sinking Muddler with a lot of movement to it.

Controlling Density and Sink Rates of Fly Patterns

—a disquisition on fly fishing and fishing muddlers

by David Allerton

Background

Standard flyfishing approaches use line density as the primary medium to control depth of presentation. Non-fly fishers tend to rely on lure density to control depth and presentation. My premise suggests that fly fishers that control the density of the fly line, leader and the fly may reach unprecedented control over their presentation.

Today fly lines come in a variety of sink rates and a fly fisher should find any density imaginable in a commercial fly line. However, judicious use of lead core, Cortland's LC13 and level lines may produce home brewed products that may solve specific problems. As many fly fishers know, line diameter affects sink rate and line control quite dramatically. Thinner lines usually sink faster than their more rotund brethren. Line diameter may be the main reason why some fanatic fly fishers still consider lead core the ultimate sinking line despite its numerous handling disadvantages. Fly fishers are predisposed to consider line characteristics as the primary means to control depth. I suspect that this is a corollary of the process of fly fishing where line manipulation controls the cast and the presentation. Manipulating line to control presentation is inherently natural and efficient. Recently, several companies, in particular Airflo, have been selling braided leaders of varying densities that fine-tune presentations and allow options not previously available to the fly fisher. In many cases, because of the thinner diameter, these leaders are more efficient than the standard sink tip lines or mini-heads that have been used in the past.

With the advent of dog nobblers, boobies, jigs, clousers and other options, fly fishers have begun to consider fly density as a component in a properly presented approach to control depth. New approaches, new materials and relaxed legislation have contributed to more efficient methods to plumb any and all depths of the water column. In the past, hook weight was the primary determinant of density control for flies. Owing to particular regulations, additional methods of weighting were particularly discouraged by the prevailing dogma. Consequently, the only way to weight a fly or change the density was to select particular hooks for specific situations in attempts to control the depth of the presentation. This method is quite limited since hook diameters are quite uniform and only appear in a limited range. In a given size, the experimenting fly fisher might only find 3 or 4 hook weights that were available commercially. Hardly the range that could provide a means to control density minutely.

The next logical approach is the addition of varying amounts of weight to reach the desired presentation. This approach can be very effective, but has some underlying problems. The concentration of weight at the working end has two primary drawbacks. The first is that the weight makes casting an ordeal that requires the modification of the timing and the motion of the casting stroke. Fly casting this concentrated weight can become hazardous to the caster, observers and the equipment. The second is that the angler has little control of the weighted fly's tendency to continue to drop until it hits the bottom. Consequently, hangups are inevitable unless the retrieve is timed perfectly to avoid them. In an unknown terrain, the probabilities are against the angler and fly loss will be high. To avoid this second problem, non-fly fishers have been experimenting with lures that are buoyant, neutrally buoyant and slightly negatively buoyant. It is interesting to note that most custom modifications by the buyer are designed to control the sink rate or presentation depth of the lure. Fly fishers usually construct their flies and so can modify them at will to meet varying presentations. Despite this ability to customize their wares, fly anglers have been slow to tinker with patterns to modify sink rates.

One strategy that has become common in controlling a presentation at a particular depth is to use buoyant flies on sinking lines. English anglers have been using boobies and Americans have been using dahlbergs or poppers in this manner to fish at a preselected depth above the bottom. Leader length determines at what depth the fly will travel. This approach is particularly effective in silty and vegetated substrates, since the fly will not be obscured by the bottom or the cover and is still within range of the fish. In addition, the buoyant nature of the fly allows a certain protection against hangups.

Although fly fishers are adept at combing the bottom and the surface of the water, fish live in a three-dimensional world and may be found anywhere in the water column. Occasionally, fish will suspend and are notoriously difficult to entice to strike. One could use the floating fly and sinking line and select a leader length that will allow the fly to travel on or near the same plane as the suspended fish. This is only effective if the fish are suspended near the bottom. Long leaders tend to be unwieldy in this situation and leader length will affect control of presentation. Another approach is to count down with a sinking fly. Unfortunately, most flies that sink are too heavy and tend to drop during the presentation, thus mitigating any presentation control gained. In addition, these flies are so negatively buoyant that the presentation has to be rather quick to avoid the tendency of the fly to drop down the water column. If the fish are aggressive, a fast presentation may elicit a strike. However, suspended fish tend to be less willing feeders and a slower presentation that remains in the strike zone longer has a better chance of success.

The Method

How does one control presentation to suspended fish? By controlling the density of the fly in relation to the water column, one can control the presentation. Line density and leader density are used to control the sink rate to the level of the fish and fly density is used to control the depth and manner of presentation. Leader length also acts as a control on micro-adjustments of depth control. Using the muddler minnow, I will describe a method to minutely control depth of presentation. The muddler minnow is an excellent fly to use because the deer hair collar provides an inherently buoyant material that can be used to control the final density of the fly. Weighting the fly, choice of hook, choice of materials and the size of the deer hair collar will determine the final density of the fly.

The tyer is trying to generate a series of patterns that vary in density. The first will be buoyant by being less dense than water, the second will be neutrally buoyant by being as dense as water and the last will be slightly negatively buoyant by being just a shade more dense than water. With these three flies, the right fly line and leader system, and patience, a fly fisher should be able to comb any portion of the water column with absolute control.

How does one achieve these expectations? By tying a muddler with an oversize collar, the fly fisher can then trim to the proper preselected density. The procedure is rather simple. A muddler is tied as needed with any recipe that has proven successful. The only exception is to trim the head marginally to produce a rather full collar. The fly is then placed in a container of water and allowed to soak for a while until it reaches maximum saturation. Once the fly has soaked long enough in the water, it is trimmed to match the density required. A buoyant fly will float even when well saturated. A neutrally buoyant fly will remain at the depth where it is placed and will not move up or down the column. The negatively buoyant fly will sink very slowly down the column. One must take into account the water temperature as the density of water will vary with temperature. So it is probably a sound idea to approximate the temperature that the pattern will be fished. Minute differences probably won't make much of a difference unless one is trying for a neutral density fly. Since water density varies with temperature, a fly can be created to be neutrally buoyant at a particular temperature.

A possible application of this phenomenon would be to create a fly that is neutrally buoyant at a temperature that matches the thermocline of a particular lake. If one knows the temperature of a thermocline that has fish suspend above it, a fly can be created to fish and suspend at that particular depth. It can be fished at that particular plane at any retrieve speed or even when not retrieved, at least until the line starts its upward climb. This method allows the construction of flies that provide absolute control of presentation in a three-dimensional world.

The Clouser Minnow

The Clouser Minnow is one of the most phenomenally successful flies ever invented—ranking right up there with the Woolly Bugger for taking more kinds of fish under all kinds of conditions. Originally developed by Bob Clouser up on the Susquehanna for smallmouth, it has spawned myriad variations that work on largemouth, stripers, saltwater fish in general, and even trout. If you're going smallmouth fishing in the Southeast, you've got to have a few of these babies along. One of the most popular colors for smallies is the Chartreuse variation given here, but it can be tied with a wide variety of colors and materials.

Hook:	Mustad 79580, TMC 300 or 3X to 4X Streamer Hook, # 2-10
Thread:	White (or Chartreuse)
Eyes:	Dumbbell eyes red with black pupils
Wing:	White bucktail, twice hook length
Overwing:	A few strands of rainbow krystal flash and chartreuse bucktail, twice hook length

Tying Instructions

1 It is important to keep in mind when tying the Clouser that the eyes are tied in on the top of the hook which makes the fly swim upside down.

This helps prevent snagging and must be considered when tying in the different colored materials.

2 Start the thread just behind the eye of the hook and wrap it to a point about 1/4 hook length behind the eye.

3 With the hook upright in the vise, tie in the dumbbell eyes to the top of the hook using figure eight wraps around the hook. Secure it tightly in place, finishing with the thread in front of the eyes.

4 Tie in a clump of white bucktail at least twice hook length on top of the hook in front of the eyes. Most Clouser devotees believe that this fly works best when tied sparse, so don't make it too big a clump of bucktail. Trim the butts of the bucktail in front of the eyes to a taper.

5 Tie in a few strands of rainbow Krystal Flash just a little shorter than the bucktail in front of the eyes on the bottom of the hook. If you're using a rotary vise, this is a good point to turn the hook upside down. You then will be tying it in the position that it will be moving in the water.

6 Tie in a clump of chartreuse bucktail at least twice hook length on the bottom of the hook in front of the eyes. Trim the butts of the bucktail in front of the eyes to a taper.

7 Wrap the tapered bucktail in front of the eyes with thread to form a nicely tapered head.

8 Whip finish and coat the head with head cement, clear acrylic or epoxy as desired.

Variations

The variations on the Clouser are almost endless:

Use different combinations of colored bucktail and Krystal Flash or flashabou. Popular combinations are: tan and white, pink and white, blue and white, green and white, red and white, green and yellow, olive and yellow, etc.

Use Ultrahair instead of bucktail. Bob Clouser likes the translucent look that this material gives to the fly.

Add a pair of press-on eyes to the head of the fly before coating it with clear acrylic or epoxy if you tie it without the dumbbell eyes.

Use a different colored thread to form the head of the fly to supply a contrast between the head and the body of the fly.

Tie the white bucktail, or whatever color is used first, down behind the eyes using a few wraps of red thread to form an imitation of gills. This variation is sometimes known as a "redneck minnow."

Fishing the Fly

While the Clouser Minnow was originally developed for Smallmouth, it is also one of the most versatile flies that anyone has ever developed, with the possible exception of the Woolly Bugger. The list of fish that have been caught on Clousers may exceed that of any other single fly. Great for Smallmouth, of course, it is also a deadly saltwater fly for a wide variety of marine species. It works on Bass, panfish, Stripers, and even on Trout. This is just an all-around versatile fly.

Fly fishing for Gar

Just returned from vacationing down in Florida for the past couple of weeks and couldn't think of a better way to start off writing about Garfish than with a tale about the exploits of friend David Allerton and myself amidst the Gators, Gars and Groupers. We spent the greater part of that time fishing along, above and below the Tamiami Trail and let me tell you that fishing the Trail takes a little adjustment to your technique. A lot of the fishing was in the canals that line the Trail and abound in an unusual mix of swamp and saltwater fish depending upon the particular location and the tides. The fish don't take too much adjustment, but fishing the Trail sure does since a lot of your casting is done with your back only a few feet from a road with cars and semi's whizzing along behind you. Rigging for the Trail means being absolutely certain that somewhere in your leader/tippet combination there is something that is considerably weaker in strength than your backing. The reason for this will shortly become evident. The next adjustment is to your timing and by this I don't mean getting a good tight loop in your cast. What I'm talking about is timing your backcast so that it comes between large vehicles that are passing right behind you. Good timing on the Trail sounds something like this: Swish, WHOOOSH! Swish, WHOOOSH! Swish, plop, retrieve, retrieve. Bad timing sounds like this: Swish, WHOOOSH! Swish, "Oh Shit!" SCHREE-EEEECH! POW! as you've suddenly had 250 yards of backing ripped off of your reel at a rate that makes a Bonefish look downright sedentary! In the meantime you realize that nice machined aluminum reel you were so proud of is beginning to glow a cherry red and rimming it is definitely out of the question. I sure don't own any reels that will slow down a Peterbilt doing 65!

One of the interesting parts though of fishing the Tamiami Trail is that the canals alongside it abound in Florida Gar, a species similar to the Shortnose Gar and we spent quite a bit of our last trip working on the techniques necessary to catch these abundant, but sometimes difficult fish. One of the greatest underdeveloped gamefisheries of the Southeast is that of the Garfish. There are at least five different species of garfish found in the Southeast ranging from the Alligator Gar that can top 100 lbs. in size to the more widely distributed Longnose and Shortnose Gars that are found throughout almost all of the area.

The garfish is a predator that attacks viciously and is a strong fighter—all of the things that we are often looking for in a gamefish. It compares in many ways to the Pike and Muskie which have been recognized as gamefish for years by fly fishermen. So why has the garfish been so neglected? There are a number of different reasons for this, not the least of which is that throughout the Southeast the garfish is not highly prized as a food fish. Garfish are certainly edible, but are not universally recognized as being so because of their somewhat strong flavor. The Cajuns of Southern Louisiana prefer to treat them as a fish to be used in court-bouillon or fish soup. They have a firm flesh that stands up well in cooking and this manner of preparation also mitigates the strong flavor. In most other parts of the Southeast though they are viewed as a trash fish and even a nuisance. Garfish can also be extremely difficult to handle once they have been caught. A long mouth filled with needle-sharp teeth can be intimidating to say the least and their habits of surface feeding lead them to strike out at any attempt at handling when near the surface. One bite by a Garfish is often enough to make any fisherman immediately refuse to deal with them again—even if any digits are not lost in the process. For those who have pursued Garfish as a gamefish, a further complication has been consistent hookups. The Gar has a very tough mouth that makes hook penetration difficult. Garfishing tactics have not been developed as yet that have been well publicized and most fishermen view them as difficult to catch. There are a number of tactics though that have been pursued by fly fishermen successfully in taking Gar.

Gar will consistently hit Clousers and other minnow imitations. The problems have been with consistency of hookups with the usual hooks employed when tying Clousers. Try tying your Clousers on hooks made of strong, but thin wire with chemically sharpened points and your hookup percentage will greatly increase. Extremely sharp hooks made of thin wire are necessary for consistent penetration in the Gar's tough mouth. Another fly that will consistently take Gar is the Dahlberg Diver, using a strip of rabbit fur for the tail rather than feathers. This fly is usually most successful when fished extremely slowly. Since the Dahlberg is a surface fly, it will also provide very spectacular slashing surface attacks by the Gar. Once again, a thin wire hook will provide better hook penetration and more consistent hookups. A difficulty with the Dahlberg is that often just the tail is hit by the fish and getting hookups can still be difficult. One method of overcoming this problem is to tie in a trailing hook when tying the Dahlberg.

Another successful tactic for Garfishing is to use "flies" which are basically frayed nylon rope such as is used for ski ropes. The Gar will pursue these crude "flies", attack them and then are fought and landed when their teeth become tangled in the rope. These "flies" do not even use hooks as a part of their construction and are nothing more than a short length of frayed nylon secured to the end of a tough tippet. Another suggested material for the construction of such "flies" has been nylon stockings. Part of the tactic of employing such flies does involve maintaining a constant tension on the line when fighting the fish as the only connection between the fish and the line is a few loops of nylon that can easily slip off of their teeth.

Proper tackle is an area that has also been neglected in the pursuit of garfish.

Since very few fishermen have deliberately set out to catch a Gar, when one is hooked it is usually on tackle that is totally unsuited to the task at hand. The result most of the time is lost fish. First one must consider the size and strength of the fish. Most of the Longnose and Shortnose Gar found in the small streams and lakes of the Southeast are not that large with one running three feet or so in length being considered a whopper. These fish can easily be handled with a five weight to six weight rod. The larger Alligator Gar of the deep south, however, can run to five and six feet in length and weigh in at over 100 lbs. Considerably heavier rods are going to be necessary to handle a fish of this size. While Gar do not make incredibly long runs like Tarpon, they are strong, hard-fighting fish and reels with good drags such as are used in saltwater fishing are necessary even for the smaller ones. Lines need be nothing more than your usual weight forward floating line. Gars are primarily surface feeders. Of critical importance, however, is your leader and tippet. Gar are not leader shy, so the leader and tippet can be strong enough to support a hard-fighting fish and stand up to heavy abrasion from the Gar's needle-sharp teeth. For the Longnose and Shortnose Gar a 1X to 2X leader is usually sufficient, but the tippet must be highly abrasion resistant. Saltwater tippets heavier than the leader are recommended. A good 20 lb. hard mono will do the job for most Shortnose and Longnose Gar. For the larger Alligator Gar it may even be necessary to go to a steel core terminal rig.

The final difficulty with pursuing garfish is successfully landing and/or releasing them without being injured yourself. As I mentioned earlier, these fish attack viciously. Their habit of surface feeding means that they will lash out as they are brought to the surface for either landing or release. Extreme caution is necessary as these fish are brought close to landing. Many Garfishers who pursue them as gamefish seriously recommend that the line simply be cut not very close to the fish's mouth if you value your hand. A strong, tough net can immobilize the fish enough to make removal of the hook or frayed rope possible with a minimum of risk. Even then a pair of long-nosed pliers are a necessity. Using barbless hooks will also make hook removal easier. No matter what method you decide upon you must take strong precautions against those slashing teeth. This is not a fish that I would recommend angling for from a float tube.

Garfish are tough fish that when treated with care and respect can reward the fisherman with powerful runs and a bruising fight. They are abundant throughout most of the warm and not so warm waters of the Southeast. They are present, for example, in many of the same waters that hold Smallmouth as well as those where Largemouth and panfish congregate. This is a gamefish that has been greatly underexploited throughout their range and deserve a much closer look by fly fishermen.

The Godawful Garish Gar Grabber

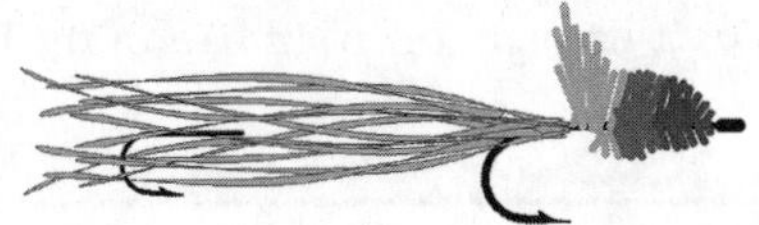

This fly combines the different methods of taking Gar all in one fly. The Dahlberg Diver is a fly that is highly successful in getting Gar to hit, but does not provide consistent hookups. This fly is basically an adaptation of the Dahlberg with the inclusion of thin chemically sharpened hooks to get better penetration in the tough mouth, the addition of a trailer hook to overcome the problem of the fish hitting just the tail of the fly, and the construction of a tail out of pantyhose to give a good grip on the teeth of the fish when neither hook has struck home. The colors chosen are especially effective in the early morning and late afternoon when Garfish are at their most active.

Tying Instructions

1 The first step for tying this fly is actually to dye some white pantyhose. Go to the store and get the cheapest white pantyhose in the largest size that you can find. While you're there pick up some yellow Rit or Tintex dye. You want to get white pantyhose because they will take the dye better than the skin colored ones. Next you'll need a bucket, crock or pot that you are never going to use for anything else to do the actual dyeing. The dye will pretty much ruin whatever you put it in so don't use anything good. It is also not recommended to try cooking in a pot or

Hooks:	One Tiemco 8089NP #2-10 or other chemically sharpened bass bug hook. One Tiemco 811S #2-8 or other chemically sharpened straight eye standard length hook
Thread:	Yellow
Weed Guard & Trailer:	Stiff heavy monofilament—20 lb. test or heavier
Tail:	Strips of white nylon pantyhose dyed yellow tied in w/some Krystal Flash
Body/Head:	Yellow, green & purple spun deer hair trimmed to a Dahlberg Diver style body/head (flat on the bottom, bullet-shaped head tapering back to a flaring collar). The back of the body is spun first from yellow hair. This will form the flaring collar and a few strands will be left tapering back over the tail. The middle part of the head is spun from green deer hair and the front part of the head from purple deer hair.

other device that you have dyed in. Bring about a gallon of water to a rolling boil on the stove and pour it into the dyeing pot. Drop in two teaspoons of dye and stir it around with some implement that you also don't mind losing to any other purpose—an old stick works just fine. Drop in the pantyhose and stir them around for a while as well. In the meantime also have a bucket or pot of cold water ready. Check the pantyhose regularly until they have turned just slightly darker than the shade that you want. Pull them out of the dye, let the excess dye drain back into the dye pot, and then plunge them immediately into the cold water and stir them around. The cold water sets the dye so that it won't fade. Hang up the pantyhose to dry and then cut into thin strips about 1/4" to 3/8" wide and about 3" to 5" long depending upon the hook size with which you are working. Grab each strip of pantyhose by one end and using your other hand slide it along the strip while stretching the strip. This will cause the strip to form into a small tube longitudinally.

2 Prepare the trailer hook and weed guard: Take one of the 811S hooks and tie about a 8" piece of 20 lb. mono onto the eye of the hook. Use a little epoxy or other glue to secure the knot.

3 Take both hooks and crimp down the barb. When it comes time to get one of these hooks out of the mouth of the Gar, you will be happy that you did.

4 Secure the bass bug hook in the vise.

5 Start the thread at the bend of the hook and wrap forward about ¼". Position the mono with the trailer hook so that the eye of the trailer hook is about 1¼" to 1¾" behind the bend of the bass bug hook depending upon the size hooks used. Lash the mono holding the trailer hook in place on top of the bass bug hook by wrapping thread back to the bend and then forward to where you had begun wrapping the thread. Use tight wraps of thread closely spaced. Grasp the butt of the mono (which now should be sticking forward toward the eye of the hook) and bend it back 180 degrees. Lash it in place with the thread wrapping tightly back to the bend of the hook and then forward again. You should now have the trailer hook in place and a long butt of monofilament sticking out the back of the hook for later use as a weed-guard. Use epoxy or other glue to further secure the thread wraps and monofilament to the hook.

6 Take 4-5 pieces of the dyed pantyhose that have previously been cut into strips and secure it in place as a tail. This should be tied in over the top of the thread and epoxy that is securing the monofilament into place. After the pieces are secure in place, trim them to ½" longer than the trailer hook.

7 Secure several pieces of yellow, green, and/or purple Krystal Flash over the top of and to the sides of the pantyhose strips as highlights. Cut to slightly shorter than the tail. Return the thread to just in front of the tail.

8 Spin yellow deer hair over about ⅓ of the remainder of the hook shank toward the eye of the hook. Pack the hair tightly as you spin it into place.

9 Spin green deer hair over about another ⅓ of the hook shank toward the eye of the hook, packed tightly.

10 Spin purple deer hair over the final ⅓ of the hook shank toward the eye of the hook, packed tightly.

11 Do a whip finish just behind the eye of the hook using only a couple of turns, just to keep the thread from unraveling and cut the thread.

12 Trim the deer hair flat on the underside of the hook. Trim the purple and green deer hair to form a tapered bullet-shaped head. Trim the

yellow deer hair to form a flaring collar. Leave a few strands of the yellow deer hair that flare toward the back of the hook untrimmed. This forms the classic Dahlberg Diver–shaped head.

13 Restart the thread just behind the eye of the hook.

14 Bend the monofilament used to form the weed guard forward underneath the hook, following the shape of the hook, but slightly below the point. Secure the monofilament in place just behind the eye of the hook and trim off the excess.

15 Whip finish and secure in place with glue.

Variations

Color can be anything that you like. If you don't want to fool with dyeing panty hose then try using Aunt Lydia's Rug Yarn for a tail.

Fishing the Fly

Be sure that you read the previous article for a more complete description of flyfishing for Gar in the Southeast. There are a few things to keep in mind when fishing this fly, however. Remember that there are three ways that you can end up with the fly attached to the fish: 1) the trailer hook (the most likely hookup), 2) the bass bug hook (less likely, but possible), or 3) with the fish's teeth tangled in the panty hose tail. The third possibility is the one for which you have to be the most careful and alert. If you get attached by the panty hose then it is extremely important to keep a constant tension on the line when fighting the fish. Since there is no actual hook sunk into the fish it is very easy for the fish to get free if constant tension is not applied.

This fly is most effective when worked with a slow, but constant retrieve. If the fish bats at the fly and misses it or just gets a bit of the tail do not stop the fly. Keep right on moving it along at the same or maybe even a little bit faster rate. Slow and steady is the story here until you finally get a hook up or a tangle up.

The Hellgrammite

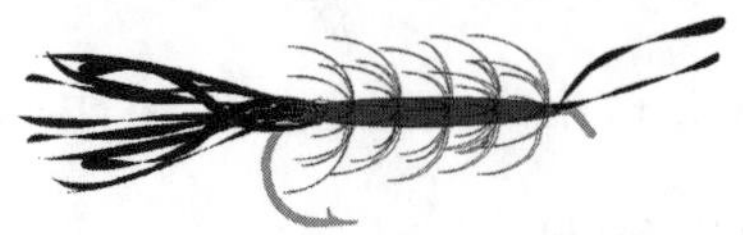

There are many patterns called a Hellgrammite that are primarily stonefly imitations, but when you mention the Hellgrammite or "Hellgrammy" in the Southeast, what most fishermen are usually talking about is a fly that is used as often for smallmouth as it is for trout. As such, it really is closer to a streamer or Woolly Bugger than it is a nymph and is usually fished more like a Woolly Bugger. The following pattern was originated by Harry Murray.

Hook:	Mustad 79580 or TMC 9394 (3X to 4X Streamer Hook) #2-12
Thread:	Black
Weight:	"Lead" wire wrapped around hook as desired (optional)
Tail:	Black ostrich herl about hook length long
Rib:	Black saddle hackle, palmered through body
Body:	Black chenille
Antennae:	Black rubber bands

Tying Instructions

1 Start the thread just behind the eye of the hook and wrap it to the bend.

2 If you want to weight the fly, take your "lead" wire and wrap it from about 1/4 shank length from the bend to about 1/4 shank length from the eye. Wrap thread over this to secure it in place and finish with your thread at the bend of the hook.

3 Tie in a dozen or so pieces of ostrich herl about the same length as the hook. These are often just tied in and then trimmed to length.

4 Tie in a piece of black saddle hackle by its tip.

5 Tie in a piece of thin black chenille, then move the thread back to about 1/4 hook shank length from the eye.

6 Wrap the chenille to the thread and tie off. Trim the excess.

7 Palmer the saddle hackle to the thread and tie off. Trim the excess.

8 Tie in two pieces of black rubber band about 1/2 hook length long so that they stick out over the front of the hook. Wrap the part of the rubber bands just behind the eye of the hook well with thread to form a "head." Whip finish.

Fishing the Fly

Fish this fly just like you would a Woolly Bugger. Great for Smallmouth, of course, it can also be effective on Stripers and Bass as well.

The Datchett Razzler

That Toast of Tinsel Town, The Datchett Razzler, was first brought to my attention in an article by Garry Trudeau in *The Wall Street Journal.* Inspired by his Purplish Prose, I proceeded to invent an appropriate pattern for this flashy fly. Then after actually catching a few fish with the darned thing, it lay dormant gathering dust somewhere down in the nether reaches of my fly box until Hilary Thompson suggested the Mardi Gras Fly Swap. I immediately realized that this was the absolutely appropriate fly for my entry. Having spent onwards of 12 years living in The Crescent City, "Nawlins," I knew that this swap called for the tawdriest, tackiest, most truly tasteless entry that I could concoct. There is no doubt in my mind that this is it. The inspirational article that follows, "Casting Call," was by Garry Trudeau, the pattern and tying instructions are my own. I can't blame him for them, just for the inspiration, and Mardi Gras for the colors.

"Trow' m' sumptin', mista!"

Tying Instructions

1 Throw any semblance of taste that you might have out the window and gather all the tying materials together in one place. Yeah, I know there's no way that you can make a good-looking fly out of that stuff, but do it

Hook:	Mustad 79580 or 9672 (3X to 4X Nymph/Streamer) # 4-12
Thread:	Yellow
Tail:	2 yellow dyed grizzly saddles
Butt:	Yellow ostrich herl
Ribbing:	Gold oval tinsel
Body:	Purple floss (preferably iridescent)
Throat:	Yellow hackle
Wing:	2 green dyed saddles
Topping:	Golden pheasant crest
Head Butt:	Yellow ostrich herl
Eyes:	Pair of mono eyes painted gold
Note:	A slight variation, but equally atrocious, is to use green iridescent floss for the body and purple saddle for the wing.

anyway. This is Mardi Gras in New Orleans—"The City That Taste Forgot."

2 Start your thread just behind the eye of the hook and wind it back to the bend.

3 Tie in two yellow dyed grizzly saddle hackle tips as a tail. The tail should be about as long as the hook. The two feather tips should be tied in back to back with the glossy side out.

4 Tie in several wraps of yellow dyed ostrich herl as a butt just in front of the tail.

5 Tie in about 3-4" of gold oval tinsel to be used as ribbing and let hang.

6 Tie in 2 long strands of purple floss to form the body. This would preferably be the iridescent variety (the tackier looking the better). Wrap the thread to about 1/8 to 1/4 hook shank length behind the eye. If you're chintzy with your floss then you can also use the thread to form an underbody that is roughly cigar shaped—tapered at both the front and the back and fatter in the middle.

7 Wrap the floss forward forming a cigar shaped body—tapered at both the front and the back. Tie off the floss with the thread and trim off the excess floss.

8 Spiral the tinsel forward as ribbing, tie off and trim the excess.

9 Tie in a throat of yellow saddle hackle fibers long enough to reach to the point of the hook.

10 Tie in a wing of 2 green dyed saddle tips. These should be tied in over the top of the body as in a classic salmon fly (quell sacrilege) and should be long enough to reach to the tip of the tail.

11 Tie in a topping of golden pheasant crest over the top of the wing.

12 Tie in a butt of yellow ostrich herl just behind the head of the fly and over the wrapping that holds all the above in place.

13 Form a pair of burnt mono eyes and paint them gold.

14 Tie in the burnt mono eyes using figure eight wraps and then continue wrapping to form the head of the fly.

15 Whip finish just behind the eye of the hook.

16 Lacquer the head with clear acrylic finish or something else glossy.

17 Take the dang thing to New Orleans for Mardi Gras where some drunken tourist will gladly pay you good money for it, but don't be caught dead near a trout stream with it if you value your reputation.

Tastelessly yours,
L.J. DeCuir

Casting Call

by Garry Trudeau

Like a large rainbow trout, *A River Runs Through It* caused a deceptively small splash when it first surfaced in October. But 14 weeks and $40 million later, Robert Redford's film adaptation of Norman Maclean's slender classic is still in wide release and starting to haul in major awards. Several explanations of "River" 's success made the rounds, including the Redford cachet and Brad Pitt's dimples, but in a film about flyfishing, any serious accounting of its charms must include its tiny, hackled stars—the flies themselves.

Indeed, it could be argued that casting the roles of the artificial flies for "River" required as much artistry as did any of the on-camera casting. From the onset, Redford insisted on using flies that mimicked natural food forms rather than those flies known as "attractors"—crass, over dressed lures which basically annoy trout into striking them. Redford's position, leaked early to the trades (Ordinary Bob Nixes Fruit Flies for Fish Pic), was part of the aura of integrity that had prevented his movie from being made for 14 years, but authenticity had its price. Indeed, the film was very nearly scuttled when a studio executive, Mark Canton, insisted that the Datchett Razzler, a hideous attractor he had picked up in Aspen, be prominently featured.

Redford held his ground. While the Razzler, with its flashy plumage and sleek, elongated shank, would undoubtedly have had greater marquee value, Redford had promised Maclean on his deathbed that he would be true to the author's 62-year-old memory of a Bunyan Bug No. 2 Yellow Stone Fly, created by the Missoulan Norman Means. Although the pattern had remained in the Means estate, securing the rights from its executors proved uniquely arduous, in that they were represented by Sam "Can He Call You Back?" Cohen, who, through a nasty coincidence, was also representing the atrocious Datchett Razzler for Orvis.

That the Bunyan ever made it into Scene 10 of "River" at all was due to Redford's perseverance—with an assist from the weather. Wicked gusts whistling through the Bitterroots made the Razzler, with the lift and stability of a dead muskrat, a moot issue. The thwarted studio mogul, who had even brought along a stylist for his tufted wannabe, left in a snit, gunning his Range Rover over a half-dozen antique wicker creels in the process.

Redford's problems, however, did not disappear with the executive. The Bunyan itself, painstakingly tied on site to mimic that day's hatch of flies, was picked off mid-cast by a passing finch, who was then hurled unceremoniously into the drink by the actor Pitt, who was only slightly less startled than the trained Rainbow waiting to greet the Bunyan. The peeved Pitt then pitched his $19,000 stunt rod into the river and roared off in HIS Range Rover, leaving Redford to explain to a visiting reporter why the incident did not constitute cruelty to three separate species, not including the actor.

If Scene 10 was problematic, then 57 was downright disastrous. In this scene, Maclean's skunked hero finally resorts to an attractor, the Bobcat Special. But while it's one thing to cast this fulsome homage to high kitsch, it's quite another to get a Montana Brown to pay it the slightest mind. From day one, Redford had been getting plenty of attitude from the location trout, but when the Bobcat Special landed in the river like a watermelon, the fish all but left the state. Other stand-in attractors were then considered—The Mink Spuddler, the Carnhill Nobbler and the Green Butt Griddle Bug—but the actor had been checked out on none of them, so the scene was dropped from the film.

What a relief it must have been then, to move on to Scene 82-A, where Brad Pitt shadow-casts with an elegant Greenwell's Glory (a dressing dating from 1854, thus easily obtained for scale), or the rapturous Scene 108 where the brothers stand at river's edge in iridescent, misty splendor filling the air with silken lines and exquisitely back-lit chenille-wrapped Parmachene Belles.

It is at such moments that the film itself takes glorious flight.

Terrestrials

Terrestrials are often a neglected area in the flyfisherman's repertoire. They are too often thought of as merely a fallback during that gap between hatches in the middle of the year. And while it is true that Terrestrials are often most useful during the summer months, it is unfortunate to think of them as deserving anything less than your full attention. To fish Terrestrials properly takes every bit as much care, observation, planning, and careful presentation as fishing any mayfly hatch. I strongly recommend that you examine Harrison Steeves' and Ed Koch's marvelous book *Terrestrials*. They treat the subject with every bit of the care, attention, and concern that it deserves and will teach you more about the tying and fishing of Terrestrials than you probably thought possible.

It is also important for the flyfisher in the Southeast to not think of Terrestrials just as Trout flies. Practically every other species of fish to be found in the Southeast adores chowing down on these normally ground-bound bugs every bit as much as any Trout does during the summer months. Whether you want to pick up a few tasty Bluegills for frying, stalk Hawgs on one of our many lakes, or pursue almost any other kind of fish around, there is probably a Terrestrial that will entice it. Explore the use of Terrestrials for any number of other species besides just Trout and you will be justly rewarded.

Besides being rewarding to fish, there is another benefit to utilizing Terrestrials—most of these flies are darned easy to tie and really don't take very long. That means that you'll be spending more time out there fishing and less time at the tying bench—a great benefit during those long lazy days of summer when you want to spend as much time enjoying the outdoors as you can.

The Deer Hair Beetle

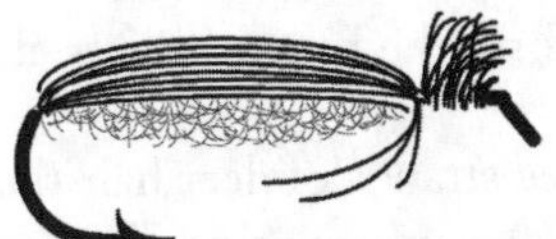

At that time of the year when terrestrials are among the major food items for fish, this beetle pattern is a simple pattern that can satisfy the dry fly addict's desire for a surface pattern. This pattern can be varied by using different colors of deer hair and by the addition of a small dot of white or fluorescent enamel on top of the body to make it easier to see.

Hook:	Mustad 94840, TMC 100 #12-18
Thread:	Black
Shell:	Black deer hair pulled forward over body
Body:	Peacock herl
Legs:	Black deer hair from the shell tied off on each side and trimmed
Head:	Butts of black deer hair from shell tied off and trimmed

Tying Instructions

1. Start the thread at a point about ⅓ behind the eye of the hook.
2. Cut off and trim the fuzz from a small clump of deer hair to form the shell top of the beetle. A clump about the thickness of a wooden kitchen match is about right for a #12 hook.

3 Stack the deer hair by its butts. Lay the deer hair along the top of the hook and lash it to the hook starting with the butts at the thread position and then ending at the bend of the hook. Take a couple of extra turns at the bend of the hook.

4 Tie in several peacock herls depending upon the size of the hook. Wrap the thread forward to the end of the hair butts. Wrap the peacock herl forward to the end of the hair butts and tie them off. Trim off the excess.

5 Pull the deer hair forward to form the top shell of the beetle. Take several tight turns of thread just in front of the hair butts to secure it in place. Whip finish. Trim the excess tips of the deer hair in front of the tie-off point to form the head of the beetle.

6 Cut through three strands of deer hair that form the shell of the beetle close to the bend area on each side. These will then flare forward to form a set of legs on each side.

Fishing the Fly

Like most Terrestrials, this beetle pattern is usually fished as a dry fly and during the summer months when Terrestrials are at their most active. For the dry fly addict, Terrestrials can help fill that long gap between the end of the hatches of the many aquatic insects at the beginning of summer and the approach of fall.

Al's Cricket

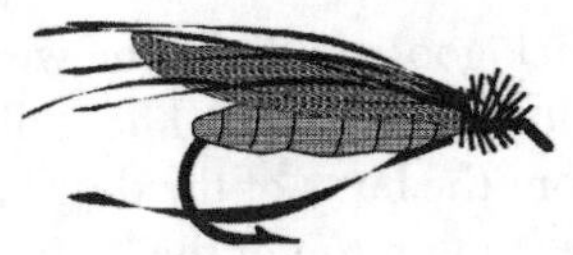

There are many cricket patterns available. This one by Al Troth is a fairly easy one to tie and a great floater.

Hook:	Mustad 9671 or TMC 5262, (2X Nymph) #10-14
Thread:	Black
Rib:	Black thread
Body:	Black deer hair
Wing:	Black goose quill section
Head:	Black deer hair
Legs:	2 single black goose wing fibers

Tying Instructions

1 Start the thread at the bend of the hook, leaving a 4-5" section dangling out the back of the hook and wind the thread forward to a point about ¼ shank length behind the eye. The excess thread dangling out the back of the hook will later be used to rib the body.

2 Select a clump of black deer hair about the thickness of a wooden matchstick for a #10 hook. Brush off the fuzz and stack it by its butts.

Tie in the clump to the top of the hook with the butts about ¼ shank length behind the eye of the hook. Wrap the thread around the deer hair and the hook back to the bend of the hook.

3 Return the thread to the butts of the deer hair. Pull the deer hair forward over the top of the lashed down body already formed and tie them down with the thread.

4 Spiral the excess thread that is dangling out the back of the hook forward as ribbing to the butts of the deer hair and take a couple of turns of thread to secure it in place. Trim off the excess thread and deer hair.

5 Take a section of black goose quill for the wing. Round the end of the section to form the tip of the wing. The quill section should be long enough to extend from the butts of the deer hair to slightly beyond the end of the hook. Tie it in on top of the body already formed.

6 Spin black deer hair in from just in front of the body to just behind the eye of the hook. In the spinning a few fibers should trail backwards toward the rear of the hook and over the top of the wing.

7 Tie in a single black goose wing fiber on each side of the head as legs. These should trail backwards to about the back of the hook. Whip finish.

8 Trim the spun deer hair on the front of the fly to a head shape, leaving several hairs trailing backward over the top of the wing.

Fishing the Fly

Cricket patterns are great flies—not just for Trout during the summer months, but for many other fish as well. Panfish love crickets, and they will provide dry fly action for Smallmouth, Bass, and other fish as well.

Foam/Latex Ants

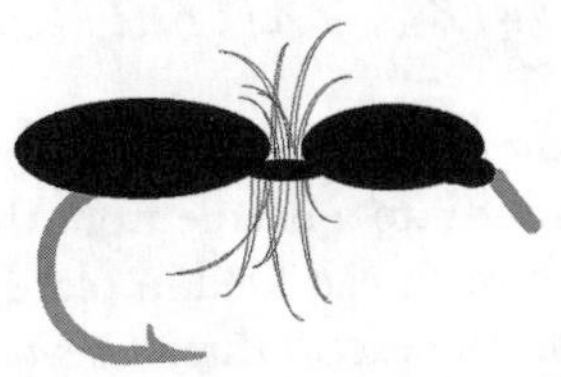

With the terrestrial season upon us once again it's time to start thinking about stocking up the old fly box with ants, beetles, and a variety of other crawlies. This might also be a good opportunity to experiment in a relatively new flytying technique that has excited a lot of interest among tyers recently—the use of liquid latex-covered foam bodies. Since Carl Richards first pioneered the use of liquid latex-covered foam bodies for

Latex/Foam Ant

Hook:	Mustad 94840, TMC 100 or any fine wire dry fly hook, #14-20
Note:	For this technique you want to select a hook that is one size smaller than you would for an equivalent fur ant, e.g., for a #14 size body you use a #16 hook.
Thread:	Same color as the ant body
Head/Abdomen:	Rainey's or other float foam, trimmed to shape and covered with colored liquid latex
Legs:	Hackle, deer hair, mono, or rubber legging material in color to match body

mayfly/stonefly/caddis imitations, a number of recipes for these foam/latex flies have begun to float around among tyers. The advantages of these foam/latex-bodied bugs are numerous: they are fast to tie (once you get the technique down), extremely durable, unsinkable, and highly realistic. Because the latex is buoyant, but not quite as buoyant as foam, the flies also float slightly into the film rather than riding high on top. This results in a more realistic presentation that can be deadly on picky fish.

The following recipe for a foam/latex ant is adapted from one developed by Jeff Clark and first published on FLYFISH@, the flyfishing listserv on the Internet.

Tying Instructions

1 Tie an overhand knot into one end of a 1' to 2' piece of heavy thread or mono and thread it into a needle from the opposite end so that you have a single strand of thread held in place on the needle by the knot on the end. Trim off the excess thread beyond the knot.

2 Cut pieces of foam for the head and abdomen of the ants in the size and shape that you need for your flies. You are going to be making a number of ant bodies at once to speed up the tying process. If you want all of your ants to be one size then cut all the foam pieces the same size or you can make different size ant bodies all at the same time. You are cutting one piece of foam for the head and another larger one for the abdomen. The two pieces together should be about the length of the hook shank. The two pieces should be roughly rounded on the sides. Don't worry if they look rough, chunky and angular; the latex will take care of that later.

3 Use the needle to thread an ant head onto your length of thread and slide the foam to near the end of the thread. Then thread an abdomen onto the thread leaving about ½" space between it and the head. Repeat this until you have all of the heads and abdomen lined up on the thread with about ½" space between them.

4 Secure the needle in your vise or stick it into something that will hold it securely and then tie the other end of the thread to something else solid so that the thread is held taut and is over the top of a surface that you don't mind dripping liquid latex onto.

5 Apply a drop of cyanoacrylate (CA) glue to the thread just beyond the first head and then slide the head over the glue. Apply another drop of CA glue about ½ hook shank length behind that head and then slide

the abdomen behind it to a point about $\frac{1}{4}$ hook shank length behind the head. You should end up with an ant body that is about full hook length with about $\frac{1}{4}$ hook shank length between the head and abdomen. Continue this process until you have all of the heads and abdomen assembled on the thread into full ant bodies with spaces of thread between each body. CA glue is available at model hobby stores that specialize in model airplanes, cars, boats, etc. At these stores you will be able to find it in a variety of consistencies: thin, medium and thick. The medium consistency works best for this technique. Thin consistency such as Super Glue or Krazy Glue tends to soak into the thread too much and thick consistency such as Zap-A-Gap tends to bead up as you slide the ant bodies around, creating glops of glue on the end of the bodies rather than securing them firmly to the thread.

6 Now you are ready to work with the liquid latex. Liquid latex is available at most hobby/craft stores and at stores that carry theatrical makeup. Brands such as Rub-R-Mold, for example, are sold for making miniature scenery for model train setups. You are also going to need some permanent markers and/or acrylic paint. The permanent markers can be used to color the liquid latex after it dries. The acrylic paint can also be used to paint the liquid latex after it dries or can be mixed with the latex to create a body that has the color throughout. Mixing the acrylic paint with the latex also speeds up the finishing time since you only have to wait for one drying process.

7 Apply the liquid latex or latex mixed with acrylic paint to the ant bodies with a fine artist's brush. The idea is to cover the foam chunks with a layer of liquid latex creating a smooth, rounded body. This is where you cover all of the dings, edges, etc., that were created in cutting the foam chunks. With a little bit of practice you will soon be creating smooth, shiny and highly realistic-looking ant bodies. Apply the liquid latex to all of the foam bodies on the thread and let them all dry. After the bodies have completely dried, color them with permanent markers or acrylic paint if necessary.

8 Cut off one complete ant body from the thread (head and abdomen plus the space in between)just behind the rear of the abdomen, leaving a little thread at the head end of the head. Place the hook in your vise and start your tying thread just behind the eye of the hook.

9 Position the head of the ant body just behind the eye of the hook and take a couple of wraps of thread over the thread sticking out of the front of the head. Whip finish to secure in place. Cut off your tying thread. Trim the excess thread sticking out over the eye of the hook. Apply a

little CA glue to the whip finish to secure it firmly in place and let the glue dry.

10 Restart your tying thread over the thread just in front of the abdomen and around both that thread and the hook. Take a couple of wraps to secure it in place and whip finish. Cut off your tying thread. Apply a little CA glue to the whip finish to secure it firmly in place and let the glue dry.

11 An alternate method of securing the ant body to the hook is to carefully work the hook through both the head and abdomen of the ant body before securing the hook in the vise. Then take a couple of wraps of thread in front of the head, whip finish and trim. Take a couple of wraps of thread just in front of the abdomen, whip finish and trim. A little CA glue then applied in both places and just behind the back of the abdomen where the hook comes out will firmly anchor the whole thing in place. Note that if you use this method, the hook should exit from the abdomen, not at the end of the abdomen, but just slightly ($^1/_4$ hook shank length) in front of the end on the underside of the abdomen. If you have trouble getting the hook through the ant body with this method, try reducing the amount of CA glue that you were using to secure the bodies to the thread in the body construction part of the technique. This method of securing the body to the hook results in a more durable ant, but is a bit more difficult than the first method.

12 Restart the thread just behind the head of the ant and add a couple of turns of hackle, 3 strands of deer hair, or other legging material. Whip finish and trim thread and deer hair or legging material. It is usually not a good idea to use CA glue to secure these in place as it will tend to stiffen up the legs unless applied VERY carefully. Head cement is usually better for this part of the process.

The end product is a foam/latex ant that is highly realistic, extremely durable and can be easily produced in large quantities. The latex/foam body also results in a body that is very realistic in feel to the fish and can increase your hookup rate.

Fishing the Fly

Latex Ants are definitely a member of the dry fly family of ant imitations. I and many other flyfishermen have pondered over the fondness that Trout seem to have for ants. For whatever reason, ants seem to attract Trout. This is a great pattern for use during the summer months on both the mountain streams and the tailwaters of the Southeast.

The Foam Hopper

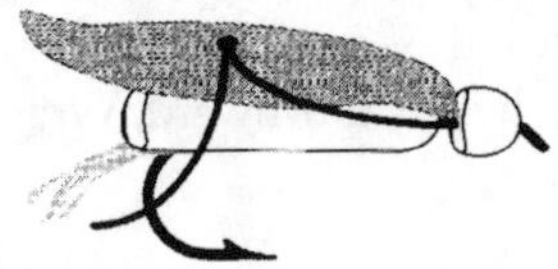

This is a very simple foam hopper pattern to tie. You can find the foam cylinders available at many fly shops in a variety of sizes; they make the job of shaping the foam even easier. Use green or yellow foam for hoppers or black foam for a cricket. The foam can also be colored using marking pens to achieve a mottled effect on the body of the hopper. In addition to the foam you will also need some CA glue (Super Glue). CA glue is available at many hobby shops that specialize in radio control planes and cars in a variety of thicknesses. I've found that the medium consistency is the easiest to control for this kind of work. These shops will also have a CA glue accelerator available that speeds the drying of the glue.

Hook:	Mustad 9671 or TMC 5262, (2X Nymph) #8-14
Head:	Foam cylinder slightly less than ¼ shank length
Thread:	Brown
Tail:	Red hackle fibers shorter than gap width in length
Body:	Foam cylinder slightly shorter than shank length
Wing:	Ringneck pheasant "church window" feather trimmed to shape and coated with head cement
Legs:	Rubber legging material

Tying Instructions

1 Cut a cylinder of foam the diameter of the head of the hopper and round it slightly on the front side. The cylinder should be slightly less than $\frac{1}{4}$ shank length long. Skewer it on the point of the hook with the rounded end toward the point. Work the foam head around to a point its own length behind the eye of the hook. Place a little CA glue in the area of the hook behind the eye where the head will end up then slide the head forward over the top of the glue. Be careful that you don't use so much glue that it will be squeezed forward and clog up the eye of the hook.

2 Now place the hook in your vise and start the thread at the bend of the hook. Tie in a short tail of red hackle fibers slightly shorter than gap length and pointing slightly downward. Wrap the thread forward to just behind the head.

3 Cut a cylinder of foam for the body of the hopper. It should be slightly rounded at the front end and cut to a wedge shape at the back. In length it should be such that when the front end is placed about $\frac{1}{16}$" behind the head the back end will be slightly longer than the hook. This usually means slightly shorter than shank length. This cylinder will form the main body of the hopper. Cut a slit into the "underside" of the body of the hopper. Place some CA glue on the shank of the hook from just behind the thread to just in front of the bend of the hook. Slip the slit of the body cylinder in place over the top of the hook, leaving about a $\frac{1}{16}$" space between the head and the body. Hold the body cylinder in place while the glue dries. Here is where some of the CA accelerator will speed up the process greatly.

4 Cut a wing from a ringneck pheasant "church window" feather. The wing should be rounded at the back and tapered toward the front. It will be tied in just in front of the body of the hopper and should be long enough to extend slightly past the back of the body. Coat this with head cement, lacquer or whatever you prefer and let dry. If you are tying a number of hoppers, it can speed up the process to make a bunch of wings of the proper lengths ahead of time and let them all dry at once. Tie in the wing so that the front end is between the body and the head and the wing extends over the body of the hopper.

5 To form a leg, take two sections of rubber legging material laid side by side and tie them in an overhand knot. At the knot trim off one of the two sections extending out of the knot in one direction. This will leave you with two sections sticking out of the knot in one direction and one

section sticking out of the knot in the other direction. The knot will be the joint of the leg. The single section will be the trailing end of the leg and the double section will be tied into the fly between the head and the wing on the side. Position a leg on one side of the fly so that the knot is in line with the bend of the hook and tie it in place. Tie in the other leg on the opposite side of the hook. Trim off the excess legging material.

6 Whip finish behind the head and add a small drop of CA glue to the thread where the wing and legs are tied in.

Fishing the Fly

Late summer and into early fall is the hopper season around most of the Southeast. This is the time when these flies can produce some slashing strikes from Trout. Don't be afraid to drop one of these bugs down with a real plop. This seems to actually attract the fish. Delicate presentations are not the approach with hoppers. These can also be great flies for panfish, Smallies, and Bass.

The Fur Ant

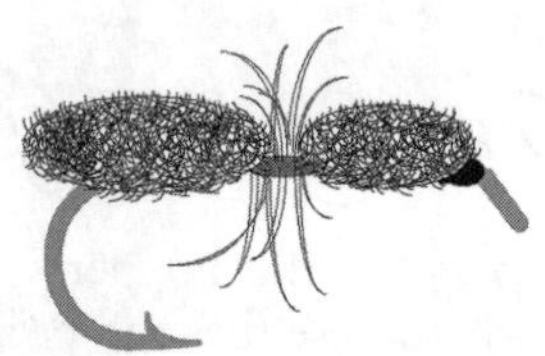

An easy-to-tie ant pattern for the terrestrial season. Southeastern ants come in a wide variety of sizes and colors. Vary the pattern to suit your locales.

Hook:	Mustad 94840, TMC 100 #14-20
Thread:	Black, red or cinnamon
Abdomen:	Black, red or cinnamon dubbing
Hackle:	A couple of turns of black or brown hackle
Head ("Thorax"):	Black, red or cinnamon dubbing

Tying Instructions

1. Start the thread at the bend of the hook.
2. Dub the abdomen forward to the midpoint of the shank. The abdomen should taper from the back to fattest in its middle and then taper down again as you get to the midpoint of the shank.
3. Tie in the hackle and take a couple of turns. Tie off and trim the excess.
4. Dub in the head ("thorax") of the ant in a dubbing ball that finishes just behind the eye of the hook. Whip finish.

The Mylar Beetle

Recently after a day of fishing the South Holston I dropped by Mahoney's in Johnson City, TN, to pick up a few items and check on the latest. I happened to glance at their tying desk and there was a really great looking Japanese Beetle. When I asked about it, George was kind enough to give me the details on a quick, very effective Beetle Pattern. It takes some braided mylar tubing, rubber legging material, a foam body and a magic marker. I'll give you the recipe for the Japanese Beetle and then you can vary the color to make June Bugs, etc.

Tying Instructions

1 For the Japanese Beetle, take some pearlescent braided mylar tubing and color it with an ordinary black magic marker. Quickly wipe off the marker and you will be left with tubing in a gorgeous Japanese Beetle mix of colors.

2 To turn this into a Beetle you then need the appropriate size hook, black thread and a foam body in the appropriate size and shape. The foam body can be purchased preshaped or you can form your own. Take the foam body and skewer it onto the hook and secure it in place with a little CA glue. It does need to be glued in place on the hook or it will twist on you later, creating problems. It should be secured so that the back of the body is right at the bend of the hook, but there is space between the front of the body and the eye of the hook for the "head" of the beetle.

3 Secure the hook in your vise in the usual manner. Take a couple of turns of thread at the back of the body and let the thread dangle below the hook.

4 Slip the tubing over the eye of the hook and slide it to the back so that the unraveled end protrudes beyond the thread. Take a couple of turns of thread around the mylar to secure it in place behind the body and whip finish.

5 Then take a couple of turns of thread around the mylar in front of the body to secure it in place and whip finish.

6 Trim off the excess tubing. Trim it very closely in the back, but leave a little of the loose braiding in the front and shape it to form the "head."

7 Now turn the body of the beetle upside down in your vise. Cut three pieces of rubber legging material 1" or more in length. They should be long enough for you to work easily with them and will be trimmed to exact length after they are glued in place.

8 Put a dab of CA (cyanoacrylate) glue on the underside of the beetle body. Place the three pieces of legging material on top of the CA glue so that they extend over both sides of the beetle. I usually use two of them to form an X and then lay the third one on crossways.

9 After the glue has dried, you can then cut the ends of the six legs sticking out to the length that you desire. Note: Do not use CA accelerator to help dry the glue on the bottom of the beetle. This causes the glue to turn opaque and ruins the look of the bottom.

Voila! You have a quick and very good looking beetle. It does take a little bit of practice to get the tie offs on the mylar tubing looking correct. The first time that I tied one I was able to turn out an acceptable beetle. The second one was even better looking. You can play around with different kinds of mylar tubing and different markers to get a wide variety of colors and form the foam body in whatever size and shape you desire for the beetle that you would like to imitate.

Fishing the Fly

Japanese beetles can be a very effective fly on both the mountain stream and the tailwaters of the Southeast. There actually is often a "hatch" of these insects during the summer when they swarm in large (and for gardeners and farmers, extremely annoying) quantities. Check with a local gardener to find out when the "hatch" usually occurs in your area and be ready with some of these easy-to-tie flies.

The Great Smokies

Origins of the Flies of the Great Smoky Mountains

The Western migration of Americans that began in the 1700s led through a path in the Blue Ridge Mountains we know as The Cumberland Gap. Formidable barriers prevented those early pioneers from taking most other routes. To the North lay the Alleghenies of Western Pennsylvania and what is now West Virginia and to the South rose the Great Smoky Mountains of North Carolina and the Eastern part of today's Tennessee. It was only after the more desirable portions of Kentucky and Tennessee were settled that our pioneers' attentions were directed back to these rugged bypassed areas of the Smokies. A few isolated valleys in the midst of otherwise inhospitable mountains offered refuge to those early settlers determined enough to seek them out. This was rocky, hardscrabble farming land and to survive, those who came to live there had to make use of whatever forms of food were available in addition to those crops that they could coax out of the ground. The Great Smoky Mountains did, however, offer abundant wildlife including numerous streams teeming with native Brook Trout. So in addition to hunting and trapping, these early settlers also became fishermen and the history of fly fishing in the Great Smoky Mountains began.

These were not displaced English gentlemen, however, carrying with them the traditions of the dry fly developed on the Test and the Itchen. These were hardy American pioneers who had to fish so that their families could survive. Most of the fishing done by these settlers was either with bait or by the use of fish traps and native poisons shown to them by the local Cherokees. It was not until the late 1800s and early 1900s that fly fishing was introduced to the Smokies along with logging and the Rainbow and Brown trout. When logging destroyed much of the habitat of the native Brookies, the Rainbows and Browns were introduced to attempt to reconstruct the fishery. The result is that even with the regrowth of the early logging areas the Rainbows and Browns are now the dominant fish of the mountain streams with the Brookies relegated to the higher altitudes.

The early flies of the Smokies were primarily wet flies or nymphs. It was not until about the 1930s that dry flies were introduced into the area by sportsmen. These early flies were developed by local fishermen or guides using readily available materials and based upon their experiences with bait fishing and the habits of the local trout. It was not until much later with the establishment of the Great Smoky Mountains National Park that many of the flies being created in the Eastern United States were introduced into the area.

Flyfishing techniques have changed in the Smokies as well. The early local fly fishermen did not have finely crafted bamboo rods and silk lines of the early 1900's or the high-tech graphite and plastics of today, but used long poles that they fashioned from cane or hickory along with lines of whatever material that was handy. Reels were unknown and "casting" was severely limited on overgrown streams in the midst of half vertical terrain. The techniques used by the early fly fishermen find their closest approximation in the "short line nymphing" of today. It is still possible occasionally to come across an old-timer working a trout stream with a 10-15' piece of bamboo cane and a line of about equal length tied to the end of it. If you watch carefully you will learn a lot about the fishing flies and presentations in these mountain streams and if you can get him to show it to you (or even talk to you) most likely the fly on the end of that line will be a "Yallerhammer."

No one knows who invented the Yallerhammer or most of the other flies that have come out of the Smokies. Even those flies of today named after or attributed to someone are in most cases codified versions of flies that had been passed on through years of verbal tradition. Eddie George, for example, when speaking of the background of his George Nymph, freely admits that it is a development of the "Cottontop" that goes back further than anyone can remember. Similarities to classic English or Eastern U.S. patterns are in most cases attributable to coincidence or parallel development rather than imitation. The Thunderhead has often been described as an Adams with a white, divided calf-tail wing, but Joe Hall who is generally given credit for the Thunderhead had never met Leonard Halladay or even seen an Adams when he produced his first Thunderhead. In its classic version it was also tied with American Possum rather than the more usual Muskrat it and the Adams are tied with today.

The classic Yallerhammer was a fly that was tied with materials that were easily available as were all of the early flies of the Smokies. The Yallerhammer derives its name from the Yellow Shafted Woodpecker or Common Flicker and uses a split wing feather of that bird to give it its characteristic shape, movement and color—"Yallerhammer" being a local name for the bird. Even though the Flicker is not endangered, it is protected in most states as a "songbird" and substitutes for the feathers have had to be developed. In Tennessee, for example, it is illegal to kill a Flicker or to sell the feathers. It is not, however, illegal to possess the feathers. The result has been the development of a lively exchange of "roadkill" feathers. The tradition being that if someone gives you some feathers you are expected to reciprocate the next time that you come across some. Flickers commonly feed on the ground and are also attracted to bird feeders.

Predation by cats is common and the leftovers are eagerly scooped up by local Yallerhammer aficionados. For the more squeamish or careful, the yellow dyed grizzly has become the most common substitute for the original Flicker wing feather. It does not have the shape, color or movement of the original though, and as a result other flies that trace their ancestry to the Yallerhammer have been developed such as the Tellico Nymph. The original Yallerhammer was a very simple fly. On a wet fly hook you secure one end of a split wing feather of the bird to the back of the hook. Then you form a body out of 2-3 peacock herls usually twisted with the thread for extra strength. The feather is palmered forward in an open spiral to just behind the eye of the hook, tied in place, trimmed and whip finished. The result when tied with a true Yellow Shafted Woodpecker feather is ugly as homemade sin. The feather is extremely difficult to work and the resulting fly is often misshapen and awkward. Yallerhammer lovers, however, claim that this is not just part of the charm of the fly, but necessary for fish to be attracted. "Purty Yallerhammers don't ketch fish." Today in the Smokies you can find the Yallerhammer being fished in its original version as a wet fly or nymph and in more modern variations as both a dry and wet fly. It is a fly that has a strong attraction for panfish as well as trout and is also a favorite among bluegill fishermen.

Probably the most famous dry fly of the Smokies is the Thunderhead. An attractor pattern developed by Joe Hall of Bryson City, North Carolina the Thunderhead is the premier dry fly pattern of the Smokies. The white Wulff-type wing combined with a body, hackle and tail similar to the Adams makes this a fly ideally suited to the rough waters and varied insect life of the mountains. Today the body of the Thunderhead is most often tied with muskrat dubbing, but has been tied in the past using local possum-making it one of the few flies to utilize this material. The Thunderhead is used year-round, but is probably best suited to the spring and early summer months. It is especially favored on the highly productive waters of Abrams Creek. While not having the notoriety or rustic charm of the Yallerhammer, the Thunderhead is an all-around better producer than any of the other dry flies of the Smokies.

Another popular dry fly of the Smokies and, for some, an even better producer than the Thunderhead, is the Brown Hackle. Originally developed from the Brown Hackle Peacock, a wet fly, the Brown Hackle is a fly that can be used year-round in the mountains. Often known locally as the Ramsey, the Brown Hackle is a simple fly to tie. A wingless fly, it is tied from back to front of the hook using a golden pheasant tippet tail, a gold tinsel or mylar tag, a body of peacock herl and a few windings of brown dry fly hackle before finishing off the head.

Two other dry flies developed originally in the Smokies are the Gray Hackle Yellow and a Smoky Mountain version of the Near Nuff. Both of these are more limited in the times when they are commonly used, being most popular in the months of May through June. The Gray Hackle Yellow is a very attractive pattern that uses a red tail, gold ribbing over a yellow body and then grizzly hackle with no wing. A very pretty pattern when properly tied, it has in more recent versions often developed a split wing of lemon wood duck. The Near Nuff is distinguished by its long forked tail usually tied from two stripped grizzly hackle stems. The wing is formed of split, divided lemon wood duck, then the body is shaped with the thread and covered with a stripped peacock herl. The addition of one golden ginger and one grizzly hackle completes the fly.

Wet flies of the Smokies that are still in use today in this age of dwindling popularity of these once common patterns include the already mentioned Yallerhammer and Brown Hackle Peacock. The Brown Hackle Peacock is a very easy fly to tie and can be extremely effective. I consider it to be even more versatile than its dry fly cousin the Ramsey. Hatches in the Smokies are sporadic and unreliable, but wet flies and nymphs are consistent producers. The Brown Hackle Peacock is tied from only three materials: soft brown hackle is used to form the tail and a soft hackle collar; the body is formed of peacock herl with a gold tinsel or mylar tag. This is an extremely simple and highly effective pattern.

Nymphs originating in the Smokies have become the most widespread of the patterns that have migrated to other parts of the United States. Of these, the one that has traveled the farthest and found the widest acceptance is the famous Tellico Nymph. Considered by many to have been developed from the original Yallerhammer, its appearance and method of employment is undeniably much closer to that classic fly than are many of the Yallerhammer's modern variations. The version of the Tellico given here is the Blackburn Tellico, developed by Rick Blackburn, a contemporary Smoky Mountains fly tyer. It can be tied either weighted or unweighted. Brown hackle fibers are tied in for the tail and then one end of the turkey wing strip for the wing case and 2-3 peacock herls to be used for the ribbing are tied in above the tail. The body is dubbed using a golden yellow dubbing material mixed with hare's ear and dubbed forward to about ⅓ of the way back of the eye. At this point a brown hackle is tied in and left hanging. The rest of the body is dubbed forward. The peacock herls are spiraled forward to where the hackle is hanging out of the body and then the hackle and ribbing are palmered forward to just behind the eye, tied off and trimmed. The hackle is trimmed flat on top of the body and the wing case is pulled forward and tied off. This produces a fly that works in many different sizes and situations.

The George Nymph is a later development of the Cottontop Nymph and because of its easy visibility is ideally suited for fishing in the shallow mountain streams of the Smokies without a strike indicator. Fished unweighted, it can even be effective as an emerger pattern. Today the white clump of fur that gives the fly its original name is mainly tied using modern acrylics, z-lon, etc. This is another fly tied from the back forward with the tail going on first followed by one end of the turkey strip for the wing case being secured. A peacock herl body is wound forward to ¼ hook shank short of the eye and then the other end of the turkey strip back is tied off and trimmed. One end of a piece of white acrylic yarn is secured to the top of the hook. A soft brown hackle collar is tied in and the top of it trimmed flat. The yarn is pulled tight over the top of this, tied off, trimmed and the fly finished. This fly is most often fished in the short line situations common in the Smokies with the white yarn top acting as a built-in strike indicator.

One last nymph from the Smokies is the Streaker Nymph which is usually used in situations where a stickbait imitation is desired. Also developed from the original Yallerhammer, this is a skinnier version of the fly to more closely resemble stickbait. For this fly, a short tail of brown hackle fibers is first tied in and then a thin piece of turkey wing strip and 1-2 peacock hackles are secured by one end just above the tail before the dubbing is applied. A lighter colored tan-yellow dubbing is used for the body and then the peacock herl is spiraled forward as ribbing. The turkey wing case is pulled forward on top, secured and the excess trimmed. Then some short brown hackle fibers are tied in underneath in the front as a throat.

Most of the flies developed in the Great Smoky Mountains were not intended to imitate specific forms of insect life, but rather to be general imitators or attractors. The hatches of the Smokies are usually limited and sporadic. There are, however, a large variety of different kinds of insect life in these mountains. Under such conditions, the most successful flies have been those that seek to suggest many of the different forms that the trout feed upon while providing something in the way of movement and/or color that the fish find enticing. The "attractors" of the Smokies are usually not the gaudy flies that go by these names in many other locations. They are more generalized patterns that export well to other areas simply because they are not that specific. The Tellico Nymph has been the most widespread of these exports with the George Nymph close behind. I would suggest that the dry fly of the Smokies that would probably be a good producer in a wide variety of situations, but has not found widespread acceptance, would be the Thunderhead. Anytime that you are looking for a generally useful pattern in a little bit faster water, the better flotation and visibility of the white calf tail wing of the Thunderhead would make it a fly worth considering. For the panfish fancier, the Yallerhammer in any of its many manifestations is also another fly worth adding to your arsenal. Until recently, the relative isolation of the Smokies from the major population centers of the Eastern United States has kept these flies from being widely known. Abrams Creek, the Little River, Hazel Creek and the numerous other streams of the Smokies have not received the publicity of the Battenkill, the Letort, the Yellow Breeches and other famous eastern streams. Because of that there is still a lot of relatively unspoiled fishing to be found in the Smokies for which many of us are very grateful.

—L.J. DeCuir
Somewhere in the Mountains of East Tennessee

Note: For those of you interested in more information on the history of fly fishing in the Smokies, Don Kirk's chapter on "Trout Fishing in the Smokies" in his book *Smoky Mountains Trout Fishing Guide* is an excellent place to begin. If you can locate a copy of Robert S. Masonin's now out of print *The Lure of the Smokies,* there is material in there as well. For the serious scholar though, often the best sources can be verbal history provided by fast disappearing local residents and materials that can be unearthed at numerous historical societies throughout East Tennessee and North Carolina.

The Yallerhammer

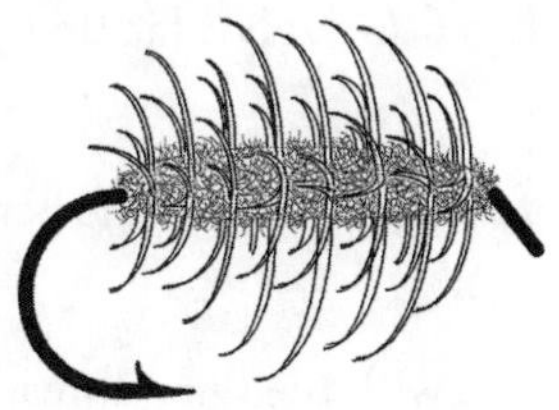

The Yallerhammer is one of the flies of the Smokies that has been around so long that no one really has any idea who might have been originally responsible for it. There is even a great deal of debate about exactly what the original fly was like because today just about everyone who ties it has their own version ranging from nymphs, through wet flies, and even dries. My own suspicion is that the nymph/wet fly version of the pattern is closest to the early fly. The original fly was tied with the split wing feather of the Yellow Shafted Woodpecker or Flicker, known locally as the Yallerhammer. Today this bird is protected as a songbird in many states. Killing the bird and/or selling the feathers is illegal. As a result fly tyers have adapted to other materials. The most common substitute for the original feather is now Yellow Dyed Grizzly Hackle.

This version of the Yallerhammer is a modern adaptation of the classic nymph/wet version of the fly. This pattern is designed to be tied with materials that are generally available to fly fishermen throughout the world.

Hook:	Mustad 9761, TMC 5262 or 2X Nymph Hook # 4-14
Thread:	Black
Weight:	"Lead" wire or substitute
Palmered Ribbing:	Yellow Dyed Grizzly Hackle
Body:	2-5 strands of Peacock Herl depending upon size of the hook

Tying Instructions

1. Start the thread just behind the eye and wrap to the bend of the hook.
2. Wrap 6-10 turns of "lead" wire around the hook, centering the on the shank.
3. Use the tying thread to form a tapered "cigar shaped" underbody, securing the "lead" in place while forming the body.
4. Tie in the Yellow Dyed Grizzly Hackle by its tip at the bend of the hook.
5. Tie in the strands of Peacock Herl at the bend of the hook and let them hang.
6. Twist the Peacock Herl with the tying thread and wrap it forward to just behind the eye of the hook. Take turns of thread to secure it in and trim the excess herl.
7. Palmer the Yellow Dyed Grizzly Hackle forward in an open spiral to just behind the eye of the hook. Take a couple of turns of thread to secure it in place and trim off the excess hackle.
8. Whip finish and trim off the excess thread.

Variations

The Yallerhammer (Classic Nymph/Wet Fly Pattern)

Hook: Mustad 3906 # 8-14
Thread: Black
Hackle: Split wing feather of Yellow Shafted Woodpecker (Flicker) palmered from back to front
Body: Peacock Herl

The Yallerhammer (Classic Wet Fly Pattern)

Hook: Mustad 3906 #8-14
Thread: Black
Body: Peacock Herl
Hackle: Split wing feather of Yellow Shafted Woodpecker (Flicker) tied on as a wet fly collar

The Yallerhammer (Modern Wet Fly Pattern)

Hook: Mustad 3906 #8-14
Thread: Black
Tail: Mixed yellow and black hackle fibers, hook gap in length
Hackle: Yellow dyed grizzly palmered from back to front
Body: Peacock Herl

The Yallerhammer (Modern Dry Fly Pattern)

Hook: Mustad 94840 #12-18
Thread: Black
Tail: Mixed yellow and black hackle fibers, 1½ times hook gap in length
Body: Peacock Herl
Hackle: Yellow dyed grizzly tied in dry fly style

The Yallerhammer (Modern Dry Fly Pattern #2)

Hook: Mustad 94840 #12-18
Thread: Black
Wing: Mixed yellow and black hackle fibers, upright and divided
Tail: Black hackle fibers, 1½ times hook gap in length
Body: Peacock Herl
Hackle: 1 yellow dyed grizzly, 1 black tied in dry fly style

Fishing the Fly

The Yallerhammer can be fished like any other weighted nymph, but is most effective when some motion is imparted to the fly either by the current in the stream or by the fisherman. In the small, swift streams of the Smokies this is usually no problem, but if you are fishing it in calmer waters you should think of it more like a Woolly Bugger that is fished slowly or a wet fly on which you are using a slow retrieve. It is a very good fly for getting down into deep holes where the big ones are hiding out. In addition to being effective on trout, it is also a deadly panfish fly.

The Tellico Nymph

The Tellico Nymph is without a doubt the most widely used fly that originated in the Great Smoky Mountains of Tennessee and North Carolina.

Its exact origins are obscure, but there are many who feel that it developed from the Yallerhammer. Wherever and however it began, it has spread throughout the country and the world to become an extremely popular "attractor" pattern that is effective in many locations.

There are also numerous versions of this popular nymph that have been developed by many different tyers around the United States. Here are a couple of different versions, just so that you can see what kind of variety there is within what is now known as the Tellico Nymph. The first of these is from Rick Blackburn, a noted tyer and fly fisher from the Smokies. Rick has been tying, fishing, and teaching others to tie for years now. The second version is from David Allerton, a friend, tyer, and fly fisher whom I've joined on expeditions all over the Southeast.

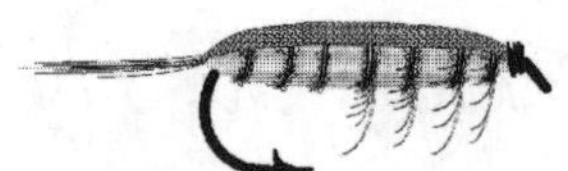

Tying Instructions

1 Cut a piece of dark brown thread about 6-8" long. Using the thread on your bobbin, tie it onto the hook just behind the eye and then wrap it onto the hook all the way to the bend. Leave most of the piece of thread sticking out the back of the hook. This will be used to twist with the peacock herl for the ribbing to reinforce the herl.

Blackburn Tellico Nymph

Hook: #6 3X to #12 2X long hook (#8 3X long is "standard")
Thread: Dark Brown
Tail: Mink fibers or brown hackle fibers
Ribbing: 2 strands of peacock herl
Wing Case: Dark Brown turkey feather section
Body: Dirty golden-yellow dubbing
Hackle: Palmered through front half of body

2 Wrap "lead" wire around the hook starting at a position about 3/16 inch behind the eye to a place in line with the point of the hook. Wrap the bobbin thread around the wire to keep it from shifting.

3 Tie in a tail of mink hairs or brown hackle fibers about 2/3 shank length long.

4 Tie in two strands of peacock herl just above the tail.

5 Tie in 1/4-inch wide piece of turkey feather just above the tail.

6 Dub the body forward using a dirty golden-yellow dubbing to a point about 1/3 hook length behind the eye of the hook. Hare's Ear Plus Golden is a good color for this. The original dubbing was 90% cottontail rabbit fur dyed golden with Rit Dye and 10% clear antron for sparkle.

7 Tie in the tip of a brown hackle feather at the point where you stopped dubbing.

8 Continue dubbing forward to just behind the eye of the hook, leaving room to tie in the ribbing, wing case, and to finish the fly.

9 Wrap the bobbin thread back through the dubbing to the point where the brown hackle feather was tied in.

10 Palmer the brown hackle feather forward to the end of the dubbing.

11 Palmer the thread forward through the palmered hackle to the end of the dubbing and tie off the hackle feather. Trim off the excess hackle feather.

12 Twist the brown thread that you earlier left dangling out the back of the hook with the peacock herl for strength and spiral them forward

together as an open ribbing to the forward end of the dubbing. Tie off and trim the excess.

13 Grasp the turkey feather and pull it over the top of the body as a wing case. Tie it off just behind the eye of the hook and trim off the excess.

14 Whip finish and lacquer the head and turkey feather wing case.

David's Tellico Nymph

Hook:	Mustad 9761 or 2X Nymph hook #4-16
Thread:	Yellow
Weight:	A few turns of "lead" wire if desired
Tail:	Several barbules of guinea breast feather
Ribbing:	One or two strands of peacock herl
Wing Case:	Four to eight strands of peacock herl
Body:	Yellow floss
Collar:	Brown hackle

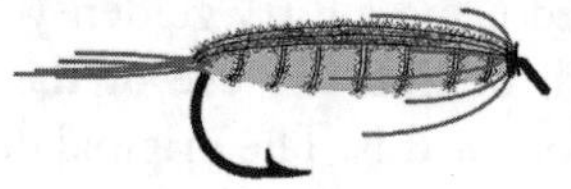

Tying Instructions

1 Start the thread just behind the eye of the hook and lay in a base of thread to the bend of the hook.

2 Wrap a number of turns of "lead" wire around the hook, centered on the hook if desired.

3 Wrap thread over the wire to secure it in place and form a body that is tapered so that it is fatter in the center and narrower at the tips.

4 Tie in several barbules of guinea feather as a tail approx. 1½ times hook gap width in length.

5 Secure the peacock herl that will be used as both the ribbing and the wing case just in front of the tail with several winds of thread.

6 Secure the floss to be used to form the body just in front of the tail and wind the thread to the front of the hook.

7 Wrap the floss to the front of the hook forming the body of the fly. Note: Leave room behind the eye of the hook to tie off the ribbing, the wing case and to tie in the collar.

8 Take a couple of wraps of thread to secure the floss behind the eye of the hook and trim off the excess floss.

9 Spiral one or two strands of peacock herl forward in an open spiral to form the ribbing. Tie off with thread and trim the excess herl.

10 Grasp the remaining strands of peacock herl and bring them forward over the top of the body to form the wing case. Tie off with thread and trim the excess herl.

11 Tie in a soft brown hackle feather by its tip and wind it around the hook just behind the eye to form a collar. Tie off and trim the excess hackle.

12 Whip finish.

Variations

1 Use soft hackle material (partridge, grouse, etc.) for the tail and collar.

2 The fly can be tied either weighted or unweighted.

3 A darker colored thread can be used to form the "head" on the fly, but don't use it underneath the floss or the color will darken when wet.

4 The color of the floss for the body can be varied as well. Pink and green seem to be the most commonly used colors other than yellow.

Fishing the Fly

This has proven to be a very effective fly on the mountain streams throughout the Southeast as well as on those tailwaters with good hatches. It can be fished either weighted or unweighted under a strike indicator or using short line nymphing technique. In the smaller sizes it is also excellent when fished under a dry fly as a dropper.

The Thunderhead

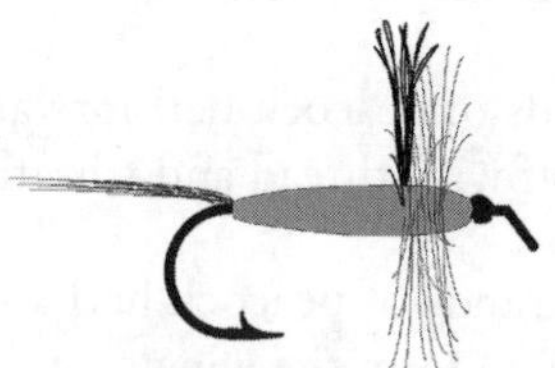

Attributed to Joe Hall of Bryson City, NC, The Thunderhead is the most popular dry fly pattern that has originated in the Smokies. While it has often been described as an Adams Wulff it was, in fact, developed completely independently of both the Adams and the Wulff style of fly. Joe Hall had met neither Leonard Halladay or Lee Wulff, nor seen any of their flies before coming up with The Thunderhead. The fly is a natural for the conditions in the Great Smoky Mountains where hatches are not heavy and this kind of generic "attractor" pattern works well year-round. The white calf-tail wing floats readily in the mountain streams and is highly visible in the quickly changing water conditions found in the Smokies. Although today it is usually tied with muskrat dubbing, it is one of the few flies that was originally tied with American Possum as dubbing.

Tying Instructions

1. Start the thread just behind the eye of the hook and wind it back to about 1/3 hook shank length behind the eye. Then wind it forward to about 1/16 inch to 1/8 inch behind the eye.
2. Lash a clump of calf tail to the top of the hook, at this point measured so that it will be the height desired for the wing when upright. Tips pointing out over the eye of the hook, butts toward the bend.
3. Grasp the calf tail by its tips and pull it upright. Take a number of windings of thread around the base of the clump of calf tail to support it in this upright position.

Hook:	Mustad 94840, TMC 100 #12-18
Thread:	Gray or black
Wing:	White calf tail, upright and divided
Tail:	Brown & grizzly hackle fibers, mixed
Body:	Muskrat (or Possum) dubbing
Hackle:	One brown and one grizzly hackle tied sparse

4 Bring your thread through the middle of and behind the calf tail, dividing it into two sections. Take one turn of thread around the hook behind the calf tail. Then further divide and separate the two sections of calf tail by taking a modified figure eight loop around both of the sections. To do this, the thread goes around the base of the far section two or three times and then back through the middle. Then it goes around the base of the near section two or three times and back through the middle, ending up behind the wing on the far side of the hook. This is similar to the method used with an upright divided wood duck flank wing, but with the addition of a couple of loops around each section of calf tail. The extra turns around the calf tail help keep this material separated and divided. Take another turn around the hook behind the wing to hold it all in place.

5 Trim the butts of the calf tail to form a taper toward the bend of the hook and lash this all in place by winding the thread to the bend of the hook.

6 Secure the tail in place with a couple of turns of thread and trim the butts.

7 Dub the body forward to just behind the wing, forming a tapered body.

8 Tie in the hackle just in front of the wing with the tips facing backward. One at a time wind the hackle around the hook taking one turn behind the wing and then two turns in front, securing and trimming each hackle as you are finished with it.

9 Whip finish just behind the eye of the hook.

Fishing the Fly

The Thunderhead is one of your classic mountain Trout stream dry flies. The calftail gives it excellent flotation in swift moving mountain streams. Fished as a dry fly, you'll find it an excellent choice in any of the Trout streams throughout the Southeast.

Other Smoky Mountain Trout Fly Patterns

Brown Hackle or Ramsey (Dry Fly) This is a very simple Smoky Mountain dry fly named after one of the earliest rod building, guiding and flyfishing families from the area.

Hook: Mustad 94840 #12-18
Thread: Black
Wing: None
Tail: 1 golden pheasant tippet
Tag: Fine, flat gold tinsel or mylar
Body: Peacock herl
Hackle: Brown

Gray Hackle Yellow (Dry Fly) This is one of the prettiest little dries to ever come out of the Smokies and is even prettier when tied with silk floss.

Hook: Mustad 94840 #12-18
Thread: Black or yellow
Wing: None
Tail: Red hackle fibers
Rib: Fine flat gold tinsel or mylar
Body: Yellow floss
Hackle: Grizzly

Gray Hackle Yellow (Dry Fly, #2)

Hook: Mustad 94840 #12-18
Thread: Black or yellow
Wing: None
Tail: None
Rib: Fine, flat gold tinsel or mylar
Body: Yellow or lemon dubbing
Hackle: Grizzly

George Nymph (Cottontop Nymph)

Developed by Eddie George from the even older Cottontop Nymph. The small white "hump" serves as a built-in strike indicator.

Hook: Mustad 94840 (dry fly) #8-12
Thread: Black
Tail: Brown hackle fibers
Wing Case: Turkey wing strip, full length top of body
Body: Peacock herl
Hump: White fur or acrylic, tied in on top as hump after turkey wing back is secured and before throat is tied in. After the throat is tied in and trimmed, then white hump is pulled forward, tied off and trimmed before whip finishing.
Throat: Brown hackle tied collar style and trimmed on top

Near Nuff (Dry Fly)

You will find many different flies all over the country called a "Near Nuff", but this is the Smoky Mountains version

Hook: Mustad 94840 #12-18
Thread: Gray
Wing: Lemon wood duck flank fibers, upright and divided
Tail: 2 stripped grizzly hackle stems tied in as a forked tail, extra long (twice shank length)
Body: Stripped peacock herl
Hackle: Golden, ginger and grizzly mixed

Streaker Nymph (Nymph) The Streaker Nymph is sometimes referred to as a "skinny Tellico." Most people familiar with the fly believe that it was intended as an imitation of "stickbait." Similar to and bearing an ancestral relationship with the Tellico Nymph, it is unclear which is older.

Hook: Mustad 9671 (2X Nymph) or Mustad 9672 (3X Nymph) #6-12
Thread: Black
Tail: Brown hackle fibers (short) or none
Wing Case: Turkey wing strip full length top of body (thin)
Rib: 1-2 peacock herls spiraled full length (under wing case)
Body: Tan or light brown mixed w/golden dubbing applied thin
Hackle: Short brown hackle fibers tied in as a throat

Brown Hackle Peacock (Wet) Another of the very oldest flies from the Smokies.

Hook: Mustad 3906 #10-14
Thread: Brown
Tail: Soft brown hackle, shank length Tag: Gold mylar
Body: Peacock herl
Hackle: 2 turns soft brown hackle tied collar style

Pat's Flies

The following three flies were first introduced to me by Pat Proffitt, a legendary fly fisherman in the mountains of East Tennessee and one of the greatest guys that you would ever want to meet. Pat knows these mountain streams like the back of his hand both when it comes to trout and smallies. Being fond of both species myself, Pat and I immediately hit it off. He often works as a guide with Bobby Schultz out of Smoky Mountain Anglers in Gatlinburg, and is one of those guides who sees their job as really helping you learn how to fish these streams. All three of these flies are mountain flies—simple, but highly effective. They are often tied weighted to help you get down into those deeper holes and pockets in these streams where the big ones may be hiding out.

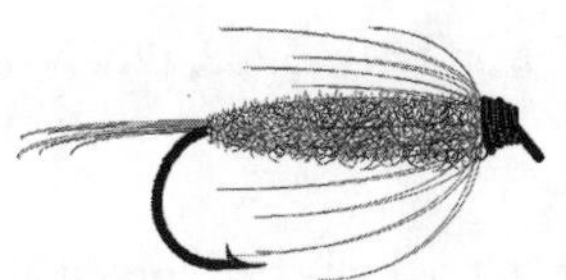

Pat's Nymph

Hook: Mustad 9671 or TMC 5262, (2X Nymph) #6-16
Thread: Black
Weight: "Lead" wire
Tail: Brown and grizzly hackle fibers
Body: Muskrat dubbing
Hackle: Soft brown and grizzly hackle tied in as a wet fly collar.

Tying Instructions

1. Start the thread just behind the eye of the hook and wind it to the bend.
2. Wrap several turns of "lead" wire around the hook to weight the fly. These should be centered on the hook. Take several wraps of thread over the wire to secure it in place and finish with the thread at the bend of the hook.
3. Tie in several brown and grizzly fibers as a tail, slightly longer than hook gap in length.
4. Dub a tapered body forward to about 1/16" behind the eye of the hook.
5. Tie in a soft brown and a soft grizzly hackle. Take a couple of wraps of each as a wet fly collar and tie off. Trim off the excess and whip finish.

Variations

1. Use some copper or gold wire to form a rib up the body of the fly.
2. Use partridge instead of soft hackle.

The Miller Nymph

Hook: Mustad 9671 or TMC 5262, (2X Nymph) #6-16
Thread: Orange
Weight: "Lead" wire
Tail: Two orange goose biots tied forked about 1½ times hook gap in length or in the smaller sizes some orange hackle fibers
Abdomen: Muskrat dubbing
Wing Case: A strip of dark mottled turkey quill
Hackle: Soft brown hackle
Thorax: Muskrat dubbing

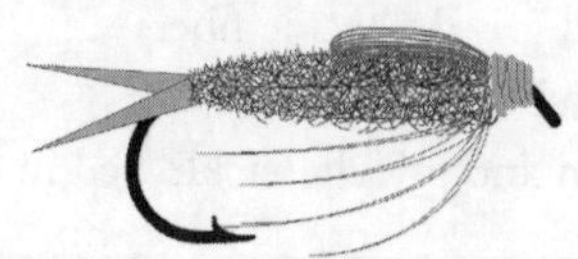

Tying Instructions

1 Start the thread just behind the eye of the hook and wind it to the bend.

2 Wind several wraps of "lead" wire around the hook as weight. These should be centered on the forward half of the hook where the thorax will be tied in later. Take several wraps of thread over the wire to secure it in place and then wrap the thread to the bend of the hook.

3 Tie in two orange goose biots as a tail, forked and about 1½ times hook gap in length. In the smaller sizes use some orange hackle fibers in place of the biots.

4 Dub a tapered abdomen about ½ way up the hook shank.

5 Tie in a strip of dark mottled turkey quill that later will have its other end pulled forward as a wing case over the top of the thorax.

6 Tie in a soft brown hackle about twice hook gap in length and take a couple of wraps around the hook. Tie off the end and trim off the excess.

7 Dub in the thorax to slightly behind the eye of the hook. The thorax should be slightly larger in diameter than the forward end of the abdomen.

8 Trim off the hackle fibers on top of the body.

9 Pull the turkey quill for the wing case forward and tie off just behind the eye of the hook. Trim off the excess.

10 Use the orange thread to form a nice-sized head on the fly and whip finish.

Fishing the Fly

Pat's Nymph and the Miller Nymph both are mountain nymphs that were designed as heavily weighted flies for fishing the deep pools of mountain Trout streams. They will sink fast and stay down there even in swift current. Detecting a strike with one of these flies can often be your biggest difficulty. It takes a sensitive eye and feel of the rod to know when there is a fish on—when in doubt, lift the rod tip. These are also great flies for use in a tandem rig, another common tactic when fishing the deep pools of the mountains.

The Smoky Mountain Blackbird

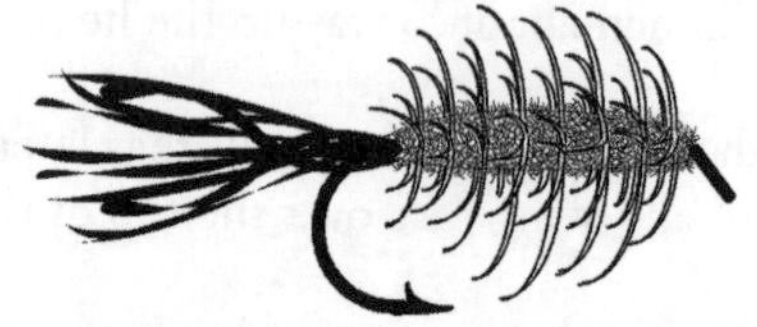

This fly is similar in many ways to the original Yallerhammer in that it utilizes the split wing feather of a bird. With the protection of the Flicker as a songbird in most Southeastern states, the Yallerhammer today is sometimes tied with a blackbird wing feather dyed yellow. This fly uses the wing feather of a blackbird in its natural state. The feeling, shape and movement of this fly is almost like that of the original Yallerhammer.

Hook:	Mustad 9672, TMC 5263 or 3-4X Streamer Hook, # 4-10
Thread:	Black
Weight:	"Lead" wire
Tail:	Barbules from the wing feather of a blackbird
Palmered Rib:	Split wing feather of a blackbird
Body:	Peacock Herl

Tying Instructions

1 Start the thread just behind the eye of the hook and wind it to the bend.

2 Wind several wraps of "lead" wire around the hook as weight. These should be centered on the hook. Take several wraps of thread over the wire to secure it in place and then wrap the thread to the bend of the hook.

3 Take several barbules from the wing feather of a blackbird about as long as the hook and tie them in as a tail.

4 Take a wing feather from a blackbird and soak it in water for a while to soften it up. Cut off the base of the quill. Using a sharp knife, cut a slit in the bottom of the quill. Carefully using the thumbnails of both hands, gently work your way up the center of the quill splitting it in half. You should end up with two usable sections. One will have the "biots" or short barbules on the top of the quill for smaller size flies and the other will have the longer barbules on the bottom of the quill for larger size flies. This is a process that will take a little practice to develop. Practice on some of the less desirable feathers till you get a feeling for splitting the feather.

5 Take one of these split wing feathers and tie it in right above the tail. Look at the barbules on the split feather before you tie it in. You are going to be palmering the split wing feather forward as "ribbing," much like the saddle hackle on a Woolly Bugger except the spirals will be closer together. Tie in the end of the split feather that will allow the barbules to "fall" to the back of the fly when you palmer the feather forward.

6 Tie in several peacock herls. Wrap your thread forward to about 1/16" behind the eye of the hook. Wrap the peacock herls forward around the hook shank to the thread. Tie off the peacock herls and trim off the excess.

7 Spiral the already tied in split wing feather forward to the thread and tie it off. Trim off the excess. The first time that you try this you will find that this is not easy to do. The feather will fight you all the way. You will need to be constantly twisting the feather as you spiral it forward to keep the split portion of the quill toward the hook shank. At first this can be difficult until you develop a feel for working with what is probably a very different type of feather than you have worked with before. It does get easier with practice.

8 Take several more wraps to firmly secure the split wing feather in place and to form the "head" of the fly. Whip finish.

Note: The technique for tying this fly (minus the tail) is identical to the method of tying the classic Yallerhammer. After you've mastered tying a few Smoky Mountain Blackbirds, you might want to try picking out some of the lighter colored wing feathers from a blackbird wing and dyeing them yellow. Then you can use them to tie up some classic Yallerhammers.

Fishing the Fly

The Blackbird is usually fished in the mountains of the Southeast like most heavily weighted nymphs, but it can also be fished like a Woolly Bugger. The tail and the way the palmered feather works will move in much the manner of the Woolly Bugger. This makes it a bit more versatile than many mountain flies and sometimes more productive as well.

Bobby's Flies

Burbling its way down a mountainside just outside of the Great Smoky Mountains National Park is one of the most beautiful streams in the Smokies—Norton Creek. As it trips its way along through 5-6 miles of pools, runs, and falls, it also flows over the top of an extraordinary number of unbelievably large mountain trout. Scattered throughout this stream are many of the fattest, largest and most unusual Rainbows, Browns and Brookies in the entire Smokies. What is most unusual about the stream itself and these fish is that this is a private stream that has been lovingly manicured and cared for by the only Riverkeeper in all of Tennessee—Bobby Shults.

Bobby also runs The Smoky Mountain Angler in Gatlinburg, ties some great mountain flies and guides through the Smokies as well. Smoky Mountain Angler is the oldest flyfishing shop in Gatlinburg and Bobby is a believer in the traditional Smoky Mountain patterns. The two flies featured here are his own creations based on years of tying and fishing these traditional patterns and are deadly patterns for mountain trout. Both flies also happen to be named after dogs. The Sunshine Fly is named after a chihuahua owned by Bobby's daughter and his son-in-law and fellow fly tyer J.C. Ramsey. The Buckwheat Fly is named after a German Shepherd owned by Tony Reagan and in its original version uses dubbing from that Shepherd.

If you're in Gatlinburg and looking for some good advice about the fishing, drop by Bobby's shop. You'll also find some of the best tied traditional Smoky Mountain patterns around.

The Sunshine Fly

Hook:	Mustad 9671 or other 2X Nymph hook #10-12
Thread:	Black
Weight:	"Lead" wire wrapped around hook
Tail:	Ginger hackle fibers (about 8-10)
Body:	Ligas March Brown dubbing
Collar:	Ginger hackle (about 4 wraps)

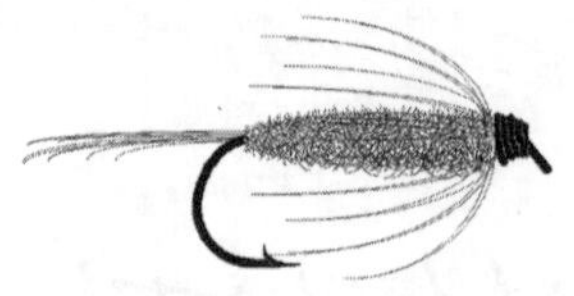

Tying Instructions

1. Start your thread just behind the eye of the hook and wrap back to the bend.

2. Take a piece of "lead" wire and start wrapping it a little in front of the bend of the hook. Wrap it forward to a little behind the eye of the hook, and then wrap it about halfway back toward the bend.

3. Lash the wire to the hook well with turns of thread and then return the thread to the bend of the hook.

4. Tie in 8-10 ginger hackle fibers as a tail about hook gap and a half again long.

5. Dub the body forward to just behind the eye of the hook. It should form a taper from the tail to the fattest part at the thorax of the fly and then taper down again slightly just behind the eye.

6. Strip down the base of a ginger hackle feather to remove the fuzz near its butt. Tie this feather in by its butt behind the eye of the hook, leaving room in front of it for a head. Take 3-4 wraps of the feather to form the collar of the fly, tie off and trim off the excess.

7. Take several more wraps of thread to form the head and then whip finish.

The Buckwheat Fly

Hook:	Mustad 9671 or other 2X Nymph hook #10-12
Thread:	Black
Weight:	"Lead" wire wrapped around hook
Tail:	8-10 barbules from a Blackbird feather
Body:	"Buckwheat" dubbing (brushed out of the coat of a German Shepherd or use a coarse gray dubbing w/bits of tan instead)
Collar:	Split blackbird wing feather (3-4 wraps)

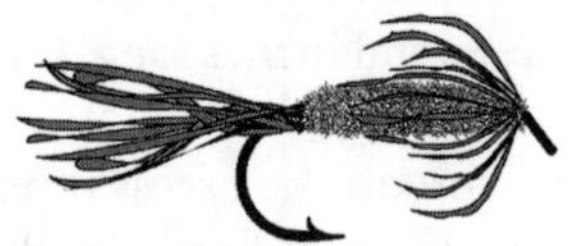

Tying Instructions

1 Start your thread just behind the eye of the hook and wrap back to the bend.

2 Take a piece of "lead" wire and start wrapping it a little in front of the bend of the hook. Wrap it forward to a little behind the eye of the hook, and then wrap it about halfway back toward the bend.

3 Lash the wire to the hook well with turns of thread and then return the thread to the bend of the hook.

4 Tie in 8-10 Blackbird feather barbules as a tail about hook gap and a half again long.

5 Dub the body forward to just behind the eye of the hook. It should form a taper from the tail to the fattest part at the thorax of the fly and then taper down again slightly just behind the eye.

6 Take a Blackbird wing feather and split it down its stem. You will be using the "short" side of the feather to form the hackle collar. It is helpful to soak the feather for a while in water before trying to split it. Begin splitting at the base of the feather and carefully work your way toward the tip. Use an X-acto knife or single-edged razor blade to start the split on the feather then carefully work your way up the feather with your thumb or fingernail, splitting the feather into two parts as you go. This will give you one piece that has the "biots" or short side barbules to use as the collar and one piece that has the longer barbules to use for the tail or for larger flies. It does take a little practice to get used to this technique. This is the same way that Yallerhammer feathers are split for that traditional Smoky Mountain fly.

7 Lash the end of the split Blackbird feather down just behind the eye of the hook. Use your thread to form the head of the fly and then take the thread back to a point that will be about 3-4 wraps of the feather behind the eye of the hook.

8 Form the collar of the fly by wrapping the split Blackbird feather back from the eye of the hook.

9 Lash the feather down with a couple of wraps of thread. Cut off the thread, leaving a piece several inches long. Using your fingers, tie off the thread at this point with a couple of knots around the hook shank and lashed down feather. Trim off the excess thread and feather. Use a little head cement to secure the knots firmly in place.

Fishing the Fly

Both of these flies are designed for fishing on the bottom of the stream. They can be fished using a strike indicator or by using short line nymphing technique. These are also great flies to use with the "all mono" system described in the chapter "Gettin' Down." Many of the traditional Smoky Mountain flies such as these, the Yallerhammer, etc., are also often fished in tandem. These two flies make a great pair to fish together. Try the Sunshine Fly as the top fly in the two, fly rig with the Buckwheat Fly tied in as a dropper, and then if that doesn't seem to be working, reverse the order. If the stream is high, you might even need to add a little extra weight to your tippet—about 6-8" in front of the top fly—to help it sink even quicker.

Larger mountain trout often are found in the deep pools just below a fall or run. You need a fly that sinks quickly to get to the bottom of these pools fast in the short distance below the fall or the run.

Fly Tying and Other Information

Basic Flytying Tools

There are hundreds of different kinds of tools that can be used for tying flies that range in price from very inexpensive to unbelievably costly. For the beginner though there are really only a very few basic tools that are necessary for starting out as a fly tyer. I do not recommend that you begin by buying one of the Fly Tying Kits that are available. These kits often contain very cheap tools that will have to quickly be replaced and the selection of materials in them is seldom suited to the kinds of flies that you will want to tie—no matter where you live. Instead I recommend that you start with a simple selection of inexpensive, but good quality tools and buy only the materials that you will need for tying the flies that interest you. You will quickly learn more about fly tying and be able to decide which tools you really need above the basic selection and which materials you want for the specific kinds of flies that you intend to tie. As you set out to tie each new fly, take the time to learn a little more about each of the new materials that you will need before you purchase them. You will find that your collection of flytying materials will grow much quicker than you would have believed and that you will develop a knowledge of each of these materials that will stand you in good stead for the rest of your life. If you have a friend who is already a fly tyer, ask them for advice. If you don't, then drop by your local fly shop and talk to the folks there—stressing to them that you are just beginning and don't want to get into expensive purchases at this point.

An even better way to begin learning about fly tying is to join a fly tying class. Here you will have the experience of a seasoned instructor to help you over the rough spots and answer the many questions that you will have. Flytying classes are often run by your local Trout Unlimited or Federation of Fly Fishers chapters as well as by many local fly shops. Most flytying classes will start off with suggestions for the basic tools and materials that you will need to begin tying flies for your area.

The following is my suggestion for a basic set of tools. You will be able to tie any fly in this book using only the tools on this list.

A Flytying Vise

The vise is the most expensive piece of equipment for the beginning fly tyer. The vise is designed to hold the hook steady while you are tying the fly. There are many different kinds of vises on the market today, from the simple and inexpensive to the extremely complex. The beginning fly tyer should start with an inexpensive, but good, quality vise. The price range for a vise like this is around $40-50. There are less expensive vises on the market, but they are usually manufactured out of cheap materials and the quality of the machine work is quite poor. There are many more expensive vises on the market ranging in price from $100 on up. You may decide later that you want to invest in one of these more expensive vises, but you should wait until you understand fly tying a little better and can make a more informed decision about what your own particular needs happen to be. Some of the most experienced fly tyers in the world are still tying their flies on the inexpensive vise that they began tying on thirty or forty years ago and feel that nothing more is necessary.

A Set of Hackle Pliers

Hackle pliers are a simple device for grasping materials such as the tip of a hackle feather without having to apply pressure with your hand. Hackle pliers consist of a pair of jaws and a spring handle. When you squeeze the handle, the jaws of the pliers open to be placed around the material. When you release the handle, the jaws close and grasp the material. These are inexpensive devices.

Scissors

You will need two pairs of scissors: a good, quality pair that come to a fine point for cutting feathers, fur, yarn, thread, etc., and an inexpensive pair for cutting wire, paper, tinsel, fishing line or other tougher material. Do not use the good ones for cutting the tough materials. This is a quick way to ruin a good set of scissors. I'm still using a set of scissors that I stole from a nail file set when I first started tying flies for this latter purpose.

A Bobbin

A bobbin is a device for holding the spool of thread that you use in tying the fly. It usually consists of two spring steel sides that grasp the spool of thread and a tube at the front that the thread runs through. You can compress or expand the steel springs to hold the proper amount of tension on the spool and control how easily the thread comes off the spool. These come in a variety of sizes designed to hold different size spools of thread. Start off with one that is properly sized for a standard spool of thread. Another simple, inexpensive device.

Tweezers

Tweezers are used for grasping small pieces of material and holding them in place. A simple, inexpensive set of tweezers will usually do the job just fine.

A Bodkin

A bodkin is a needle with a handle on it. The handle can be made of wood, plastic or metal. This is used for picking out dubbing on the fly, moving fine pieces of material out of your way, applying glue and a variety of other purposes. They usually don't cost very much, but you can also make your own by gluing a needle into a wooden dowel.

A Single-Edged Razor Blade

Available at your local hardware, drug store, etc. A very useful tool for cutting thread when you have finished the fly and for trimming all sorts of other materials.

Some Pins and Needles

These can be used for applying glue, cleaning out the eyes of your flies when you have slopped glue into them, holding materials in place, etc. I've found that the pins that come in men's dress shirts are excellent for this because they have a nice round end that is easier to grasp than the straight pins used in sewing.

A Whip Finishing Tool

It can be very difficult for beginners to grasp the intricacy of how to whip finish a fly by hand. This simple tool makes the job much easier and is usually well worth its cost. There are two kinds on the market. One kind is manufactured by Matarelli and is more expensive. It looks like a bent piece of wire that rotates in a tubular brass handle. It comes with an easy to follow set of instructions and produces perfect whip finishes. The second kind looks like a metal handle with a hook on the end and a bent piece of wire in a "V" shape attached perpendicular to the tool. This second kind is manufactured in India by a variety of companies and is less expensive, but don't even bother with it. I've never met anyone who has ever been able to successfully master how to make the second kind work.

If you can get an experienced fly tyer to demonstrate to you how to do a whip finish by hand, then I would recommend that you attempt to master the technique. Doing the whip finish by hand is much more versatile than using the whip finishing tool and can be used in a much wider number of circumstances. It can, however, be a difficult technique to conquer and will usually take a good deal of practice. It is also a technique that is very difficult to understand just by reading instructions. Learning how to whip finish by hand is seldom conquered without the assistance of an experienced instructor.

A Hair Stacker

There is some debate about whether a hair stacker is really necessary or not. Many fly tyers use old shell casings to stack hair. The purpose of a hair stacker is to align the tips of hair so that they can then be used for building wings and other parts of the fly. Most commercial hair stackers come in two parts: a weighted base and a removable top that is simply a cylinder that fits precisely into the base. You put the hair to be stacked into the stacker with the tips down. Tap the stacker on a hard surface a couple of times and the hair is stacked. The removable top or cylinder can then be separated from the base to help you grasp the hair by its stacked tips. I've found that a hair stacker is a really useful tool for the beginning fly tyer. The people who don't need one are usually the old pros who have already been doing it for years.

An Old Toothbrush

Most hair comes still attached to a part of the skin of the animal. It is cut off that skin before use. Before it can be stacked, spun or otherwise employed, however, it needs to be cleaned of the small fuzz that is attached. An old toothbrush is one of the best tools for cleaning off this fuzz. Grasp the hair by the tips and brush the fuzz off the base of the clump, then grasp it by the base and clean the fuzz off the tips. Stack the hair after you have cleaned it.

A Good Light

Fly tying is precise, small-scale work and you need a strong light so that you can see what you are doing. A goose neck lamp or other lamp that can be positioned close to your work is a very useful kind of lamp to have. If your eyesight is not that good, you might also want to consider a lamp with a built-in magnifier. These can also be helpful for tying very small flies. There are some very expensive lamp/magnifier combinations that are manufactured specifically for fly tying, but there is also a relatively inexpensive lamp/magnifier that uses an incandescent bulb on the market and can be found at larger office supply stores for around $20. There are other models with a fluorescent lamp in the $60 range.

That's It!

Those should be all the tools that you are really going to need to start tying flies. Sure, there are lots of other toys out there that you may decide at some later point in time that you want or need, but you can begin tying flies with just the simple tools that I have outlined above.

The Anarchist Fly Swap

I recently took part in a fly swap with tyer's from around the country that was labeled "The Anarchist Fly Swap." The idea behind the swap was that all of the patterns had to be original patterns that primarily featured items that were scrounged, found, made, stolen or borrowed, but that kept the use of commercially available materials to an absolute minimum. In keeping with the spirit of the swap, this article features tips on tools and materials for fly tying that you do not have to buy at your local fly shop. The pattern for the fly that I entered is The Bulldog Scud immediately following. You may not want to incorporate all of these ideas into your tying, but with a little bit of imagination you will find solutions that work for you.

Tools

Scissors

My first pair of flytying scissors was lifted from my wife's manicure set. When she found out what I'd done I had to replace hers with a better pair, but I still use those scissors as my wire-cutting scissors to spare my good scissors the dings, chips and misalignments you get from cutting wire.

Hair Stacker

Many tyers that I know swear by cartridge cases as hair stackers. A variety of calibers will give you everything from a small hair stacker to a large one and all sizes in between.

Bodkins

I've never bought a commercial bodkin. Yet mine still looks pretty classy. Took a dowel and cut it to the length that I wanted. Drilled a hole in one end and glued in a needle, then sanded it down to a shape that I liked and finished it. I added a soft copper wire loop to the opposite end from the needle that has also proved handy on numerous occasions.

Tweezers

My first set of tweezers came from that same manicure set that I raided for my first pair of scissors. I still like them best for some jobs such as making mono eyes because they come to a point rather than being blunt on the end.

Hemostats

Invaluable tools for the fisherman. What you may not know is that many of the hemostats used in doctors' offices, emergency rooms, etc., are disposables that you might be able to get for free from a medical worker that you know. Many of the medical ones do not have serrated tips. These smooth-tipped ones are very handy around the tying bench. Caution: Be sure that you sterilize them before using.

Shirt Pins

The pins that come stuck in dress shirts are great for fly tying. They have nice little balls on the dull end that makes them easier to grasp than regular straight pins. Perfect for applying just a little dab of head cement.

An Old Toothbrush

Ideal for brushing the fuzz off that hunk of deer hair that you're about to stack before spinning.

That should give you some kind of an idea about tools that you can find, adapt and/or modify for fly tying. Flytying materials are limited only by your imagination. Keep your eyes open and it is amazing what you can find that is applicable to fly tying. In the Bulldog Scud pattern next, for example, there is not a single material that was purchased commercially. Everything was scrounged, found, etc. Here's some ideas about the kinds of things to think about.

Materials

Dubbing

The undercoats of many domestic pets make great dubbing. If you don't care for the texture that comes from picking up "dust bunnies" then you might want to consider getting what is known as a "slicker brush" from a pet store. These are designed to brush out this undercoat. Your pet will usually love the attention and you've got an unlimited supply of whatever color your particular pet happens to be. The "red" of one of my Bulldogs happens to make a perfect Light Hendrickson Nymph and isn't too bad for a scud either. The "gray" of a Himalayan Cat is delightful for a Thunderhead or Adams. If the consistency isn't quite right, then chopping it in one of the mini food processors will get it just as fine as you could care for.

Whiskers

The whiskers of many dogs and cats are great for the antennae of Stone Flies and other nymphs. Don't go around trimming or pulling out your poor dog's or cat's whiskers; they will fall out regularly and all you have to do is be alert and pick them up.

Guard Hairs

The long coat hairs or guard hairs of many pets also can be used in fly tying. Black Labs are famous for participating in the construction of many Stonefly Nymphs. Once again, don't trim your poor pet bald; just be patient and they will fall out regularly or you can pick them out of a comb or brush after you've groomed your pet.

Various Found Plastics

Plastic materials around the house have innumerable flytying uses. Easter Grass makes great scud backs as do strips cut from plastic bags. Check out the wrapping and decorative materials that are available at holidays such as Christmas. Many of these have properties that will make them very useful in fly tying.

Found Feathers

If you've got a cat that is like mine, they will regularly present you with "gifts" that were formerly one of our feathered friends. Take a good look at the feathers before you clean up the mess. Many of them would be useful in fly tying. Need some natural colored goose biots? The Giant Canadian Geese that are local in many parts of the Southeast shed their wing feathers all the time and the back half of that feather is exactly that. Got a duck pond near your house? Walk around it a little bit and you can pick up feathers of all kinds that will make good tying material. "Nuking" these feathers in a microwave will quickly kill any of the bugs and beasties that may inhabit them.

Wires

Electrical wire of various gauges will make different sizes of copper ribbing for nymphs, streamers, etc. Before you toss out old electronic devices, check them over for useful wires in a variety of sizes and colored coatings.

"Metallic Threads"

Fabric scraps with "metallic threads" in them can yield very interesting ribbing for flies. It can be worthwhile sometimes just to browse around your local fabric store. The bargain bin may yield more ribbing material than you can use in a lifetime for a buck or two.

Old Monofilament Line

Don't throw out the line on that old spinning reel. You've got an unlimited source of ribbing, burnt mono eyes, and all kinds of other uses.

These are just a sampling of some of the materials that are often just lying around your house waiting for you to make use of them. Keeping your eyes open and thinking about things that you find will often yield a source of flytying materials that you hadn't dreamed existed. I first discovered Easter Grass as a great material for scud backs when I was sweeping the house one day after Easter and found some of it tangled up in the broom. As I was picking it out it hit me that this would be perfect for that purpose.

The Bulldog Scud

This pattern actually resulted from my wife's suggestion after she had swept up the latest collection of "dust bunnies" that our dogs had generously deposited on our floors. When she said, "Isn't there something that you could use all of this hair for?" that set me looking at it a little closer. The first thing that I thought of was that the underfur from one of our dogs (Rocky) happened to be the perfect color for a Light Hendrickson Nymph (I never have been too good about running around after Vixens trying to trim their urine-stained pubes), but then as I started looking at it a little closer I started thinking about other uses as well.

This particular pattern was originally developed for the Anarchist Fly Swap since EVERYTHING that I'm using to tie it is recycled, left over or scrounged. Heck, for this swap I even finally scraped down those old hooks that I've been meaning to clean the chewed-up flies off of. It is, however, a tried and tested pattern, having caught fish in tailwaters and ponds all over the United States. Wherever you find scuds, this pattern is worth trying.

Tying Instructions

1 Prepare, find, scrounge, steal, etc., all of the materials below and have them ready.

Hook:	Tiemco 2487 (scud) or equivalent #12-16 (or whatever old hooks you have lying around the house that you can scrape old flies off of).
Thread:	Black, Brown or whatever is left on old, almost empty spools that you've lifted from your wife's sewing area.
Ribbing:	Old mono line that's still on that spinning reel you don't use anymore.
Weight:	Scrape the insulation off copper wire that's been lying around your workshop. #22-28 gauge from old electronic projects work best.
Scud Back:	Easter Grass stolen from your kid's Easter Basket (leave that half eaten Chocolate Bunny alone!).
Body:	Dubbing combed from the undercoat of a "red" Bulldog—or dog hair swept up in dust bunnies from around the house—or whatever you can scrounge from the beasts in your particular menagerie.
Eyes:	More of that old mono line, cut in short lengths and burnt to form a pair of eyes.

2 Place the hook in the vise and start the thread just behind the eye.

3 Tie in a 2-3" piece of mono onto the top of the hook and wrap the thread back to where the curve of the hook is almost vertical, securing the mono in place underneath the thread. The excess mono will stick out the back of the hook for later use as ribbing.

4 Wrap 6-10 turns of the copper wire around the body of the hook for weight and then wrap the thread back and forth over it, securing it in place.

5 Secure the Easter Grass in place over the top of the hook with more wraps of thread. Finish your winding at the back of the hook with the excess Grass sticking out behind the hook, ready for later use as the scud back.

6 Dub whatever material you are using onto the thread and wrap the dubbing forward to just behind the eye of the hook.

7 Pull the Easter Grass forward over the top of the hook and take a couple of wraps of thread to secure it in place. Trim off the excess.

8 Spiral the mono forward in 4-7 turns, making the ribbing and secure it in place with the thread. Trim off the excess.

9 Form a set of eyes by taking a short (½"–¾") piece of mono. Hold in the center with a pair of tweezers. Burn one end at a time with a cigarette lighter to form a pair of eyes. Tip: Just as the burning end approaches the tweezers, flick that end down to extinguish the flame and then hold it downward for a few seconds to help the eye form into a nice round shape as the mono cools and hardens.

10 Tie in the pair of eyes just behind the front of the hook using figure eight wraps to secure it in place.

11 Whip finish.

12 Pick out the dubbing to form "legs" and/or "tail."

Fishing The Fly

Most scud patterns are fished dead drift close to the bottom under a strike indicator. In still water you might want to try imparting some movement to the scud, imitating the movement of the real thing darting around near the bottom of the pond.

Parts of the Hook and Fly Proportions

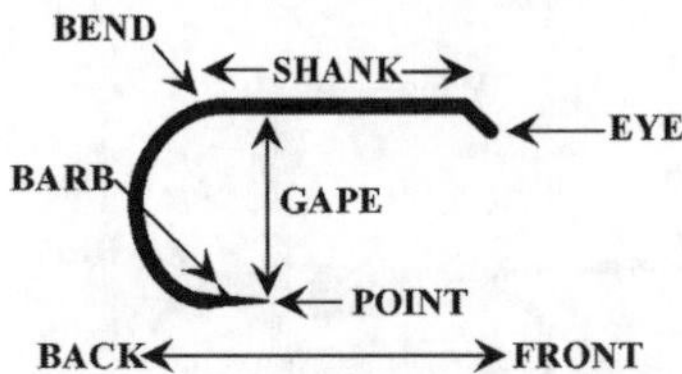

Fly Proportions

Traditional Dry Fly Proportions

Tail Length = Wing Length
Hackle Length = $\frac{3}{4}$ Wing Length or $1\frac{1}{2}$ Hook Gap
Body Length = $\frac{2}{3}$ Hook Shank

Traditional Wet Fly Proportions

Tail = Shank Length
Hackle = Shank Length
Wing = Midpoint of Tail

Typical Nymph Proportions

Nymph proportions are not standardized. There is too much variation both in the nymphs themselves and the creatures that they seek to imitate. Refer to the particular pattern.

Typical Streamer/Bucktail Proportions

Once again, refer to the particular pattern for proportions. These flies also vary considerably in the relative length of materials employed.

Parts of Flies

Parts of the Dry Fly

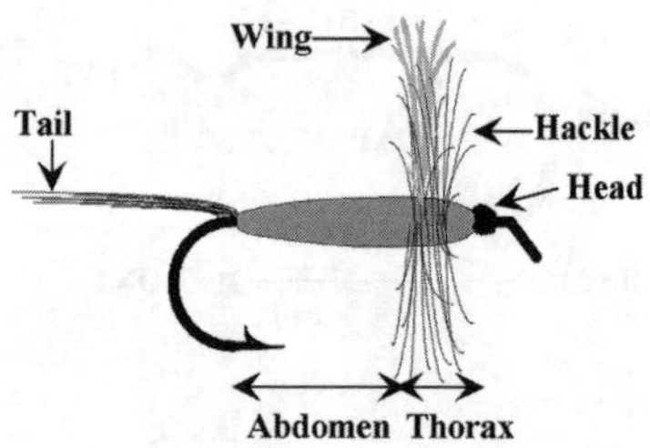

Parts of the Wet Fly

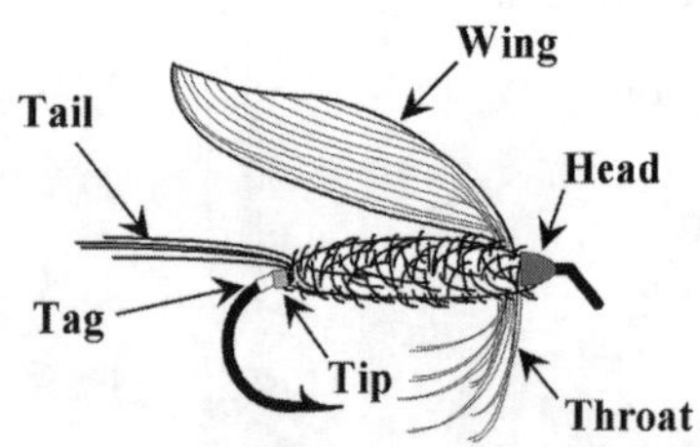

Parts of the Nymph

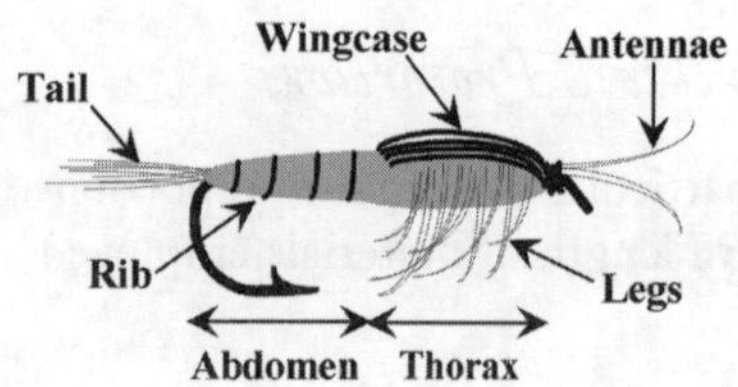

Glossary and Fly Tying Techniques

If you are not familiar with a term found in the book or do not know how to perform a particular technique, check for information here. For example, if the text calls for you to do a "figure-eight knot," this section will explain the knot in detail.

Abdomen: That portion of the body of an insect from the tail to the thorax. Sort of like from the "waist" down.

Antron: Originally manufactured by Dupont as a carpet fiber, it is now a fiber popular with fly tyers. It has a translucent sparkle to it that makes it attractive for flytying use. Available in dubbings, yarn, etc. in a wide variety of colors.

Attractor: A fly that does not seek to imitate any specific insect. Often a brightly colored fly that calls attention to itself.

Back: A direction in fly tying. Moving from the eye of the hook toward the bend. Can also refer to the upper portion of an insect's body or that part of a fly that imitates that portion of the insect's body. Many nymphs and scuds, for example, may have a "back" formed by tying a strip of material over the top of the hook from the tail to just behind the eye.

Badger: A feather with a black center stripe. Can also refer to the guard hairs of the animal. These guard hairs are a creamy color with black and white bars at the tips.

Barb: The upward projection just behind the point of the hook that holds it in the fish's mouth when hooked. This is also the technically correct name for the individual fibers attached to the stem or quill of a feather, though these fibers are more commonly called a barbule today.

Barbless: A hook without a barb.

Barbule: The most common name for the individual fibers attached to the stem or quill of a feather. The more technically correct use of this term is for the yet smaller fibers on the individual fibers or barbs attached to the stem or quill. Note: I will be employing the term barbule in its more common usage.

Barred: A feather with dark parallel markings across its width.

Beads: Metal beads are a popular item for weighting nymphs and other sinking flies. They are usually positioned immediately behind the eye of the hook with the body of the fly formed behind the bead. Available at most fly shops in a variety of diameters and colors. Most of the popular nymph patterns such as the Pheasant Tail and the Gold Ribbed Hare's Ear now have a beadhead version. Glass beads are also becoming items of interest to fly tyers. Often used to form part or all of the body of a nymph, they give it a translucency that cannot be achieved with dubbing. Formerly available only through hobby or craft stores, they are beginning to appear in fly shops (usually at a much higher price than in the hobby and craft stores).

Bend: The place on the hook where it begins to turn downward from the shank toward the point.

Beard: This is a clump of hackle or hair that has been applied just behind and underneath the eye of the hook. See *Throat*.

Beaver: Used as dubbing. The gray underfur is very water resistant and is excellent for dry flies. The guard hairs are dark brown.

Biot: An individual barbule from the top side (short side) of a large feather or quill such as a goose wing feather.

Bobbin: A tool used to hold and dispense tying thread. Adjust the tension on the bobbin by expanding or compressing the spring sides so that the spool of thread is held in place, but will still be able to turn and release thread as you wind the thread around the hook.

Bodkin: A tool that looks like a needle sticking out of a piece of wood, plastic or metal that serves as its handle. Used for picking out dubbing to make a coarser body, removing small unwanted items from the fly, applying glue and numerous other things.

Braided Tubing: A woven tubing material made from mylar or metallic fibers braided around a cotton core. The cotton core is removed before use. Available in pearlescent as well as other colors. Useful for forming bodies of streamers and many saltwater flies. Can also be used to form the body of beetles and some terrestrials.

Bucktail: Hair from the tail of a deer. Available dyed in a variety of colors. Also a fly that imitates a baitfish constructed from this hair.

Butt: The base or bottom of a feather or section of fiber, the heavier end. The butt end is most often either clipped off or tied under when building the fly. This term is also used, particularly in Salmon Flies to indicate a material (usually ostrich herl) that is tied in at a point on the shank directly over the point of the hook.

CA: Cyanoacrylate glue. A generic name for the "super glues." They come in a variety of consistencies from thin to thick. The thick varieties are often referred to as "gap fillers."

CDC: Cul de Canard: a feather from the duck's rump near their oil glands. Soft and extremely oily. Floats readily.

Caddis: A common aquatic insect. It holds its wings down over the top of its body rather than having them project upward as in a mayfly.

Calftail: The tail of a calf that has been dyed. The hairs from this are usually used to construct wings on flies. These hairs are finer than bucktail and do not flare or bend when pressure is applied with thread.

Cape: The skin and feathers from the neck and head of a chicken or other bird. Hackle feathers and many other types of tying feathers come from this area.

Catskill Dry Fly: A "traditional" dry fly. It is tied with upright wings, tapered body, long tail and a hackle collar. This is the most common style of dry fly sold in fly shops.

Cement: Often called head cement. Used to secure the last windings of thread just behind the eye of the hook to form the "head" of the fly and for other purposes as well.

Cheek: Feathers tied along the side of the hook usually just behind the eye.

Chenille: A tufted cotton or rayon cord. Available in a variety of colors. Used to form the body of some flies such as Woolly Buggers. Absorbs water readily.

Clipped Body: A fly body that has been formed by spinning hair (usually deer hair) around the shank of the hook. This spun hair is then trimmed to the shape desired. See *Spinning*.

Clump: A group of fibers, usually feather or hair. These fibers have been bunched together to form the tail, wing or beard of a fly.

Coachman Brown: A very dark brown color. Usually used to refer to hackle.

Collar: Hackle or hair wound just behind the eye of the hook or just behind the "head" of the fly.

Comparadun: A style of tying a dry fly that uses hair that has been spread in a fan-like shape as a wing.

Covert: A small feather from a bird's wing, or a wingcase on nymphs.

Cree: A feather with mixed white, brown and/or gray markings.

Cressbug: A sowbug. Insect of the order Isopoda.

Crest: A feather from the top/back of the neck of a Golden Pheasant.

Crystal Chenille: See *Estaz.*

Crystal Flash: See *Krystal Flash.*

Cul de Canard: A feather from the duck's rump near their oil glands. Soft and extremely oily. Floats readily.

Cut Wing: A wing for a fly that is formed by taking a feather and trimming it to shape.

Deer Hair: The body hair of deer is a hollow hair that floats very well. Used to form the body of flies (see *Spinning*). Available dyed in a variety of colors. Also available in a wide variety of thicknesses. Coastal Deer, for example, is a very fine deer hair that is often used for the wings on flies.

Divided Wing: A wing for a fly that is formed by taking a clump of feather barbules, fur or fibers. These are tied to the shank of the hook and then divided into two equal parts to form the two wings. See *Figure Eight.*

Domestic Hackle: Hackle from a chicken grown in the United States or Canada. The best quality "dry fly" hackle is domestic from "genetic" stock specially bred for this purpose. Imported hackle is often much less expensive, but also usually of considerably lower quality.

Downwing: A fly style, such as a caddis, with wings that project backward from the head over the top of the body rather than sticking upright.

Dry Fly: A fly that floats on the surface of the water.

Dubbing: Any material that can be spun onto the tying thread and then wrapped around the hook to form the body of the fly. Note that the thread is often coated with Dubbing Wax before the material is applied to help the dubbing stick to the thread. Dubbing can be finely chopped material of many different kinds: fur, feather, or synthetic. There are a large number of prepared dubbings available commercially. These come in a wide variety of colors and consistencies from very fine to coarse. You can also prepare your own dubbing from fur or synthetic materials by chopping them in a small food processor. To apply dubbing to the thread: hold the thread taut with the bobbin, apply a little dubbing wax to the thread, take a small amount of dubbing material and spread it out along the length of the thread, then using your thumb and forefinger, twist the dubbing material onto the thread. Note: You must twist only in one direction. Do not twist back and forth. At first only apply small amounts of dubbing until you get a feeling for how much is needed. A little dubbing goes a long way. TO DUB is also a verb meaning to transfer dubbing material onto the shank of the hook through the use of the thread to which it is attached.

Dubbing Loop: An open loop of thread. Coarse dubbing material is placed in the middle of this loop. The loop is then twisted to form a rope with the dubbing material trapped between the twists of the rope. This is a technique used with very coarse dubbing material that will not adhere easily to thread that has been coated with dubbing wax. You can create a dubbing loop with your fingers, using a set of hackle pliers to grasp one end of the loop, or there is a special tool available at many fly shops for this purpose.

Dubbing Wax: A specially prepared wax that is used to coat thread before spinning dubbing onto the thread. Note that dubbing wax should be applied very lightly. It doesn't take much for it to do its job.

Dumbbell Eyes: A pair of artificial eyes formed in the shape of a dumbbell. Usually made of a heavy material and used to weight the fly in addition to representing eyes. See Figure Eight.

Dun: A bluish-gray color. Also the first adult stage of the mayfly.

Egg Sack: Imitates the eggs sometimes found near the rear of a female insect.

Elk Hair: The hair from the body of the Elk is a very fine hair that also has the property of floating well. Used for wings on flies. Available in light, medium and dark shades. Fine deer hair such as Coastal Deer makes an effective substitute.

Emerger: An insect that is changing from its nymph or pupa state to its adult state. They are usually found right at the surface of the water in the film or meniscus. At this stage the insect is highly vulnerable to fish and often very attractive to them as well.

Epoxy: A two-part very strong cement. The two parts must be completely mixed together before being used.

Estaz: A chenille-like material that is made from plastic rather than cotton. Sometimes also referred to as Ice Chenille or Crystal Chenille.

Eye: The circular piece of metal at the front of the hook. This is where the tippet is tied onto the fly.

Extended Body: A pattern or fly in which the body of the fly extends beyond the bend of the hook.

Eyes, Artificial: There are a large number of artificial eyes that can be purchased at fly shops for use in fly tying. These include dumbbell eyes that are in the form of a dumbbell and weighted, eyes made from bead chain, doll eyes that are three dimensional, and press on self-adhesive eyes with a variety of optic qualities.

Eyes, Mono: You can also form eyes for your flies from a short piece of heavy (20-30 lb. test) monofilament fishing line. Take a piece of mono about ¾" in length and grasp it in the middle with a pair of tweezers. Using a cigarette lighter or match, set one end of the mono on fire and allow it to burn down until it almost reaches the tweezers. Just as the burning mono approaches the tweezers, quickly rotate the tweezers so that the burning end of the mono is downward. This quick rotation also should extinguish the flame. Hold the mono in this position for a few seconds until the now liquid nylon forms into a globe just below the tweezers. Repeat for the other side of the mono and you will have two round eyes formed from the mono joined by a short piece of line. These can be attached to the fly by using a figure eight just like you would a set of dumbbell eyes. See *Figure Eight.*

Fanwing: A style of dry fly wing. Uses wide fan-shaped breast feathers from a duck. Sometimes is also used to refer to the fan-shaped spread hair wing of a comparadun.

Felt Pens: Marking pens are often used by fly tyers to make color adjustments to materials. If you need a yellow dyed grizzly feather, for example, you can use a felt pen to color a regular grizzly feather yellow. Be sure that you use a waterproof pen and not a washable one.

Fibre or Fiber: An individual filament of a feather, fur or synthetic.

Figure Eight: A double loop of thread in the shape of the number eight on its side. This is a method used to hold divided wings separated from one another or to attach a set of dumbbell eyes to a hook. The figure eight is formed by coming up from underneath the hook with the thread through the middle of the divided wing, then around that side of the divided wing and again through the middle. The thread is then taken around the side of the other wing and then again through the middle. Finally it goes underneath the hook and comes up on the other side. It may take several of these figure eight turns to completely secure a divided wing in place.

When used to attach a dumbbell eye, the technique is only slightly different. Hold the dumbbell eye in place with the shank of the dumbbell perpendicular to the shank of the hook using tweezers. Bring the thread up from underneath the hook and over the shank of the dumbbell to the opposite side of the hook from which you started. Then take the thread underneath the hook to the position in which you began the thread. Again go over the top of the dumbbell shank, but then this time come under the shank of the dumbbell rather than the shank of the hook and then over the top of the dumbbell shank to the side of the eyes on which you began. Take the thread under the hook ending up with the thread on the opposite side of the hook from which you originally began. Repeat this process several times on both sides of the hook and dumbbell shank and hook. Once you have loosely secured the eye in place, remove the tweezers and keep repeating the process, pulling more tightly on the thread to hold the eyes securely in place. When you finish the fly, some head cement on these wrappings is usually a good idea.

Fishair: See *Ultrahair.*

Flank Feather: A feather from the body, under the wings of a bird. Wood duck flank, for example, is a popular winging material for dry flies.

Flare or Flaring: Constricting a clump of hair against a hook with thread so that it sticks out in all directions. See *Spinning*.

Flashabou: Mylar that has been cut into long, thin strips. Available in a wide variety of colors. It usually has a metallic sheen to its surface.

Floating Yarn: A yarn made of Polypropylene or polyester that does not absorb water.

Floss: A material used in fly tying usually for the construction of bodies on flies. The appearance is that of thick or multi-strand thread with a sheen to it. Like thread, it usually comes wound on spools and may be made of rayon, acetate or silk.

Flourescence: Fluorescent materials are materials that when struck by ultraviolet light convert those wavelengths into visible light. Since ultraviolet wavelengths are shorter than visible light wavelengths, they are bent less in refraction and will usually penetrate water to a greater depth. This means that fluorescent materials are often visible deeper than regular materials and may be more visible and attractive to fish. Many types of flytying materials incorporate fluorescence in the material itself.

Fly Tying Kits: Most experienced fly tyers do not recommend that you buy a fly tying kit. You usually are much better off having an experienced tyer recommend a basic set of tools and materials that will fit your needs more closely than the tools and materials that come in a kit.

Forward: Moving from the bend of the hook toward the eye.

Furnace: A brown feather with a black center stripe.

Fur Rope: Another name for a dubbing loop. See *Dubbing Loop*.

Furry Foam: A foam material covered with a soft short fuzz on both sides. Can be used for nymph and wet fly bodies.

Gallows Tool: A device that is attached to the vise to hold the post while tying a parachute-type fly.

Gape: The vertical distance between the point of the hook and the shank. A distance that is often used in fly tying to measure proportions. The Gape also determines the "size" of the hook such as a #10, #12, etc.

Golden Pheasant Crest: See *Crest*.

Goose: The primary flight feathers are the part of the goose that are of most interest to fly tyers. The barbules on the short side of these feathers are called biots and used as a tailing material on nymphs and sometimes as a body material. The barbules on the long side of the feather are used as a winging material. Available dyed in a wide variety of colors.

Grizzly: Feathers that are barred black and white. They may also be dyed so that the white part becomes a color.

Grouse: See *Partridge.*

Guard Hair: Stiffer, longer hairs on a furred animal. The underfur beneath these guard hairs usually provides very fine consistency dubbing. If a coarser dubbing is desired then the guard hairs are mixed with the underfur. Guard hairs may also be used by themselves to form a tail or beard on a fly.

Guinea: Speckled feathers from a guinea fowl.

Hackle: Feathers from the neck or back of a bird, most commonly a rooster. When the word "hackle" refers to a part of the fly itself, it means the part that is tied on behind the eye of the hook. A stiff hackle such as is used on a dry fly to help support it on the water is usually a feather from the neck of a rooster. It is wound around the hook in front of the wings and behind the eye. This is where a good-quality hackle such as from a domestic bird is usually desired. See also *Soft Hackle* and *Saddle Hackle*.

Hackle Colors: Rooster hackle comes in a wide variety of colors both natural and dyed. Some colors that are available are: NATURAL: White, Cream, Ginger, Brown, Coachman Brown, Dun (ranging from dark to light), Black, Badger (white or cream with a black center stripe), Furnace (brown with a black center stripe), Cock-Y-Bondhu (furnace with black tips), Variant (any color with color variation in the barbules), Ginger Grizzly (ginger barred with reddish-brown), Red Grizzly (brown with light ginger bars), Grizzly (black with white barring), Cree (black, brown and pale ginger). DYED: Dyed Dun (a variety of gray to blue/gray shades), Olive, Silver Doctor Blue (a light, but not pale blue), Green, Claret (burgundy).

Hackle Guard: A hackle guard is a device to help hold hackle out of the way while you are forming a whip finish knot. It is especially useful when you are tying a parachute-type fly where the hackle extends over the eye of the hook. There is a set of hackle guards that is available commercially. They consist of three disks, each of which has a handle on it, a hole in its center to slip over the eye of the hook, and a slit cut from the edge of the disk to the hole in the center to allow you to slip the disk over the tying thread. Each of the three disks in the set comes with a different size hole in the center for use with different size hooks. You can also form a set of hackle guards yourself from clear stiff plastic by cutting a disk, punching a hole in the center of the disk and then cutting a slit from the edge of the disk to the hole in the center.

Hackle Pliers: A tool used to grip the tip of hackle while winding it around the hook. Pressure on the body of the hackle pliers cause the jaws to separate. When this pressure is released the jaws will come together and grip.

Hackle Preparing: See *Preparing Hackle.*

Hackle Size: For traditional dry flies, the length of the barbule measured from the stem or quill of the feather should be about $1\frac{1}{2}$ times the gap width of the hook. For other flies see information in the individual patterns.

Hair Packer: See *Packer.*

Hair Stacker: A tool used to align hair tips. Usually in two parts. The hair is first cleaned of fuzz using a toothbrush then placed tips down into the hair stacker. It is gently tapped on a hard surface. This causes the tips to align with one another. The hair stacker is carefully twisted apart and the aligned hair can then be removed with the tips still aligned.

Hair Wing: A fly that uses some kind of hair to form the wing. Calftail is commonly used on Wulff-style dry flies, for example.

Half Hitch: The simplest knot used to secure thread when finishing the fly. Simply form a loop with the thread coming off of the body of the fly, slip this loop over the hook just behind the eye and pull the thread taut. It usually takes two to three half hitches to really secure this thread before the end can be cut off completing the fly. There is also a simple half hitch tool that can be used to help with this process. The commercial tool is nothing more than a metal rod, the end of which has an indentation. The rod is used to form the loop and then the indentation helps to slip the loop over the eye of the hook. The butt of a large peacock tail feather or goose quill with the tip trimmed off will serve exactly the same purpose.

Hare's Ear: The guard hairs and underfur are chopped together to form a coarse dubbing used in many nymphs and wet flies. Available dyed as well. Hare's ear and hare's mask are often used interchangeably.

Hare's Mask: Underfur and guard hairs from the face of a hare are chopped together to form coarse dubbing for wet flies and nymphs. Available dyed also. Hare's ear and hare's mask are often used interchangeably.

Head Cement: A liquid glue that is designed to penetrate thread and secure the last windings of thread that form the head of the fly into place. Head cement has a flat finish.

Hen: A female chicken, pheasant, or duck.

Herl: The shorter fibers (usually 3-6") on the stem of a long peacock or ostrich plume. The herl has still smaller fibers ($\frac{1}{16}$–$\frac{1}{8}$") sticking out of its sides as well.

Hot Colors: Colors with a high fluorescent content.

Ice Chenille: See *Estaz.*

Jungle Cock Eye: Black feathers with yellow/orange spots that resemble an eye. Used as cheeks on many streamers to resemble the eyes of baitfish. True Jungle Cock is expensive. Substitutes include: Starling body feathers, Quail neck feathers and Lady Amherst body feathers. There are also some artificial imitations available.

Krystal Flash: A highly reflective material that comes in long, thin strips. Similar to flashabou except that the strips have kinks or twists built into them that further reflect and/or refract light.

Lacquer: Similar to head cement, but with a glossy finish.

Larva: The first immature stages of an insect after emerging from the egg.

Larva Lace: A thin flexible translucent plastic tubing used to form the body of nymphs. Comes in a variety of colors and diameters. When wound around the hook it forms an excellent imitation of a segmented body.

Latex: A rubber-like material. Available as a liquid or preformed into sheets.

Lead Wire: You will find that many patterns call for the use of "Lead" Wire as a weighting material. While it is still generally referred to in this manner, it no longer is actually made out of lead. Real lead is a poisonous material that can damage the reproductive cycle of many fish and other wildlife. All so-called "Lead" wire sold in fly shops today is made from a heavy, but non-toxic compound.

Legs: The legs of insects are imitated in fly tying through a number of different methods. The legs of an adult mayfly or caddis are usually imitated through the use of a stiff hackle wound around the body or behind the head of the fly. The legs of a nymph or subsurface insect are often imitated by the use of a softer hackle tied in as a collar or throat. Rubber legging material (like rubber bands) are often used to imitate the legs of terrestrial insects.

Lemon Wood Duck: See *Wood Duck Flank.*

Mallard Flank: Feathers from the side of the Mallard under the wing. Slightly grayish feathers with fine black bars. Used in wings, tails, and other places. Available dyed to resemble Wood Duck Flank.

Mallard Quill: Gray feathers from Mallard Wings. Used for winging material in dry and wet flies. Usually sold in pairs (one from the left wing and one from the right wing).

Marabou: Very soft feathers. Originally from the Marabou Stork, now most commonly from a Turkey.

Mayfly: A family of insects common in fresh water. Most examples of these have tapered bodies with long tails and two wings that ride upright on top of the body.

Microfibbets: Fine, stiff nylon bristles available in a variety of colors. Usually used to imitate the tail of mayflies.

Midge: Very small insects of the order Diptera. Usually have two wings that ride flat on top of the body.

Mink: The underfur which is available in a variety of natural shades makes very good dubbing. Can also be found dyed. Tail guard hairs make a stiff material for winging.

Monocord: A flat, untwisted nylon thread.

Monofilament: Single strand, clear or colored nylon fishing line.

Moose: Long, heavy moose hair is often used for tailing, antennae, etc.

Mottled Turkey: Feathers from the wing of a Brown Turkey or a Wild Turkey. This feather has a speckled pattern that runs throughout and makes it extremely useful for wing cases on nymphs.

Muskrat: Has a light to dark blue/gray underfur that is a very popular dubbing. The guard hairs are also sometimes used for tails, beards, etc.

Mylar: Flat metallic colored thin plastic ribbon. Usually comes wound onto a spool.

Neck: The complete skin of a chicken (usually a rooster) including the feathers from its neck all the way down its back.

No-Hackle: A style of dry fly tied without hackles.

Nymph: The immature stage of an aquatic insect. Also refers to any artificial fly that imitates the underwater stage of an insect.

Opossum (American): The underfur is sometimes used for dubbing in certain Smoky Mountain patterns.

Opossum (Australian): A very easy dubbing material with which to work. Available in a range of colors from gray to cream to reddish-brown.

Ostrich Herl: Individual fibers (3-6 inches long) from an Ostrich Plume (large tail feather). These have yet smaller fibers all along their length. Available dyed in a wide variety of colors.

Packer: A tool used to tightly pack bunches of deer hair on a hook after spinning. See *Spinning*.

Palmer: Tying any material around an already formed body in an open spiral. The saddle hackle of a Woolly Bugger, for example, is Palmered forward in an open spiral after the body has been formed out of chenille.

Parachute: Any fly in which the hackle is wound on a horizontal plane above or below the shank of the hook.

Partridge Hackle: Body feathers from the European Grouse or Partridge. The feathers are speckled gray or brown with fine black bars. American Grouse can be an effective substitute. This is a softer hackle than from chickens and is usually used in wet flies and nymphs.

Peacock Quill: A peacock herl stem stripped of its very tiny fibers.

Peacock Eye: The tail feather of a peacock with an eye-like coloring near the tip. Often also used to refer to a piece of peacock herl that comes from the portion of the tail feather that contains the eye.

Peacock Sword: Side tail feathers from a peacock with shorter green fibers than found on the full eyed feather.

Pheasant Tail: The tail feather from the Ringneck Pheasant. Used extensively in nymphs and wet flies. An essential feather. Inexpensive and readily available. Also available dyed in a variety of colors.

Polar Bear: Formerly prized for use in the construction of streamers and salmon flies. Now protected under federal law. See *Ultrahair*.

Prewaxed: Thread that has been waxed at the factory.

Primary Feather: A long flight feather from the wing of a bird.

Proportions: Refers to the relationship between the size of the different parts of a fly. See the figures given earlier in this book on fly proportions. Note, however, that these proportions are just a generalization. Proper use of proportions are something that mostly comes with experience with tying and observing insects in nature.

Point: The sharp end of the hook.

Post Wing: A wing on a dry fly that is formed by a single clump of material such as hair or floating yarn that sticks straight up out of the body. This kind of wing is used on parachute flies.

Preparing Hackle: The hackle used for dry flies is usually selected from the neck or back of a rooster and has stiffer barbules that most other kinds of hackles. For most dry flies, you want a hackle feather that has barbules that are the same length as the gap of the hook that you are using. If you have trouble measuring the length of the barbules, there are several gauges that are easy to use and available at most good fly shops. Once you have selected a hackle feather with barbules of the proper length, then you need to prepare the feather before it is tied onto the hook. The base of the feather contains barbules that have a webby connection rather than being stiff individual fibers. Gently strip away all of these webby barbules with your fingers until you are left with a feather containing stiff individual barbules and just a short shaft at the base. You may need to trim the shaft left at the base after you have stripped off the webby barbules to get the shaft length that you need for the fly that you are tying. This shaft is what is lashed onto the hook before winding the hackle feather around the hook shaft, post wing, or other part of the fly.

Pupa: The second stage in the life cycle of insects having a complete life cycle. Often used to refer to the immature stage of the midge before emerging from the water.

Quill: This word has a number of different meanings in fly tying: a) A complete feather, b) a section of fibers cut from a complete feather, often referred to as a piece of quill or a quill section, c) the outer layer of the center stem of large feathers such as from a duck or goose, d) a rooster or hen hackle feather from which the barbules have been removed, e) the center stem of a peacock or ostrich herl from which the tiny fuzz has been removed. Quills as defined in b) – e) usually are used to form the body of a fly by being wrapped around the hook. They imitate the segmentation commonly found in insect bodies.

Rabbit: Rabbit underfur makes dubbing that is not as water resistant as the fur of water mammals such as muskrat, beaver, mink, etc. More useful for wet flies than for dry flies. Available dyed in many colors.

Red Fox: The underfur makes excellent dubbing. Natural colors range from cream to beige, gray, and occasionally pinkish.

Rib: An open spiral of material that forms an imitation of the segments of the body of an insect. To rib a fly means to wind a material in an open spiral.

Saddle or Saddle Hackle: Feathers taken from the back portion of a chicken. These are longer and softer than the hackle feathers taken from closer to the neck of the chicken.

Schlappen: Very long feathers from the extreme back portion of a chicken. Even longer and webbier than Saddle.

Scissors: A good pair of flytying scissors with fine points is one of your most important tools. It is worth the investment to buy a good pair. Do not use these scissors to cut wire, tinsel, paper or monofilament. Use an older pair of scissors that you've stolen from a nail file set for this.

Scud: A freshwater crustacean of the family Amphipoda.

Sculpin: A small, broad headed baitfish, usually inhabiting the bottom area of streams.

Seal: Seal fur was once a very popular dubbing material because of its translucency. It is now illegal to import. There are a number of artificial substitutes that are available on the market.

Secondary Feather: Shorter flight feathers from the wing of a bird.

Secure: To fasten any material into place, usually with a wrap or two of thread.

Segment: To suggest separation in the body of a fly. Ribbing, for example, may suggest the segmentation in the body of a nymph.

Shank: The long, straight portion of the hook beginning just behind the eye and continuing to the bend. An important distance in determining proportions.

Shellback: A material that is pulled over the top of the body of a fly and secured at the back and front. Used to imitate the shell of a freshwater crustacean such as a scud.

Shuck: The shed exoskeleton of an insect. Often tied in at the tail of an emerger or fly to suggest an insect that is just emerging from its underwater state.

Soft Hackle: A hackle feather from a upland game bird, usually a grouse or partridge. As the name implies, these feathers are much softer than the rooster hackle used on a dry fly and are primarily used for wet flies and nymphs. A type of wet fly that has been tied with one of these feathers.

Soft Loop: A method used to tie materials onto a hook. This method is used to hold materials such as hairs in place that will flare or bend if too much pressure is applied. A couple of loops are taken around the material using very little pressure—just enough pressure to gently hold it into place, but not enough to cause it to flare. Then a tighter loop is taken to hold it securely in place.

Sowbug: A member of the order Isopoda. Cressbug.

Sparkle Yarn: See *Antron*.

Sparse: Use the materials involved very sparingly. There's an old saying among fly tyers that materials applied heavily catch fishermen in fly shops, but those applied sparsely catch fish.

Speckled Turkey: See *Mottled Turkey*.

Spent Wing: A wing that is tied so it is flat with the surface of the water rather than upright on top of the body of the fly. Usually tied so that one wing is coming out of each side of the body of the fly. See *Spinner*.

Spey Hackle: Very long, thin hackle usually palmered over the body of a fly.

Spinner: A dry fly that imitates the mayfly that has completed mating and drops back down onto the water to die. Spinners are often of a very different coloration from the dun stage of the fly and are often tied with spent (horizontal rather than vertical) wings.

Spinning: The method of applying hair (usually deer hair) to the shank of a hook. When pressure is applied to a piece of hair, it will splay or bend at the point where the pressure is applied. This will cause the hair to stick out from the shank of the hook. This method is used to produce bodies for flies that float easily. After the hair has been spun onto the hook shank it then can be trimmed to the shape desired. To spin deer hair onto the shank of a hook: first cut a clump of fibers about the thickness of a kitchen match from the skin, remove the fuzz from these fibers with a toothbrush, lay the clump diagonally across the shank of the hook, take two full turns with the tying thread around the clump and the hook, pull the thread tight in a downward direction, causing the hair to flare out perpendicular to the shank of the hook, take another turn of thread in front of the flared hair, push the flared hair tightly toward the back of the fly with your fingers or a packer tool. Repeat this process until you have the complete length of the body formed and then trim to shape. Spinning can also refer to the process of attaching dubbing to thread. See *Dubbing*.

Splayed: A position of wings or tail of a fly that forms a "V" shape. Usually the point of the "V" is at the hook shank with the tips out to the sides.

Squirrel Tail, Gray: The tail of the gray squirrel contains long hairs that are speckled gray in color, often with a white tip. Sometimes used to form the wings of flies and used chopped to form very coarse dubbing.

Squirrel Tail, Red: The tail of the red squirrel (or fox squirrel) contains reddish-brown and black barred hairs that are used for bucktail and streamer patterns. Sometimes used chopped to form very coarse dubbing.

Stem: The center portion of a feather; the shaft or quill.

Stacker: See *Hair Stacker*.

Stonefly: A family of large aquatic insects. The nymph stage is often imitated by fly tyers.

Streamer: A style of fly designed to imitate small baitfish. Usually constructed from feathers.

Stripped: A feather from which the barbules have been removed.

Synthetic: A material that is manmade as opposed to natural.

Swannundaze: A flat plastic-like material that is softer than fishing line. Comes in a variety of colors and is often used as ribbing on very large nymphs such as stoneflies.

Tailing: Any material used to form the tail of a fly.

Tandem: Two hooks joined by monofilament or wire. Often used in the construction of baitfish imitations.

Taper: To form the body or head of a fly by gradually increasing or decreasing its diameter from front to back. The bodies of dry flies, wet flies and nymphs generally taper from back to front with the fattest portion being toward the front. The heads of flies are usually tapered toward the front of the fly with the thickest portion being toward the back of the fly.

Teal Flank: Feathers from the side of the Teal under the wing. White/gray feathers with black bars. Well marked Mallard flank may be substituted.

Terrestrial: A non-aquatic insect or a fly that imitates one.

Thorax: The portion of an insect's body between the head and the abdomen. The "chest" of the insect.

Thread: Thread comes on spools and is used as the basic material that holds all the parts of our flies together. Flies are tied with a continuous piece of thread that is usually the first thing secured to the hook and the last thing secured in place and then trimmed when the fly is completed. Thread comes in a wide variety of colors, sizes and materials. The thickness of thread is indicated by a scale such as 3/0, 6/0, 8/0, etc. The larger the number in front of the /0, the thinner the thread. A spool of thread will last you through many flies and is relatively inexpensive. Don't try to save money by buying cheap thread. It will break more easily and usually at the most crucial part of the tying process. Good-quality thread will save you many frustrations in the long run.

Most of the flies in this book can be tied using a good-quality 6/0 to 8/0 thread. Thicker thread is most often used for very large flies and salt-water patterns. Thinner thread such as 12/0 can be useful when tying very small patterns such as midges.

Most tying threads today are made of nylon, though it is available made from other materials. Silk thread has a lovely translucency to it, but can be hard to find and is usually expensive. Kevlar thread is employed where extreme strength is desired.

Thread, Starting: Starting the thread on the hook is usually the first step in tying a fly. Lay the thread alongside the shank of the hook and then using the bobbin wrap the thread around the hook and back over itself several times. Trim off the excess. This sounds simple, but may take a little practice to master.

Throat: Hackle or other fibers tied only on the underside of the hook just behind the eye. See *Beard.*

Tinsel: Metal or plastic material formed in a thin ribbon. Usually comes on a spool and is used for ribbing.

Tip: A word with a number of possible meanings: a) the end of a feather that is farthest away from the body of the bird, b) the end of a hair that is the thinnest, c) either end of a material of uniform thickness such as tinsel, d) the loose end of the thread coming off the bobbin.

Tippet: A feather from the lower neck and upper back of a Golden Pheasant or the very thin monofilament that is tied to the end of your leader and to your fly.

Topping: A feather from the crest of a Golden Pheasant. See *Crest.*

Ultrahair: A translucent, relatively stiff artificial fiber. Used as a substitute for Polar Bear or Bucktail in the construction of streamers, Clouser Minnows, etc. Available in a wide variety of colors and usually packaged in a clump of 6-8" lengths.

Underbody: A material that is not visible, but is used to build up the shape of the body of a fly.

Underfur: Soft fur nearest the skin of an animal. Shorter and softer than the guard hairs.

Underwing: A portion of a wing for a fly that is underneath another material. The material that covers the underwing is often of a more translucent nature.

Upright: A style of dry fly wing that projects upward from the body of the fly.

Variant: A multi-colored hackle feather. Also a style of dry fly that uses two different colors of hackle, often in a size larger than the hook gap.

Vise: A device for holding the hook securely while you are tying the fly. If you are just getting started in fly tying, talk to your local fly shop and have them recommend a vise that is of good quality, but not too expensive. Wait until you have gained some experience with fly tying before deciding upon a more expensive brand of vise. I know many fly tyers who are still tying with the inexpensive, but good-quality vise that they first purchased thirty years ago and see no need to invest in one of the fancier and more expensive ones on the current market.

Web: The part of a feather closer to the base that contains softer fibers. This part absorbs water and needs to be trimmed off of hackle to be used for dry flies. Hackle feathers with a lot of webbing are considered lower quality and should be priced accordingly.

Weedguard: An attachment to the hook that attempts to prevent it from catching on weeds. Usually constructed out of monofilament or wire.

Weighted: A fly that has "lead" wire wrapped around the shank of the hook before tying to help it sink.

Wet Fly: The oldest form of fly. This fly sinks in the water rather than floating on the surface.

Whip Finish: The whip finish is a technique for securing the thread just behind the eye of the hook before trimming off the last of the thread and applying head cement to finish the fly. I will give you instructions on how to whip finish by hand, but quite frankly it is extremely difficult to learn how to do by reading instructions. The best way to learn how to whip finish by hand (without tools) is to get an experienced fly tyer to teach you by demonstrating the technique. It is a worthwhile technique to learn. There are some flies such as parachutes where whip finishing by hand is much easier than using a tool. However, if you don't have an experienced fly tyer to teach you, or even after trying to learn it from one you still can't master the technique, then there is an excellent whip finishing tool on the market that would be worth your investment. It even comes with a set of instructions on how to use it that is relatively easy to understand. This tool is manufactured by Matarelli and looks sort of like a bent wire that rotates inside a metal handle. Do not be confused by another whip finishing tool that is cheaper and made in India. I've never met anyone who actually got this second tool to work for them.

To whip finish by hand: Pull about 6-7 inches of thread off of the bobbin by pulling it downward from the hook. Grab the thread at the bobbin tip with your left thumb and forefinger. Spread the first two fingers of your right hand into a slight "V." Bring the first two fingers of your right hand up behind the thread with the back (the side with the fingernails) of the fingers facing you. The thread should be between you and the two fingers on your right hand. Your forefinger should be in the lower position. Roll the two fingers toward you and in a clockwise direction until the forefinger is in the upper position with the underside of the fingers facing you. The lower finger should actually pick up the thread and form a loop of the thread. It can usually be helpful to move the left hand that is holding the bobbin and the thread coming out of it slightly to the left during this process. The left hand will also have to move to ease the tension on the thread so that the loop can be formed. At the base of the loop there will be an "X" formed by the thread coming off of the hook, the bobbin, and the loop. Keeping your fingers spread, move them and the bobbin so that the "X" is against the side of the hook where you want the whip finish knot to begin (right behind the eye). Move your fingers back so that the "X" is on your side of the hook, but the thread forming the loop and your fingers are on the other side of the hook with one piece of thread coming off of the "X" over the top of the hook and one piece of thread coming off of the "X" under the bottom of the hook. The bobbin is still on your side of the hook. Let your fingers slide together and at the same time rotate them a half turn counterclockwise. This will reverse the loop strands so that the one that went over the top of the hook is now on the bottom and the one that went under is now on the top. The tricky part of this last move is maintaining just the right amount of tension on the thread so that the thread turns as you turn your fingers. If the tension is too light your fingers will turn inside the thread loop. In effect what you are doing here is forming another "X" with the thread on the far side of the hook. Now bring your fingers down under the hook and up again until the thread is again in front of the hook and your fingers behind the hook with one strand that forms the loop coming off over the top of the hook and the other strand that forms the loop coming off under the bottom of the hook. Repeat this process four times, forming five loops of thread around the hook. After you have finished the last loop around the hook, use your right thumb and forefinger (or a pointed object such as a bodkin) to steer the loop into place on the far side of the hook while pulling the loop down tight with the bobbin. Trim off the excess thread and use a little head cement to finish.

If you are still with me after those instructions you will begin to understand why I say that the best way to learn this technique is to have someone with a lot of patience demonstrate it and work through it with you step by step—or go out and buy yourself one of the Matarelli whip finishing tools and follow the instructions that come with it carefully.

Wing Burner: A tool used to trim feathers into a winglike shape. Formed from copper or brass to resemble the shape of a fly wing, it acts as a heat sink that lets you burn away the excess feather leaving you with the shape of the wing burner itself.

Wingcase: On a nymph the case that holds the unformed wings or on an artificial a material that imitates the wingcase of a natural.

Winging/Winging Material: "Winging" a fly is the process of forming the artificial wings on the fly. "Winging Material" is any material natural or artificial that is used in this process.

Wood Duck Flank: Feathers from the side of the Wood Duck under the wing. These feathers are a lemon/brown in color with fine black bars. Used for wings, tails and a variety of other purposes.

Wulff: When used in reference to a fly, it refers to a wing style that uses hair (usually calftail) to form a divided upright wing. Thus a Royal Wulff is a Royal Coachman with this style of wing. This style of fly was developed by Lee Wulff.

Fly Selections for Specific Purposes

Specific Species & Types

Mountain Trout

Dry Fly

5 - Hair-Winged Caddis, 10 - Henryville Sp.,
12 - The Parachute, 22 - Catskill Style,
27 - Wulff Style, 31 - The Humpy,
34 - Quill Gordon, Red Quill, 36 - The Variants,
38 - Blue Quill, 39- Royal Coachman,
42 - The American Express, 45 - Green Drake,
48 - Thorax Fly, 50 - Black Fly, 52 - Trico,
54 - P.W. Midge, 59 - Quigley Em.,
62 - Klinkhammer
209 - Yallerhammer, 216 - Thunderhead,
218 - Ramsey, Gray Hackle Yellow,
219 - Near Nuff

Wet Fly

71 - Soft Hackle, 74 - GRHE Wet,
78 - Silk Midge, 80 - Belle Watling,
83 - RAPT Wet, 85 - Ark. R.B.,
87 - H.B. Ant, 90 - McGinty,
209 - Yallerhammer, 218 - B.H. Peacock

Nymph

99 - B.H. Pheasant, 102 - Pheasant Tail,
105 - P & P, 108 - Olive B.H., 110 - Prince,
112 - GRHE, 114 - Red Fox, 122 - Caddis SP,
124 - Glass Bead, 127 - Midge, 132 - PT Midge,
135 - Muskrat, 137 - Stonefly, 139 - Hell/Stone,

141 - Montana, 144 - Woolly Worm,
146 - Zug Bug, 148 - Damsel Wiggle,
209 - Yallerhammer, 212 - Tellico,
218 - George, 219 - Streaker,
221 - Pat's Nymph, Miller Nymph,
224 - S.M. Blackbird,
227 - Sunshine, Buckwheat

Streamers
153 - Woolly Bugger, 159 - Booby,
163 - Muddler, 179 - Hellgrammite,
181 - Datchett Razzler, 224 - S.M. Blackbird,

Terrestrials
189 - DH Beetle, 191 - Al's Cricket,
193 - Latex Ant, 197 - Hopper, 200 - Fur Ant,
201 - Mylar Beetle

Tailwater Trout

Dry Fly
5 - Hair-Winged Caddis, 10 - Henryville Sp.,
12 - The Parachute, 19 - Comparadun,
22 - Catskill Style, 38- Royal Coachman,
42 - The American Express, 48 - Thorax Fly,
50 - Black Fly, 52 - Trico, 54 - P.W. Midge,
59 - Quigley Em., 62 - Klinkhammer

Wet Fly
71 - Soft Hackle, 78 - Silk Midge,
80 - Belle Watling, 87 - H.B. Ant

Nymph
99 - B.H. Pheasant, 102 - Pheasant Tail,
108 - Olive B.H., 112 - GRHE, 116 - Scud,
119 - Sowbug, 122 - Caddis SP,
124 - Glass Bead, 127 - Midge, 132 - PT Midge,
146 - Zug Bug, 148 - Damsel Wiggle,
240 - Bulldog Scud

Streamers
153 - Woolly Bugger, 159 - Booby,
163 - Muddler, 169 - Clouser,
181 - Datchett Razzler

Terrestrials
189 - DH Beetle, 191 - Al's Cricket,
193 - Latex Ant, 197 - Hopper, 200 - Fur Ant,
201 - Mylar Beetle

Smallmouth

Dry Fly

12 - The Parachute, 27 - Wulff Style,
31 - The Humpy, 62 - Klinkhammer,
198 - Thunderhead, 200 - Ramsey,
216 - Gray Hackle Yellow, 218 - Near Nuff

Wet Fly

71 - Soft Hackle, 80 - Belle Watling,
83 - RAPT Wet, 85 - Ark. R.B.,
90 - McGinty, 209 - Yallerhammer,
218 - B.H. Peacock

Nymph

99 - B.H. Pheasant, 102 - Pheasant Tail,
105 - P & P, 108 - Olive B.H., 110 - Prince,
112 - GRHE, 114 - Red Fox, 122 - Caddis SP,
124 - Glass Bead, 135 - Muskrat,
137 - Stonefly, 139 - Hell/Stone,
141 - Montana, 144 - Woolly Worm,
146 - Zug Bug, 148 - Damsel Wiggle,
209 - Yallerhammer, 212 - Tellico,
218 - George, 219 - Streaker,
221 - Pat's Nymph, Miller Nymph,
224 - S.M. Blackbird,
227 - Sunshine, Buckwheat

Streamers

153 - Woolly Bugger, 156 - Worm Bugger,
159 - Booby, 163 - Muddler, 169 - Clouser,
175 - Gar Grabber, 179 - Hellgrammite,
181 - Datchett Razzler

Terrestrials

189 - DH Beetle, 191 - Al's Cricket,
197 - Hopper, 201 - Mylar Beetle

Bass

Dry Fly

5 - Hair Winged Caddis, 62 - Klinkhammer

Wet Fly

71 - Soft Hackle, 80 - Belle Watling

Nymph

114 - Red Fox, 139 - Hell/Stone,
141 - Montana, 144 - Woolly Worm,

148 - Damsel Wiggle, 209 - Yallerhammer,
212 - Tellico

Streamers
153 - Woolly Bugger, 156 - Worm Bugger,
159 - Booby, 163 - Muddler, 169 - Clouser,
175 - Gar Grabber, 179 - Hellgrammite,
181 - Datchett Razzler

Terrestrials
189 - DH Beetle, 191 - Al's Cricket,
197 - Hopper, 201 - Mylar Beetle

Panfish

Dry Fly
5 - Hair Winged Caddis, 10 - Henryville Sp.,
27 - Wulff Style, 31 - The Humpy,
42 - The American Express, 48 - Thorax Fly,
50 - Black Fly, 62 - Klinkhammer,
209 - Yallerhammer, 216 - Thunderhead,
218 - Ramsey, Gray Hackle Yellow,
219 - Near Nuff

Wet Fly
69 - L.W. Coachman, 71 - Soft Hackle,
74 - GRHE Wet, 78 - Silk Midge,
80 - Belle Watling, 83 - RAPT Wet,
85 - Ark. R.B., 87 - H.B. Ant,
90 - McGinty, 209 - Yallerhammer,
218 - B.H. Peacock

Nymph
99 - B.H. Pheasant, 102 - Pheasant Tail,
105 - P & P, 108 - Olive B.H., 110 - Prince,
112 - GRHE, 114 - Red Fox, 116 - Scud,
119 - Sowbug, 122 - Caddis SP,
124 - Glass Bead, 127 - Midge, 132 - PT Midge,
135 - Muskrat, 139 - Hell/Stone,
144 - Woolly Worm, 146 - Zug Bug,
148 - Damsel Wiggle, 209 - Yallerhammer,
212 - Tellico, 218 - George, 219 - Streaker,
221 - Pat's Nymph, Miller Nymph,
224 - S.M. Blackbird,
227 - Sunshine, Buckwheat
240 - Bulldog Scud

Streamers

153 - Woolly Bugger, 156 - Worm Bugger,
159 - Booby, 163 - Muddler, 169 - Clouser,
181 - Datchett Razzler

Terrestrials

189 - DH Beetle, 191 - Al's Cricket,
193 - Latex Ant, 197 - Hopper, 200 - Fur Ant,
201 - Mylar Beetle

Stripers

Streamers

153 - Woolly Bugger, 156 - Worm Bugger,
163 - Muddler, 169 - Clouser,
175 - Gar Grabber, 179 - Hellgrammite,
181 - Datchett Razzler

Gar

Streamers

153 - Woolly Bugger, 156 - Worm Bugger,
159 - Booby, 163 - Muddler, 169 - Clouser,
175 - Gar Grabber, 179 - Hellgrammite,
181 - Datchett Razzler

Generic & Attractor Patterns

Dry Fly

12 - The Parachute, 19 - Comparadun,
22 - Catskill Style, 27 - Wulff Style,
35 - The Variants, 38- Royal Coachman,
42 - The American Express, 48 - Thorax Fly,
59 - Quigley Em., 62 - Klinkhammer,
209 - Yallerhammer, 216 - Thunderhead,
218 - Ramsey, Gray Hackle Yellow,
201 - Near Nuff

Wet Fly

69 - L.W. Coachman, 71 - Soft Hackle,
74 - GRHE Wet, 78 - Silk Midge,
80 - Belle Watling, 83 - RAPT Wet,
85 - Ark. R.B., 87 - H.B. Ant,
90 - McGinty, 209 - Yallerhammer,
218 - B.H. Peacock

Nymph

99 - B.H. Pheasant, 102 - Pheasant Tail,

105 - P & P, 108 - Olive B.H., 110 - Prince,
112 - GRHE, 114 - Red Fox, 122 - Caddis SP,
124 - Glass Bead, 135 - Muskrat,
139 - Hell/Stone, 141 - Montana,
144 - Woolly Worm, 146 - Zug Bug,
148 - Damsel Wiggle, 209 - Yallerhammer,
212 - Tellico, 218 - George, 219 - Streaker,
221 - Pat's Nymph, Miller Nymph,
224 - S.M. Blackbird,
227 - Sunshine, Buckwheat

Streamers

153 - Woolly Bugger, 156 - Worm Bugger,
159 - Booby, 169 - Clouser,
175 - Gar Grabber, 179 - Hellgrammite,
181 - Datchett Razzler, 224 - S.M. Blackbird

Imitator Patterns

Dry Fly

5 - Hair Winged Caddis, 10 - Henryville Sp.,
12 - The Parachute, 19 - Comparadun,
22 - Catskill Style, 27 - Wulff Style,
34 - Quill Gordon, Red Quill, 38 - Blue Quill,
45 - Green Drake, 50 - Black Fly, 52 - Trico,
54 - P.W. Midge

Nymph

116 - Scud, 119 - Sowbug, 127 - Midge,
132 - PT Midge, 137 - Stonefly,
148 - Damsel Wiggle, 240 - Bulldog Scud

Streamers

163 - Muddler

Terrestrials

189 - DH Beetle, 191 - Al's Cricket,
193 - Latex Ant, 197 - Hopper, 200 - Fur Ant,
201 - Mylar Beetle

Hook Equivalency Chart

Dry Fly

Daiichi	Mustad	Orvis	Eagle Claw	Partridge	Tiemco	VMC	Draikii
Standard Dry							
1170	94840 AC 94840	J1876 J1523	59	L2A	5210	9280	305
Light Wire Dry							
1180	94833 AC 94833			K1A	5290		300
Wide Gape Dry							
1100	AC 80000 BR	J4864			100		
2X Short Dry							
1310	94838	J1509			921		
Up Eye Dry							
1330	94842		159		500	9289	
Barbless Dry							
1190	94845	J1877	61	E1AY	900		

Daiichi	Mustad	Orvis	Eagle Claw	Partridge	Tiemco	VMC	Draikii
Straight Eye Dry							
1640	94859				101		
1480					501		
2-3X Long Dry							
	94831				2312 2302 5212		

Wet Fly/Nymph

Daiichi	Mustad	Orvis	Eagle Claw	Partridge	Tiemco	VMC	Draikii
Standard Wet							
1550	3906 AC 3906	J1461	57	G3A	3769	8527	070
Heavy Wet							
1530	3908	J1642				8526	075
1X Nymph							
1560	3906B AC 3906B				3761		
2X Nymph							
1710	9671 AC 9671	J1524	63	D4A	5262	9279	730
3X Nymph							
1720	9672	J1526			5263		710
Shrimp/Scud							
1130	AC 80250 BR	J1639		K4A	2487 2457		135
Swimming Nymph							
1770		J1512			4001		

Streamer/Bass

Daiichi	Mustad	Orvis	Eagle Claw	Partridge	Tiemco	VMC	Draikii
4X Streamer							
2220	79580 AC 79580	J1511	281	D4A	9394		700
6X Streamer							
2340	3665A AC 36890	J1511			300		
Straight Eye Streamer							
1750	9674	J0167		D3ST	9395	9295	
Special Streamer							
2461	3262		22B				
Bass Bug							
2720	37187	J1878					

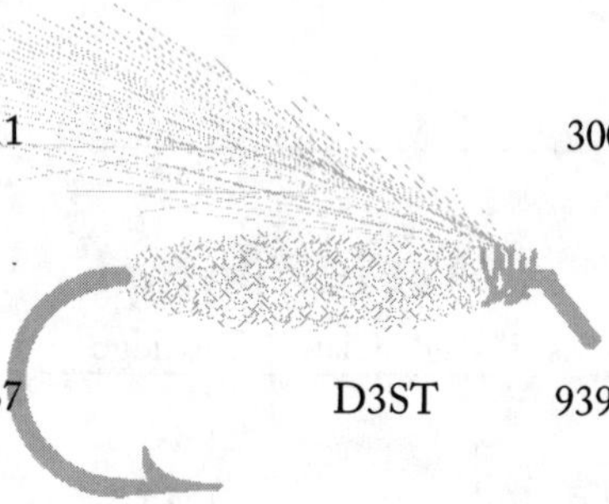

A Smoky Mountains & Southern Appalachians Stream Insect List

Remember that any Insect List is just an approximation of the times at which these particular insects usually hatch. Weather conditions from year to year and day to day will greatly affect the emergence of any insect. You shouldn't count on any of these bugs being there at the times given. Most of the Southern Appalachians also do not usually get heavy hatches, with a few notable exceptions. The result is that at any given time of year attractor and generic patterns are often your best producers. I would always have some Thunderheads, Adams, a light-colored mayfly imitation, a dark-colored mayfly imitation, a light caddis, a dark caddis, a Humpy and a midge pattern ready in dry flies in a variety of sizes. In nymphs, a Bead Head Pheasant Tail, a GRHE, a Montana, a Tellico, a Prince Nymph, a Zug Bug, and some midge pupa in a variety of sizes should cover most any time of the year. Check the list and have a few of the specific flies for that time of the year along as well, but most of the time you will do just as well if not better on generics and attractors. If you have some of your own favorite generic or attractor patterns from where you live already tied up, bring them along too. The odds are pretty good that they might work.

Mayflies

- Blue Quill #16, late February through April and October through mid-November
- Blue-Winged Olive #18, early February to early April and mid-October through November (also sometimes in December during warm spells)
- Dun Variant #10-12, early June to early September
- Green Drake #8-10, late April to Early June
- Grey Fox #14, mid-April through mid-May.

- Hendrickson & Red Quill #12-14, late March to early May
- Light Cahill # 12-16, late April through mid-August
- Little Dark Olive #16-18, late June through September
- March Brown #12-14, early April to early June
- "Orange Spinner" (descriptive name) #14, late April through early September
- Quill Gordon #12-14, March through early May
- Sulphur # 14-18, late April through June
- Tiny Olive #22-24, mid-April through mid-June and October and early November
- Trico #22-24, late June through early September

Stoneflies

- Brown Stone #12-14, mid-May through July
- Early Black Stone #14-16, February through early April
- Early Brown Stone #12-14, late February through early April
- Giant Black Stone #4-8, April through June
- Golden Stone #4-8, June through early September
- Tiny Winter Black Stone #18-22, January and February
- Yellow Stone & Green Stone (also Olives) #14-18, April through August. Pale Yellows and Olives hatch early in the season, soon followed by the brighter flies and a larger (#10-12) medium-yellow stonefly with brownish wings.

Caddis Flies (descriptive names)

First color is wing color, second is abdomen color; colors in parentheses are abdomen colors.

- Black or Black & Dark Dun Caddis #18-22, late May and early June
- Dark Dun & Black Caddis #12-14, May
- Dark Dun & Yellow Caddis #18-22, late June through August
- Dun Caddis #18, adults observed throughout the year, with concentrations late Jan. through mid-April, and July through August (also may describe several kinds of Caddis flies)
- Gray-Brown or Dun & Green Caddis (deep green or olive) #16-20, May through early August

- Large Ginger Caddis #6-8, September through October
- Mottled Brown & Green Caddis (pale yellow-lime or grayish olive) #10-12, adults observed late May through early September with concentrations late May and early June, late June, and mid-August through early September
- Mottled Tan/Brown & Yellow Caddis #14-16, mid-September through mid-November
- Speckled Gray-Brown Caddis (pale yellow-brown or grayish-tan) #12-16, late April through August
- Tan Caddis #1-16, July and August

Midges

Adult midges range in size from #18 to #28 or smaller and are present throughout the year. Typical colors are black, gray, brown, olive, cream, tan or combinations. In general, the larger and darker ones will appear during the cooler months; the smaller and paler ones in warmer months.

Terrestrials

Ants, Bees, Beetles, Caterpillars, Crickets, Inchworms, Jassids, Yellow Jackets, etc.—Mostly May through September.

This insect listing and its abbreviated calendar of information are distilled from notes that are the basis of *A Smoky Mountains & Southern Appalachians FLY HATCH SCHEDULE*, produced by Ken Snelling and published by Graphic Spirit. The 16-page, laminated, pocket-size booklet provides times of month and times of day throughout the year for both the emergences and egg-laying phases of common trout stream insects in the region, and suggests a complete selection of artificial flies for the different phases. It is widely available at fly tackle dealers throughout the Southeast and also at some book stores in the region.

Southeastern Fly Fishing on the WWW

One of the greatest resources for fly fishermen to come along in years has been the World Wide Web on the Internet. You now can quickly and easily find all kinds of information that was probably extremely difficult to track down before about regional resources. The following is a listing of URLs for information about fly fishing in the Southeast. One of the greatest advantages of the WWW, the availability of extremely current information, may sometimes turn into one of its greatest disadvantages, namely that the resources located there move about often, change location quickly and sometimes just completely disappear. All of the following locations were active as this book went to the printer, but that doesn't mean that they were still there the next day.

Southeastern Flyfishing Pages on the WWW by State

Alabama

State Game and Fish Dept
http://www.dcnr.state.al.us/agfd

Bass Anglers Sportsman Society
http://www.bassmaster.com

Merlinn Southern Outdoor
http://www.homestead.com/merlinn

Arkansas

Andy's Arkansas Fly Fishing Page
http://kanweb.com/fly

Snugg Brown's Homepage
http://www2.arkansas.net/~snuggs

TroutNet
http://home.lunaweb.net/~troutguy

Florida

Game and Fish Com.
http://www.state.fl.us/fwc/fishing

Central Florida Flats Angler
http://members.aol.com/GNewGnu/CFFA.html

Coastal Angler Magazine
http://www.camirl.com

Cyberangler
http://cyberangler.com/fishing.html

Gainesville Offshore Fishing Club
http://www.afn.org/~gofc/gofc.html

South Florida Saltwater Fishing
http://www.aksi.net/fishing

S.W. Florida: A Guide to Saltwater Flyfishing
http://www.marco-island-florida.com/don/home.htm

Georgia

Georgia Wildlife Resources
http://www.dnr.state.ga.us/dnr/wild

Georgia Women Flyfishers
http://www.accessatlanta.com/community/groups/gawomfly

North Georgia Trout
http://www.georgia-outdoors.com/ngto

Tim's Coastal Georgia Fishing Page
http://www.geocities.com/Yosemite/Trails/1000

Jim Teffeteller's SE FF'ing Guides
http://www.olfart.com

Kentucky

Fish & Wildlife Resources
http://www.state.ky.us/agencies/fw/kdfwr.htm

Louisiana

Department of Wildlife & Fisheries
http://www.wlf.state.la.us

Maryland

Maryland Department of Natural Resources
http://www.dnr.state.md.us

Flystream.com
http://flystream.com

Isaac Walton League
http://www.iwla.org

Mississippi

Mississippi Gulf Coast Fishing
http://www.datasync.com/~dbb/welcome.htm

North Carolina

Joel's Flyfishing North Carolina
http://www.adp.unc.edu/~longlegs/ff_in_nc.html

Guide to Western NC Trout
http://wnctrout.com

Joe's Fish Stories
http://cool.virtual-pc.com/~papadisc/swfishing/fishing.htm

Trout, NC: Guide to North Carolina's Public Mountain. Trout Waters
http://www.troutnc.com

South Carolina

Department of Natural Resources
http://www.dnr.state.sc.us

Tennessee

State of Tennessee Dept. of Wildlife Resources
http://www.state.tn.us/twra

L.J.'s Homepage: The Author's Page w/lots of info and up-to-date links on flyfishing sites on the WWW
http://web.utk.edu/~ldecuir/home.htm

Hiwassee River Homepage
http://members.aol.com/dd37312/hiwservr.htm

Smoky Mountain Field School
http://www.outreach.utk.edu/Smoky

Steve Kulpa's Homepage: E. Tennessee Flyfishing
http://www.usit.net/public/skulpa/index.html

T.V.A. Homepage: Lots of power hype, but there is info on the telephone "information line" that gives you generation schedules.
http://www.tva.gov

Fly Fishing Upper East Tennessee
http://ourworld.compuserve.com/homepages/flyfishntn

Virginia

Department of Game and Inland Fisheries
http://www.dgif.state.va.us

The Virginia Fly Fishing Page
http://www.iradiant.com/vaflyfish

Southeastern Flyshops and Guides on the WWW by State

Alabama

Riverside Fly Shop
http://personal.lig.bellsouth.net/lig/1/f/1flyfish/page2.html

Arkansas

Al Blanton's Guide Service
http://www.blantons-guide-service.com
Cane Island Fly Shop
http://caneislandflyshop.com
Rivercliff Cabins
http://www.rivercliff.com
Tailwaters Trout
http://www.tailwaterstrout.com
White River Homepage
http://www.crl.com/~ozark/mtnhome/trout.html
White River Trout Fishing
http://www.troutfin.com

Florida

Backcountry Fly Fishing Flyfishing Instruction
http://www.verobackcountry.com
Blue Seas Deepsea Fishing—Venice
http://www.acun.com/~blueseas
Charlotte Harbor Guide Services
http://explorer.gls3c.com/guides/guidepage.html
Chaser Tango
http://www.keywestparadise.com/chaser.html
Clewiston Guide Service's Bass Fishing
http://wmi.cais.com/bassfish/index.html
Capt. Scott Graham
http://cyberangler.com/guides/graham
Capt. Dexter Simmons: Key West & Marquesas
http://pages.prodigy.com/captdexter
Fishing Guides Northeast Coast
http://www.floridafish.com/ieguidenes.htm
Fishing Marco Is, Everglades & 10,000 Islands
http://www.marco-island-florida.com/fish/home.htm
Sanibel Fly Shop (saltwater fly fishing)
http://www.flytackle.com
The Tropical Angler
http://www.cyberisle.com/tropical/angler.htm

Georgia

West Point Lake
http://www.mindspring.com/~kje

Maryland

Chesapeake Fly and Bait Co.
http://members.aol.com/gr8flyz/index.html

On The Fly Flyshop MD, Gunpowder River
http://www.onthefly.com

North Carolina

Davidson River Outfitters
http://www.davidsonflyfishing.com
Flyfish NC
http://www.geocities.com/Yosemite/Rapids/3853
Hunter Banks Co.
http://www.hunterbanks.com
Smoky Mountains On The Fly
http://www.smokyonthefly.com
The Waterfront
http://www.jef.com/waterfront

Tennessee

Old Smoky Outfitters: Fly fishing in the Smoky Mountains National Park and East Tennessee
http://www.thesmokies.com/oldsmoky_outfitters

Virginia

Canoe Virginia
http://canoevirginia.com
Chesapeake Bay Guide and Charter Service
http://patriot.net/~bayfish
Murray's Fly Shop
http://www.murraysflyshop.com

Bibliography

For the serious student of fly tying and fly fishing, one of the outstanding collections of flytying and flyfishing books has long been the Milne Special Collection at the University of New Hampshire Library. This collection holds over 3500 works on the subject. The catalog for the collection is now available on the World Wide Web at http://www.izaak.unh.edu/specoll/milne.htm

Almy, Gerald. *Tying and Fishing Terresterials.* Mechanicsburg, PA: Stackpole Books, 1978.

Atherton, John. *The Fly and the Fish.* Rockville Centre, NY: Freshet Press, 1971.

Bates, Joseph. *Atlantic Salmon Flies and Fishing.* Harrisburg, PA: Stackpole Books, 1970.

———. *Streamers and Bucktails: The Big Fish Flies.* New York, Alfred A. Knopf, 1979.

Bay, Kenneth E. *The American Fly Tyer's Handbook.* New York: Winchester Press, 1979.

Bergman, Ray. *Trout.* New York: Alfred A. Knopf, 1938.

Best, A.K. *Production Fly Tying.* Boulder, CO: Pruett, 1989.

———. *A.K.'s Fly Box.* NY: Lyons & Burford, 1996.

———. *Dyeing and Bleaching.* NY: Lyons & Burford, 1993.

Betts, John. *Synthetic Flies.* John Betts, 1980.

Blades, William F. *Fishing Flies and Fly Tying.* Harrisburg, PA: Stackpole Books, 1979.

Borger, Gary. *Naturals.* Harrisburg, PA: Stackpole Books, 1980.

———. *Nymphing.* Harrisburg, PA: Stackpole Books, 1980.

———. *Designing Trout Flies.* Wausau, WI: Tomorrow River Press, 1991.

Boyle, Robert H., & Dave Whitlock. *The Fly Tyer's Almanac.* New York: Crown, 1975; Nick Lyons Books, 1982.

———. *The Second Fly Tyer's Almanac.* Philadelphia: Lippincott, 1978.

Brooks, Charles. *Nymph Fishing for Larger Trout.* New York: Crown, 1976.

———. *The Trout and the Stream.* New York: Crown, 1974.

Caucci, Al, and Bob Nastasi. *Hatches.* New York: Comparahatch, 1975.

Combs, Trey. *Steelhead Fly Fishing and Flies.* Portland, OR: Salmon-Trout-Steelhead, 1976.

Dennis, Jack. *Western Trout Fly Tying Manual, Vol. I.* Jackson Hole, WY: Snake River Books, 1974.

———. *Western Trout Fly Tying Manual, Vol. II.* Jackson Hole, WY: Snake River Books, 1980.

Dubois, Donald. *The Fisherman's Handbook of Trout Flies.* New York: A.S. Barnes, 1960.

Ellis, Jack. *The Sunfishes.* Bennington, VT: Abenaki Publishers, Inc., 1993.

Fish, Frederic F. *Trout Fishing Waters of North Carolina.* Raleigh, NC: The Graphic Press, Inc. 1971.

Flick, Art. *Art Flick's New Streamside Guide.* New York: Crown, 1969; Nick Lyons Books, 1982.

———. *Art Flick's Master Fly Tying Guide.* New York: Crown, 1972.

Fling, Paul N., & Donald L. Puterbaugh. *Expert Fly Tying.* New York, Sterling Publishing Co., 1982.

Harder, John R. *The Orvis Fly Pattern Index.* New York: Penguin Books, 1990.

Harvey, G[illegible]rge W. *Techniques of Trout Fishing & Fly Tying.* NY: Lyons & P[illegible]ubl., 1990.

[illegible]v. *Popular Fly Patterns.* Salt Lake City: Peregrine-Smith,

[illegible]

[illegible]*Vol. 1.* Portland: Frank Amato Publ., 1995.

[illegible]*ad Fly Tying Guide.* Portland, OR: Frank Amato

Hughes, Dave. *American Fly Tying Manual.* Portland, OR: Frank Amato Publications, 1989.

———. *Wet Flies.* Mechanicsburg, PA: Stackpole Books, 1995.

Jacobs, Jimmy. *Trout Streams of Southern Appalachia.* Woodstock, VT: Backcountry Publications, 1994.

———. *Tailwater Trout in the South.* Woodstock, VT: Backcountry Publications, 1996.

———. *Trout Fishing in North Georgia.* Atlanta: Peachtree Publ., 1993.

Jennings, Preston. *A Book of Trout Flies.* New York: Crown, 1970.

Jorgensen, Poul. *Modern Fly Dressings for the Practical Angler.* New York,: Winchester Press, 1976.

———. *Modern Trout Flies.* New York: Doubleday, 1979, Nick Lyons Books, 1982.

Kaufmann, Randall. *American Nymph Fly Tying Manual.* Portland, OR: Frank Amato Publications, 1975.

———. *The Fly Tyer's Nymph Manual.* Portland, OR: Western Fisherman's Press, 1986.

———. *Tying Dry Flies.* Portland, OR: Western Fisherman's Press, 1991.

Keith, Tom. *Fly Tying and Fishing for Panfish and Bass.* Portland, OR: Frank Amato Publications, 1989.

Kirk, Don. *Smoky Mountains Trout Fishing Guide.* Hillsborough, NC: Menasha Ridge Press, 1985.

Knopp, Malcolm & Robert Cornier. *Mayflies.* Helena, MT: Graycliff Publ., 1997.

Koch, Ed. *Fishing the Midge.* Harrisburg, PA: Stackpole Books, 1988.

Lafontaine, Gary. *Caddisflies.* New York: Nick Lyons Books, 1981.

———. *The Dry Fly.* Helena, MT: Graycliff Publishing Co., 1990.

———. *Trout Flies: Proven Patterns.* Helena, MT: Graycliff Publishing Co., 1993.

Leisenring, James, & Vern Hidy. *The Art of Tying the Wet Fly and Fishing the Flymph.* New York: Crown, 1971.

Leiser, Eric. *The Book of Fly Patterns.* New York: Alfred A. Knopf, 1987

———, *The Dettes - A Catskill Legend.* NY: Willowkill Press, 199

Leonard, J. Edson. *Flies.* New York: A.S. Barnes, 1950.

Lively, Chauncy. *Chauncy Lively's Fly Box.* Harrisburg, PA: Stackpole Books, 1980.

Marbury, Mary Orvis. *Favorite Flies and Their Histories.* Edison, NJ: The Wellfleet Press, 1988.

Marinaro, Vincent. *A Modern Dry Fly Code.* New York: Crown, 1970.

———. *In the Ring of the Rise.* New York: Crown, 1976.

McKim, John F. *Fly Tying: Adventures in Fur, Feathers and Fun.* Missoula, MT: Mountain Press, 1982.

Migel, J. Michael, ed. *The Masters on the Dry Fly.* NY: Lyons & Burford Publ., 1977.

Morris, Skip. *Tying Foam Flies.* Portland: Frank Amato Publ., 1994.

———. *The Art of Tying the Bass Fly.* Portland: Frank Amato Publ., 1996.

Murray, Harry. *Trout Fishing in the Shenandoah National Park.* Edinburg, VA: Shenandoah Publishing Co., 1989.

———. *Fly Fishing for Smallmouth Bass.* New York: Lyons & Burford, 1989.

Nemes, Sylvester. *The Soft-Hackled Fly.* Old Greenwich, CT: The Chatham Press, 1975.

———. *Spinners.* Bozeman, MT: Publ. by the Author, 1995.

Perrault, Keith E. *Perrault's Standard Dictionay of Fishing Flies.* Orlando, FL: Daniels Publishing Co., 1984.

Pfeiffer, C. Boyd. *Bugmaking.* NY: Lyons & Burford Publ., 1993.

Richards, Carl & Bob Braendle. *Caddis - Super Hatches.* Portland: Frank Amato Publ., 1997.

Richards, Carl & John Krause. *Tailwaters of Southern Appalachia.* Kentwood, MI: Anteheier & Krause Publ., 1996.

Roberts, John. *Collins Illustrated Dictionary of Trout Flies.* London: Collins W... 1995.

... H. "Polly." *Tying and Fishing the Fuzzy Nymph.* Harrisburg, ...le Books, 1978.

... *...nphs and the Trout.* London: A & C Black, 1970.

... *...Matching the Hatch.* New York: Macmillan, 1955.

... York: Winchester Press, 1973.

Shaw, Helen. *Fly Tying.* New York: Ronald Press, 1963, Wylie, 1981.

Slone, Harry. *Virginia Trout Streams.* Woodstock, VT: Backcountry Publications, 1994.

Smedley, Harold Hinsdale. *Fly Patterns and Their Origins.* Muskegon, MI: Westshore Publications, 1943.

Steeves, Harrison R., III & Ed Koch. *Terrestrials.* Mechanicsburg, PA: Stackpole Books, 1994.

Stewart, Richard. *Universal Fly Tying Guide.* Brattleboro, VT: Stephen Greene Press, 1979.

Stewart, Richard & Farrow Allen. *Flies for Bass and Panfish.* Intervale, NH: Northland Press, 1992.

Stoltz, Judith & Judith Schnell, eds. *Trout.* Mechanicsburg, PA: Stackpole Books, 1991.

Surette, Dick. *Trout and Salmon Fly Index.* Harrisburg, PA: Stackpole Books, 1978.

Surette, Dick, ed. *Fly Tyer Pattern Bible.* North Conway, NH: Saco River Publishing Corp., 1985.

Swisher, Doug & Carl Richards. *Selective Trout.* New York: Crown, 1971.

Talleur, Richard. *Mastering the Art of Fly Tying.* Harrisburg, PA: Stackpole Books, 1979.

———. *The FlyTyer's Primer.* Piscataway, NJ: Winchester Press, 1986.

———. *Modern Fly Tying Materials.* NY: Lyons & Burford, 1995.

Veniard, John. *Fly Dresser's Guide.* London: A.C. Black, 1952.

Waterman, Charles F. *Fly Rodding for Bass.* NY: Lyons & Burford Publ., 1989.

Williams, A. Courtney. *A Dictionary of Trout Flies.* London: A.C. Black, 1949.

Wilson, Bob, & Richard Parks. *Tying and Fishing the West's Best Dry Flies.* Portland OR: Frank Amato Publications, 1978.

Wulff, Lee. *Lee Wulff on Flies.* Harrisburg, PA: Stackpole Books, 1980.

Index